IMAGES
of America

ACCOKEEK

On the Cover: Taken on June 1, 1923, this photograph shows workers restocking the dwindling population of shad with fry raised at the Bryan Point shad hatchery in Accokeek. (Courtesy of the Library of Congress, Prints and Photographs Division.)

IMAGES
of America

ACCOKEEK

Kenneth Bryson

ARCADIA
PUBLISHING

ISBN 978-0-7385-9757-7

Published by Arcadia Publishing
Charleston, South Carolina

Printed in the United States of America

Library of Congress Control Number: 2012937896

For all general information, please contact Arcadia Publishing:
Telephone 843-853-2070
Fax 843-853-0044
E-mail sales@arcadiapublishing.com
For customer service and orders:
Toll-Free 1-888-313-2665

Visit us on the Internet at www.arcadiapublishing.com

This book is dedicated to Robert "Papa" Tilch (1895–1974) and the members of the Tilch family who continue to support the preservation of Accokeek heritage.

Contents

Acknowledgments

I wish to thank Brinkley Gary, associate publisher, and Lissie Cain, my editor at Arcadia Publishing, for their patient responses to my questions. Their advice has been invaluable in guiding me through the intricacies involved in producing a book of high quality within the deadline.

Libraries and archives in the metropolitan Washington area have shared their immense resources with me. They include the Accokeek Branch Library (Anne-Marie Ramsey and Kamaria Hawkins), the Library of Congress (Kristi Finefield and Jan Grenci), the Maryland Historical Society (Eben Dennis), the Maryland State Archives (Maria Day, Joseph Leizear, and Dan Ramirez), the National Archives and Records Administration (Holly Reed, Meghan Ryan, and Joseph Schwarz), the Prince George's County Historical Society (Susan Pearl), Surratt House Museum (Joan Chaconas and Sandra Walia), and University of Maryland Libraries (Liz Novara).

Government agencies, foundations, citizen associations, and other institutions sharing their expertise with me include the United States Census Bureau (Joshua Coutts and Ashleigh Perry), the Accokeek Foundation (Lisa Hayes, Laura Ford, and Anjela Barnes), the Alice Ferguson Foundation (Lori Arguelles, Doris Sharp, Laura Gillespie, and Libby Campbell), the British Museum (Christopher Sutherns), Christ Episcopal Church (Wes Courtney and Brian Vander Wel), the Ciesla Foundation (Aviva Kempner and Andrew Geyer), the Corcoran Gallery of Art (Linda Crocker Simmons), Fort Washington Baptist Church (Darin Poulard), the Maryland–National Capital Park and Planning Commission (Greg Kearnes and Howard Berger), the Moyaone Association (George Hanssen), the National Oceanic and Atmospheric Administration (NOAA) (Skip Theberge), the Silesia Citizens Association (Carol Tilch and Karen Tilch), the Prince George's County Planning Department (Jill Kossack and Michelle Reidy), St. Mary's Catholic Church of Piscataway (Bill Keimig), and St. Mary's College of Maryland (Julie King).

Special thanks are due to Adelaide Copeland, Nancy and Holly Wagner, and others who allowed me to scan photographs from their personal collections. They are named in the credits throughout the book.

INTRODUCTION

Recognition often comes belatedly. When Capt. John Smith visited the upper Potomac River in 1608, he discovered the Piscataways and other Algonquian-speaking indigenous people. At one time, they were the most populous and powerful inhabitants of the Chesapeake Bay region. But, by the 1800s, the Piscataway nation had declined dramatically. On January 12, 2012, Maryland governor Martin O'Malley issued an executive order giving state recognition to the Piscataways. By that time, few residents of Accokeek identified themselves as American Indians.

Accokeek has had its share of controversies and scandals. The official history of Christ Church relates that the first pastor of the church, Rev. George Tubman, had been rector for only a short time when the Maryland Council found him guilty of bigamy. He had married a woman in Charles County while he was still the husband of a woman in England. Reverend Tubman was banished for this offense; but soon, he was back as rector, serving again briefly until he died in 1701. In the late 1600s and early 1700s, conditions in this area were not conducive to religion. One missionary wrote to the Archbishop of Canterbury: "Also the Lord's Day is profaned, religion despised, & all notorious vices committed as that it has become a Sodom of uncleanness and a pest house of iniquity." Later, the American Revolution led to a rift between the rector, Rev. Jonathan Boucher, who defended the established Church of England, and the congregation, who were growing tired of taxation and other oppressive policies of Great Britain. The situation was such that Reverend Boucher armed himself with two loaded pistols when he held services.

The chapter Our African American Heritage includes images of a slaveholder's account book, a notice from 1775 seeking the capture and return of a runaway slave, and a freedom certificate from 1813. There also is a portrait of John Edward "Grit" Bruce, who was born a slave near Piscataway Creek. After he gained his freedom, he became a prominent newspaperman and author. In 1860, the area around Accokeek had 142 slaveholders and 1,600 slaves out of a total population of 3,040. The 1864 Constitution of Maryland, sponsored by radical Republicans, freed the state's slaves. Immediately after the Civil War, Democrats gained control of the Maryland legislature, and Oden Bowie, formerly a large slaveholder, was elected governor. Former slaveholders sought compensation for the loss of their "property," but this failed.

Maryland, a border state, had divided loyalties in the Civil War. Accokeek, like most of southern Maryland, was more sympathetic to the Confederacy. It is not surprising that a few prominent citizens were Confederate spies. One, Thomas Harbin, operated a hotel in Piscataway. Plots to kidnap or assassinate Abraham Lincoln swirled around him. Nonetheless, he was never convicted of a crime. On the Union side, Charles H. Baldwin, a Congressional Medal of Honor winner, is buried in the graveyard of Christ Church.

Alice Ferguson and her husband, Henry, bought Hard Bargain Farm in 1922. The farm attracted many who shared Alice's talents and interests. Her passion for archeology was shared by friends who looked for Indian artifacts. She organized a comprehensive dig that involved many organizations and resulted in significant scientific and historical results. Weekends at the farm attracted a diverse collection of friends from the city. The group, which came to be known as "Fergie's gang," enjoyed polo and volleyball. The spirit of that time is captured in Alice's paintings *A Day at the Farm* and *The Frog Pond*. Following Alice's death in June 1951, her bequest resulted in the establishment of the Moyaone Reserve and the Alice Ferguson Foundation.

The Moyaone is only part of greater Accokeek. Calvert Manor is another enclave that was founded after World War II. A community organization, the Calvert Manor Garden Club, was established 60 years ago. Other parts of old Accokeek continued the rural, farming tradition, but, with the end of tobacco farming, this industry died out. Hard Bargain Farm and a few other operating farms remained. Today, the Accokeek Foundation operates National Colonial Farm as a living history museum depicting life on a farm of the middling sort at the time of the American Revolution. The building of Indian Head Highway, connecting Accokeek with the Indian Head Naval Reservation to the south and Washington, DC, to the north, opened up opportunities for growth outside the traditional limits of old Accokeek. Since 1990, rapid growth of Accokeek has occurred, mainly to the east of Indian Head Highway.

Silesia is another enclave located outside the boundaries of Accokeek. This community was founded by emigrants from Silesia, which was then part of Prussia in the German Empire. Robert Stein was the first person to come to America from Silesia. He was a linguist and arctic explorer. Stereo photographs from his 1899–1901 expedition document that aspect of his life. Another was Robert "Papa" Tilch, who played an important role in the greater Accokeek community.

Residents of Accokeek have been prominent in the worlds of art and music. The house at Hard Bargain Farm contains several of Alice Ferguson's paintings and her piano. Paintings of Henry Ferguson by Richard Kenah and Lenore Thomas Straus and examples of Straus's sculpture can be seen around the house, which is now occupied by the staff of the Alice Ferguson Foundation. The chapter Where the Arts Come Out highlights three Accokeek musicians with national reputations: Danny Gatton, Grace Griffith, and Lynn Hollyfield. Today, a new generation of artists, writers, and musicians continues to bloom in this unique community.

The chapter Old Family Photographs preserves the memory of families of old Accokeek residents. Some of these families were living in Accokeek in the 1800s, and their descendants continue to live in the community.

Accokeek itself was given official recognition in 1990 when the US Census Bureau made this area a Census Designated Place with clearly identified boundaries. This enables the gathering of comparable data covering the most recent decades. Before that, Census data were available for Election District 5 (Piscataway), of which Accokeek was and still is a small part. The final chapter, Modern Times, touches on a few aspects of the emerging story of Accokeek and its residents. A prominent theme is preservation. As Accokeek has grown rapidly, many are working to maintain a link with the past. Nonetheless, development will continue in the future as it did in the past.

One

Early Days

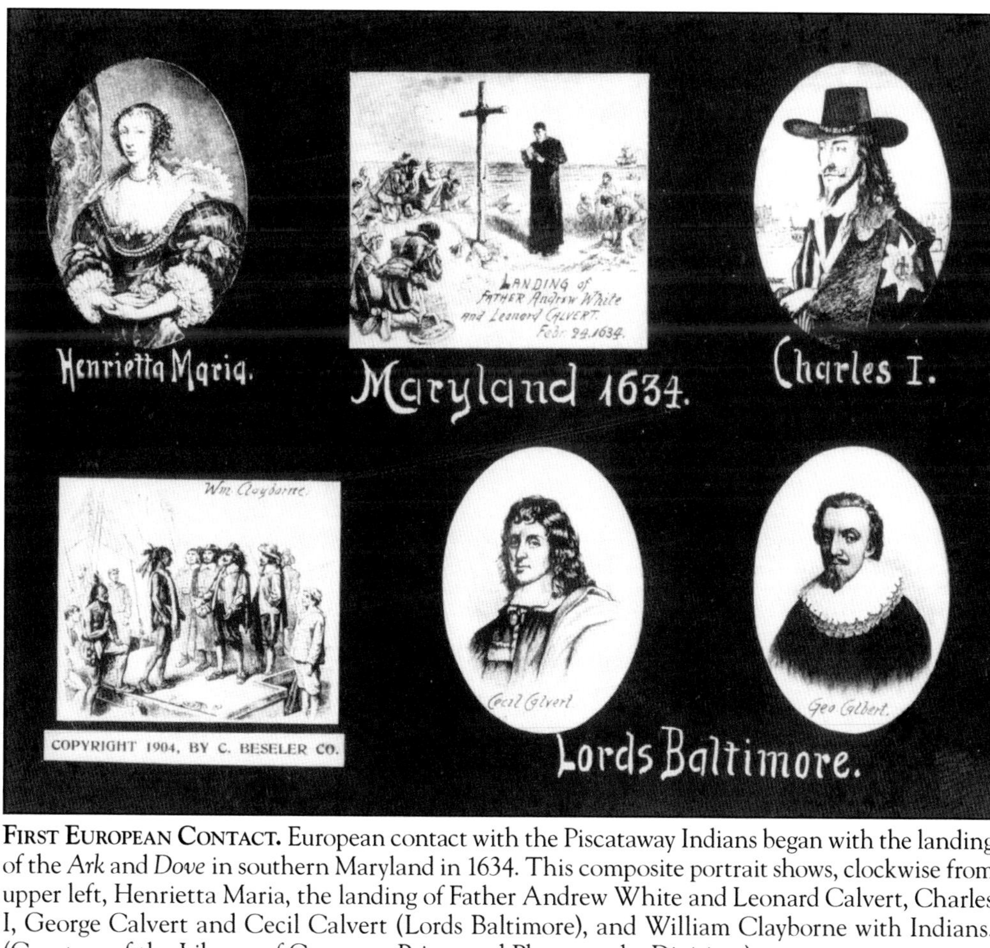

First European Contact. European contact with the Piscataway Indians began with the landing of the *Ark* and *Dove* in southern Maryland in 1634. This composite portrait shows, clockwise from upper left, Henrietta Maria, the landing of Father Andrew White and Leonard Calvert, Charles I, George Calvert and Cecil Calvert (Lords Baltimore), and William Clayborne with Indians. (Courtesy of the Library of Congress, Prints and Photographs Division.)

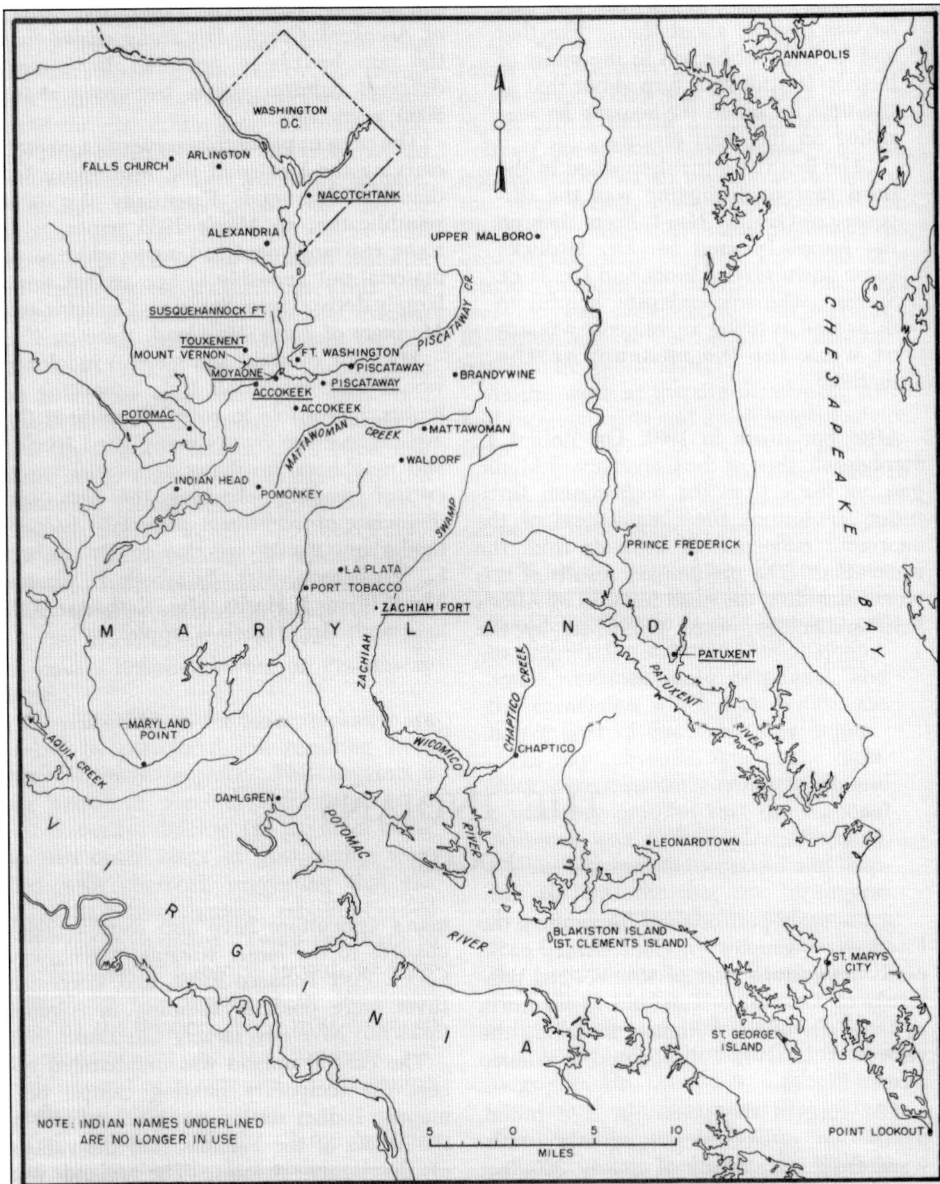

Piscataway Empire. The word Piscataway is thought to mean "where salt and fresh waters meet" in the Algonquin language. It refers to both a place and to the indigenous people living there. The Piscataway *tayac*, or emperor, ruled over 130 miles of native territory and villages on both shores of the Chesapeake Bay. For the purposes of this book, the focus will be on the villages of Moyaone and Piscataway. The Piscataway village, on the Potomac River below the mouth of Piscataway Creek, was called Moyaone by Capt. John Smith. It may have been in existence for 300 years before Smith's visit in 1608. Its exact location is unknown despite extensive archeological investigations at the Accokeek Creek site. The village of Piscataway is thought to have been farther inland on Piscataway Creek. Pending archeological studies in the current Piscataway historic village, its nature remains to be discovered, but there is good reason to associate it with the "palace" of Piscataway emperor Kittamaquund in 1639–1640. (Courtesy of the Alice Ferguson Foundation.)

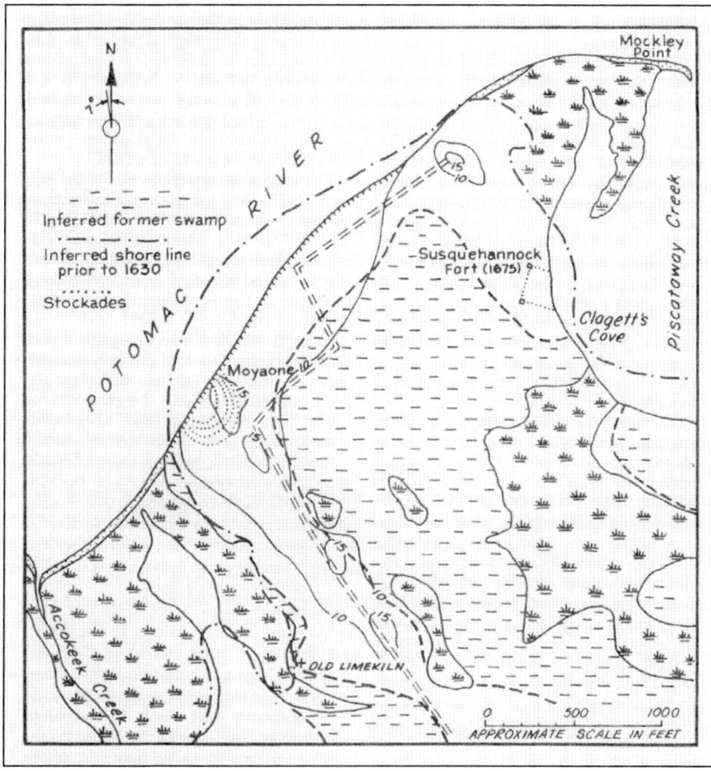

VILLAGE OF MOYAONE. This map shows the location of the Piscataway village of Moyaone according to the booklet *The Prehistoric People of Accokeek Creek* by Robert L. Stephenson. Note the location of Susquehannock Fort (1675). Conflict between the Piscataway and Susquehannock people may have prompted the Piscataways to move to a safer location, such as Zachiah Fort, which is seen on the map on the opposite page. (Courtesy of the Alice Ferguson Foundation.)

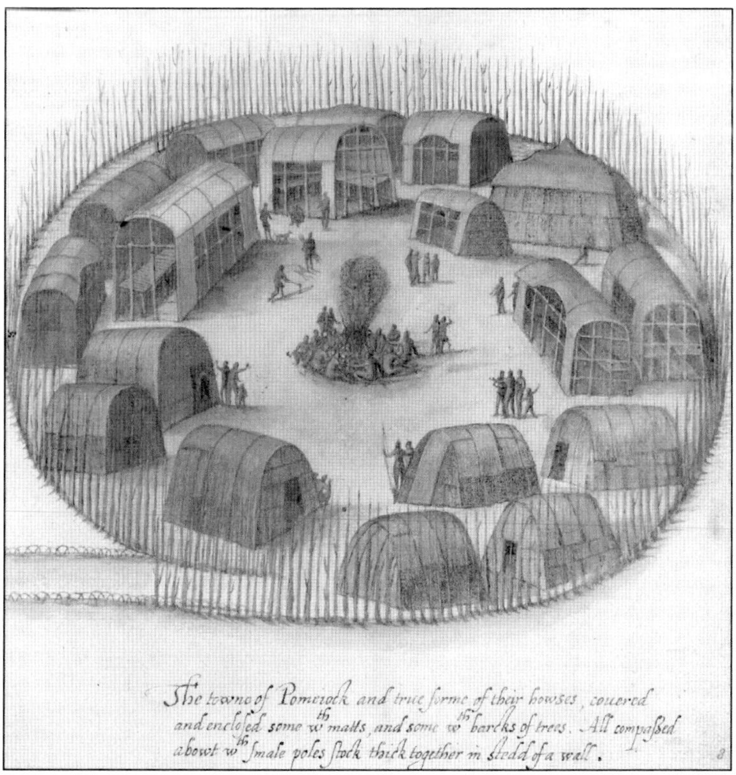

ALGONQUIN VILLAGE. This drawing by John White, the governor of the so-called Lost Colony in what is now North Carolina, shows the kind of village believed to have been at Moyaone. White was the first Englishman to paint the people and natural life of the American continent. This and other watercolors are reproduced in Paul Holton's book *America 1575*. (Courtesy of the trustees of the British Museum.)

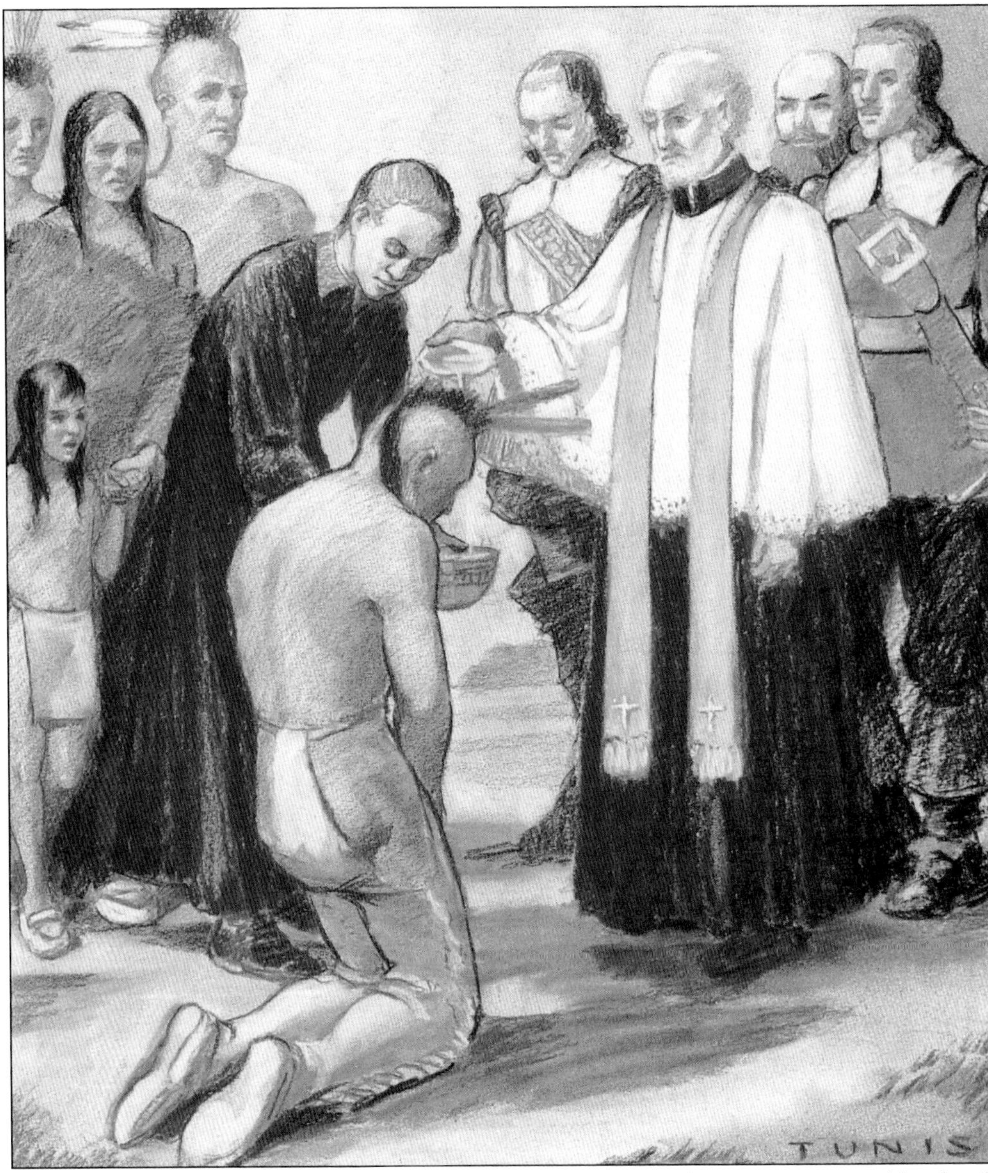

BAPTISM OF KITTAMAQUUND, 1640. Kittamaquund, the *tayac* of the Piscataways, and his family were baptized on July 5, 1640. Father Andrew White, a Jesuit, performed the baptism. Gov. Leonard Calvert attended the ceremony along with other Maryland officials and Piscataway leaders. The scene is represented in this charcoal drawing by Edwin Tunis, an American illustrator of Colonial life, drawn between 1925 and 1935. During the baptism, Kittamaquund was given the Christian name Charles and his wife and one of his daughters were given the name Mary. Kittamaquund adopted the colonists' style of dress and learned to speak some English. Princess Mary went to live with a colonist family, the Brents. She later married Giles Brent. Kittamaquund died in 1641. Father Andrew White, who had learned some of the native language, first visited Kittamaquund in June 1639. The tayac, who liked Father White, invited him to live in his palace with him and his family. (Courtesy of the Maryland State Archives.)

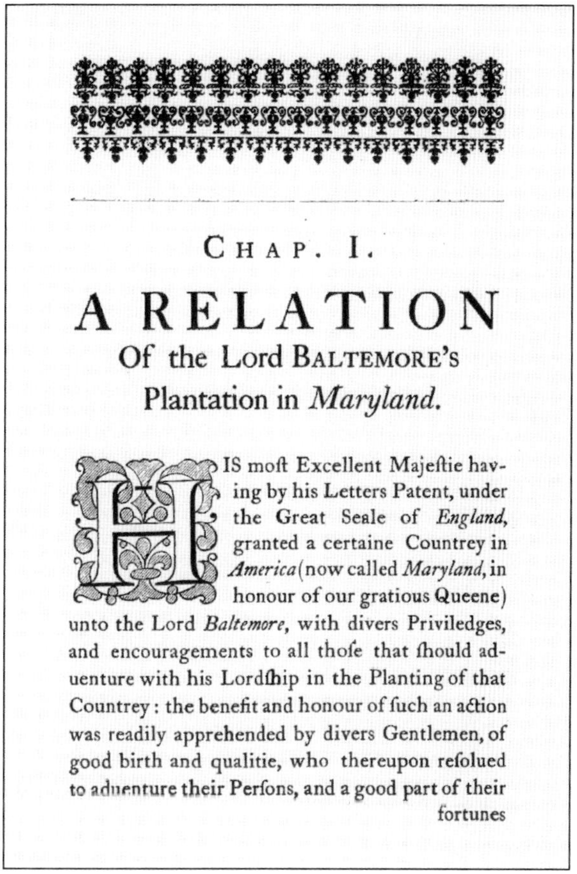

CHAP. I.

A RELATION
Of the Lord BALTEMORE'S
Plantation in *Maryland.*

HIS moſt Excellent Majeſtie having by his Letters Patent, under the Great Seale of *England,* granted a certaine Countrey in *America* (now called *Maryland,* in honour of our gratious Queene) unto the Lord *Baltemore,* with divers Priviledges, and encouragements to all thoſe that ſhould aduenture with his Lordſhip in the Planting of that Countrey: the benefit and honour of ſuch an action was readily apprehended by divers Gentlemen, of good birth and qualitie, who thereupon reſolued to aduenture their Perſons, and a good part of their fortunes

PISCATAWAY, 1635. This documents the visit of Gov. Leonard Calvert to "Paschatoway" in 1635. Here, he met with Capt. Henry Fleet, who had lived for many years among the Indians, spoke their language very well, and was esteemed by the natives. The governor asked the *werowance* if he and his people could set down there. The werowance replied that the governor should use his own discretion in the matter. (Courtesy of the Maryland State Archives.)

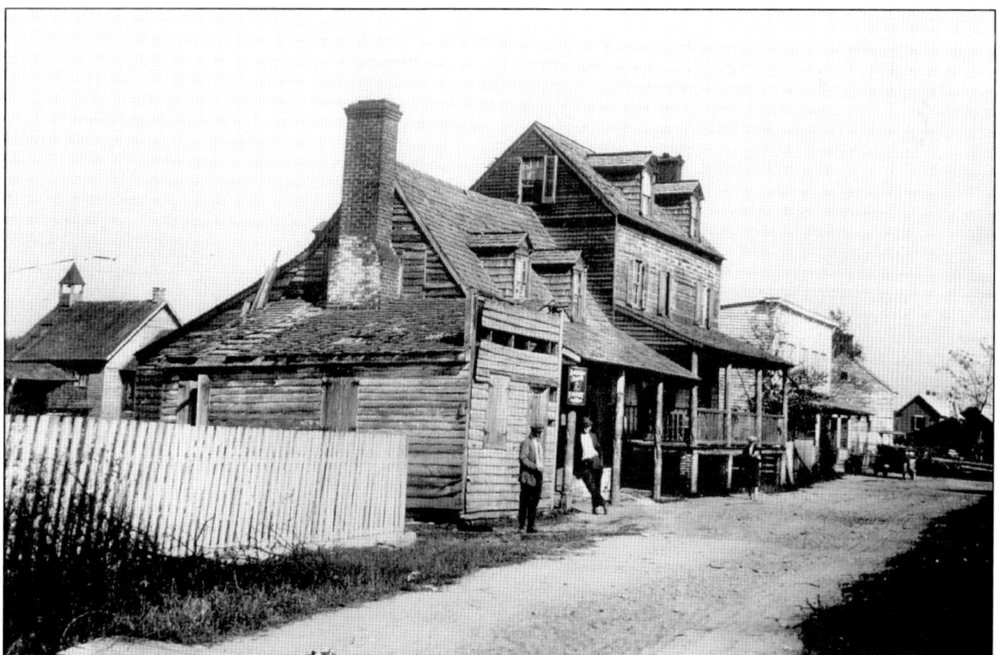

PISCATAWAY, 1910. Piscataway was established in 1707 as a port by the Maryland Colonial Assembly and designated as a tobacco inspection station in 1747. With siltation of Piscataway Creek in the 1800s, the tobacco inspection point was transferred downstream. The village continued to serve as a local commercial center into the early 1900s, with taverns, stores, schools, residences, a hotel, a church, and a telegraph and post office. (Courtesy of the Maryland State Archives.)

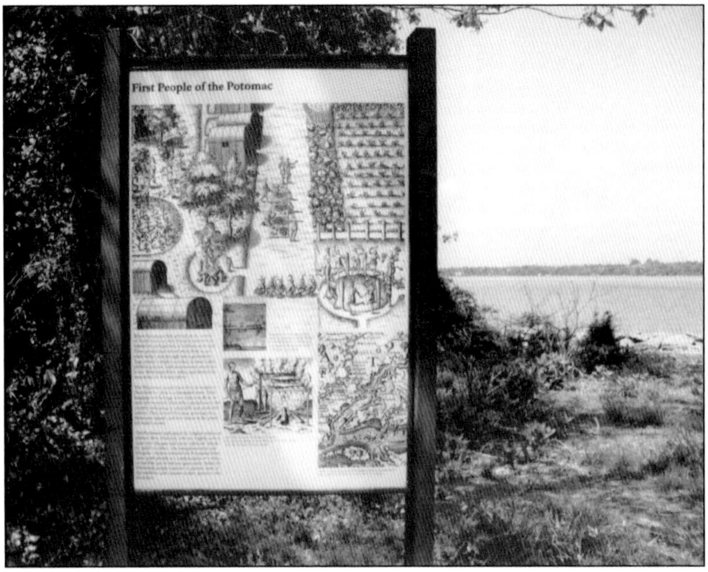

PISCATAWAY PARK. Piscataway Park is named after Piscataway Creek, itself named after the Piscataway Indians. The park is home to bald eagles, beavers, osprey, and other wildlife. It encompasses areas of wetland, meadow, and woodland. It is administered by the National Park Service. This sign is one of the ways that the park pays tribute to the first inhabitants of the Potomac. (Author's collection.)

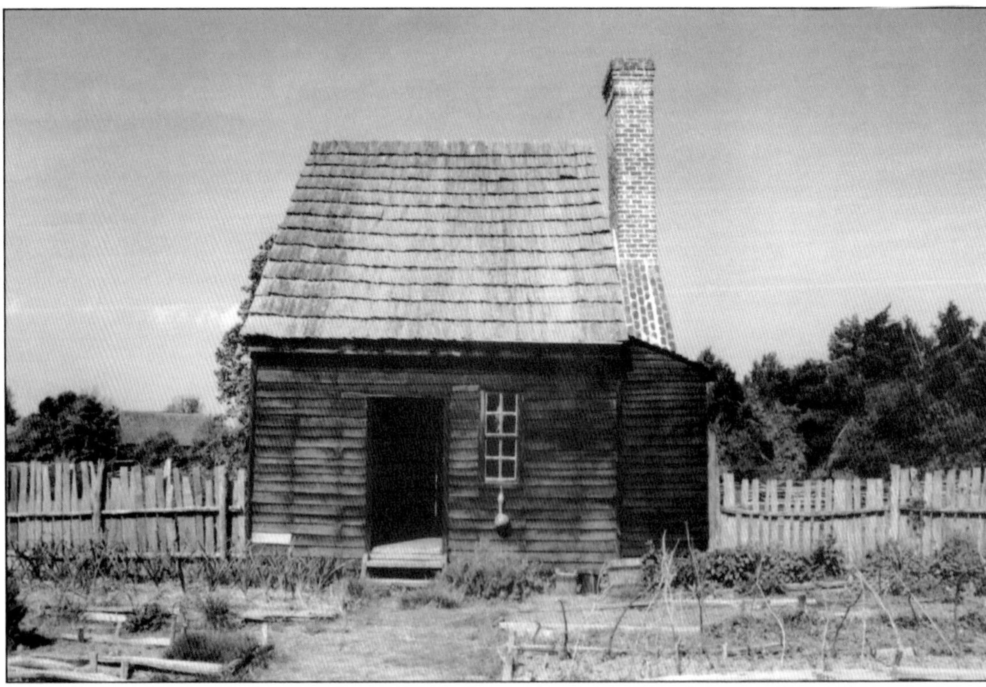

NATIONAL COLONIAL FARM. The Accokeek Foundation manages the National Colonial Farm, a living history museum established in 1958. It depicts a middling Maryland family farm on the eve of the American Revolution. Through heritage breed livestock and seed-saving programs, it preserves nearly extinct heritage animals and crops for future generations. Visitors to the National Colonial Farm can experience how ordinary people lived during this period. (Author's collection.)

MATT MATTINGLY. The manager of the National Colonial Farm, Matt Mattingly, says that for most Americans, their primary understanding of the Colonial period is the history of the gentry class. Part of the mission at the National Colonial Farm is to present an alternate view of our history through the lens of a so-called ordinary family in this region on the eve of the American Revolution. (Author's collection.)

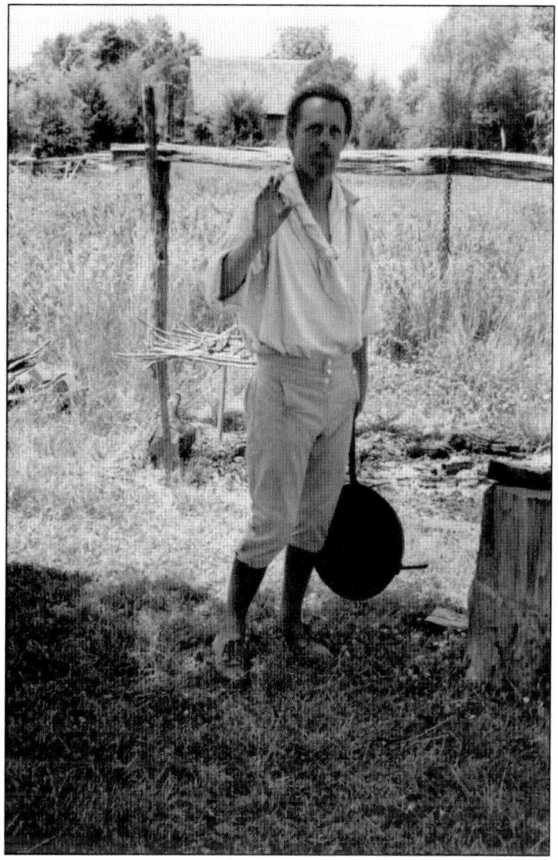

COLLEEN WALTER. As the site interpreter, Colleen Walter assists Mattingly in the Foodways demonstrations conducted monthly throughout the year. Foodways is an introduction to the epicurean delights of Colonial Marylanders. Visitors to the National Colonial Farm learn how people's tastes and the food itself have changed over 300 years by exploring "receipts" (recipes) and meal preparation. (Author's collection.)

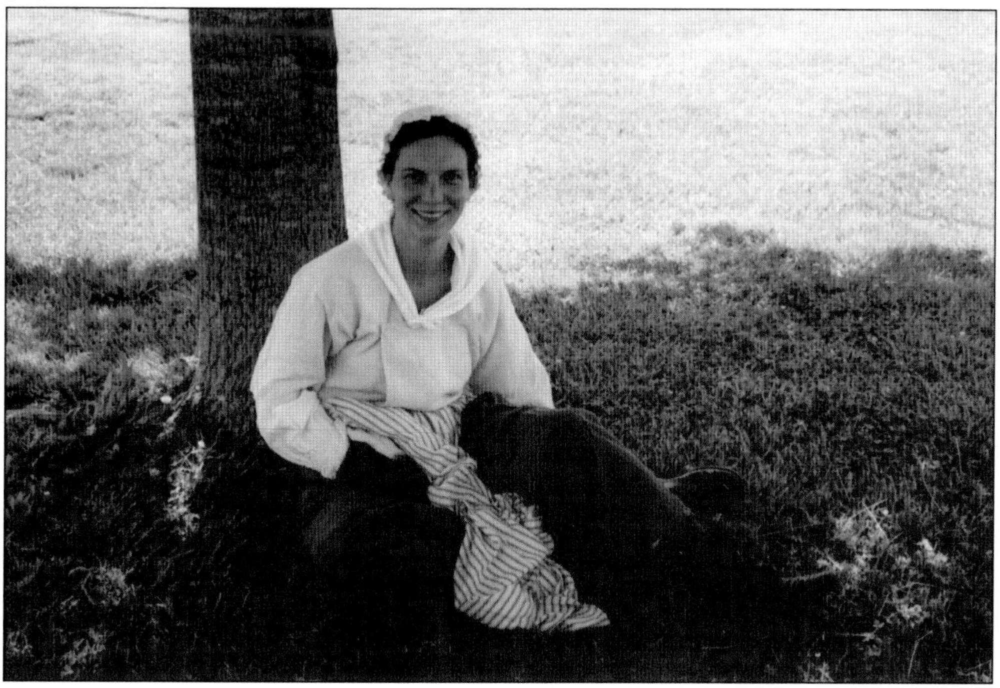

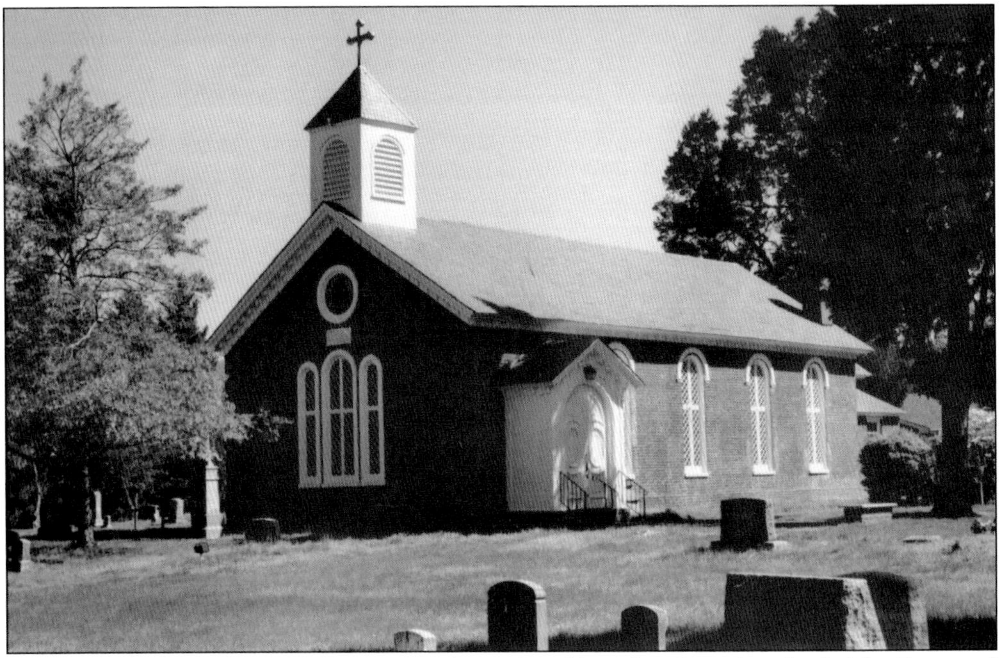

Christ Episcopal Church, Accokeek. This is the oldest church in Accokeek. The Episcopal congregation in Accokeek dates back to 1698. Traveling to the nearest church, St. John's, Broad Creek, was a hardship for people in Accokeek. So, in 1745, the Maryland General Assembly authorized the building of a "chapel of ease" in Accokeek. The present brick church was built in 1857. (Author's collection.)

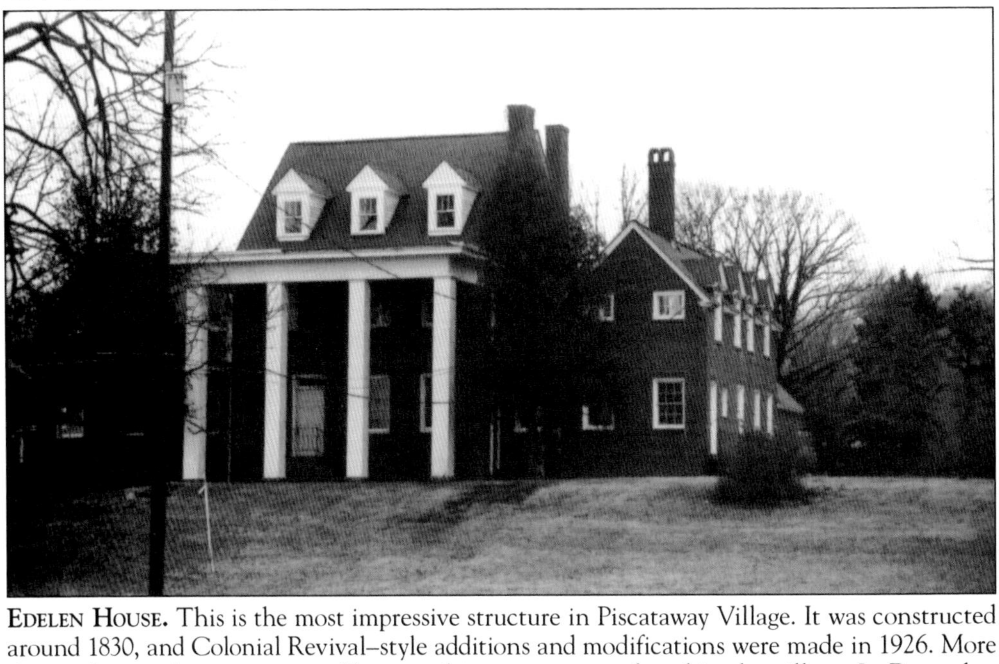

Edelen House. This is the most impressive structure in Piscataway Village. It was constructed around 1830, and Colonial Revival–style additions and modifications were made in 1926. More than a dozen other structures of historical importance are found in the village. In December 2011, Piscataway Village Historic District was listed in the National Register of Historic Places. (Author's collection.)

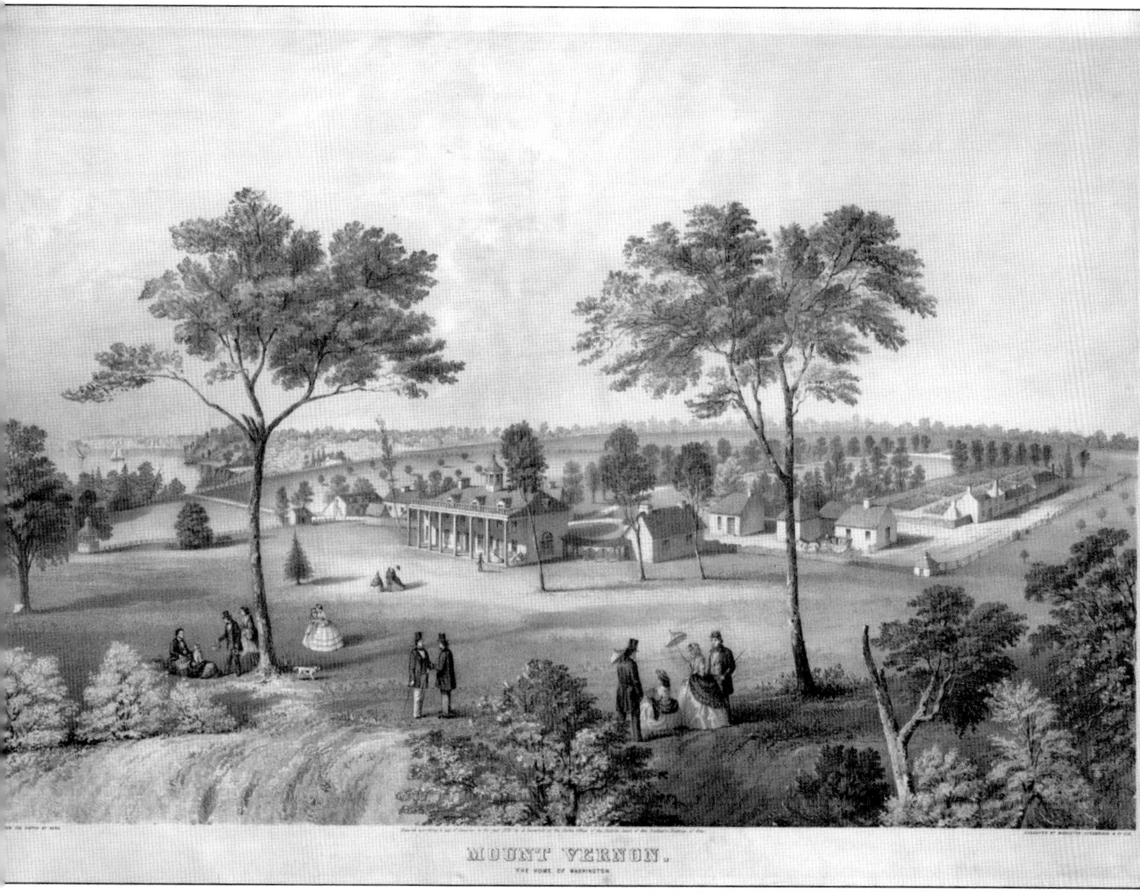

The George Washington Connection. Accokeek is directly across the Potomac River from George Washington's Mount Vernon. Washington's diary records that he fished along the Maryland shore of the Potomac as far south as Broad Creek. A marker at St. John's Church, Broad Creek, reads, "Credible evidence and honest tradition record that Washington attended services here on numerous occasions." Enoch Magruder, a large landowner, was a fellow parishioner. Through this connection, the Maryland Council, meeting on May 18, 1778, ordered a sloop to Magruder's fishery on Broad Creek to load 280–300 barrels of fish. These were to be taken to Charlestown, in Cecil County, at the head of the Chesapeake Bay. They were then to be forwarded "with all expedition" to Valley Forge. The encampment at Valley Forge had been chosen to take advantage of the shad migration in the Schuylkill River. However, the British had constructed a barrier at Philadelphia to block the shad migration in the spring of 1778. This necessitated the request for fish to be shipped from Broad Creek. (Courtesy of the Library of Congress, Prints and Photographs Division.)

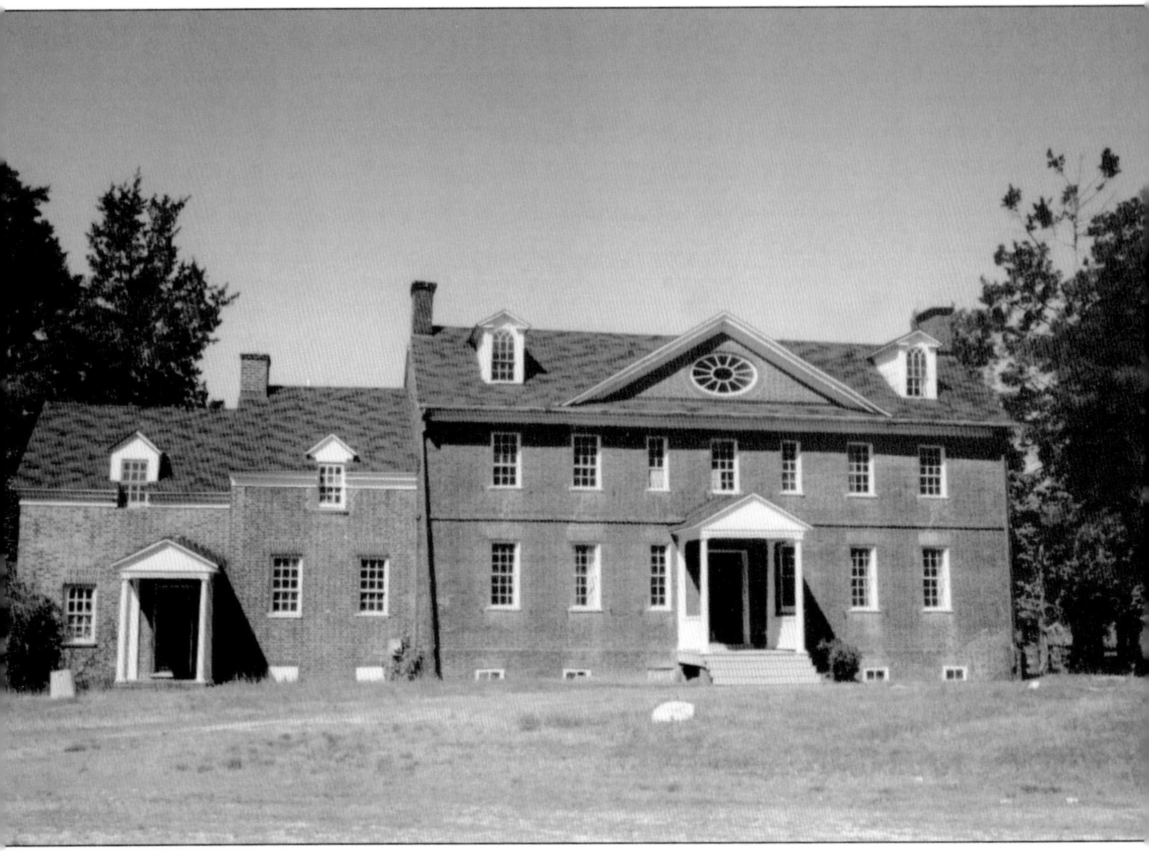

ENOCH MAGRUDER AND BATTERSEA. In 1769, Enoch Magruder purchased the Battersea property from James Marshall. Magruder is listed in the bill of sale as a merchant. Just prior to his purchase of Battersea, he purchased an adjacent property known as Want Water. The 1776 Colonial census of Maryland lists Enoch Magruder as 53 years of age; his wife, Meek, as 54; their son Dennis as 18; their daughters Elizabeth and Eleanor as 24 and 22, respectively; and another boy, Thomas Noble, as 14. There were also 26 African Americans listed by name as members of the Magruder household. Enoch Magruder died in 1786. His daughter Sarah Magruder Lyles inherited a portion of the Battersea property. Magruder's properties passed through many hands in the following years. Battersea is now known as Harmony Hall. In 1966, Harmony Hall and adjacent land containing Want Water were sold to the federal government to be administered by the National Park Service. (Author's collection.)

Two

Our African American Heritage

Census of August 31, 1776 in St. John's and King George's Parishes

Total black and white	8,441
Total black	3,455
Total free blacks	55
Total slaves	3,400
Total white	4,986

Accokeek in 1776. At the time of the American Revolution, slaves greatly outnumbered free blacks in the area of Accokeek. Slaves constituted 41 percent of the total population of St. John's and King George's Parishes, and free blacks less than 1 percent. The Continental Congress intended to raise \$3 million by levying a tax on each colony according to a quota to be determined by the 1776 population census. (Author's collection.)

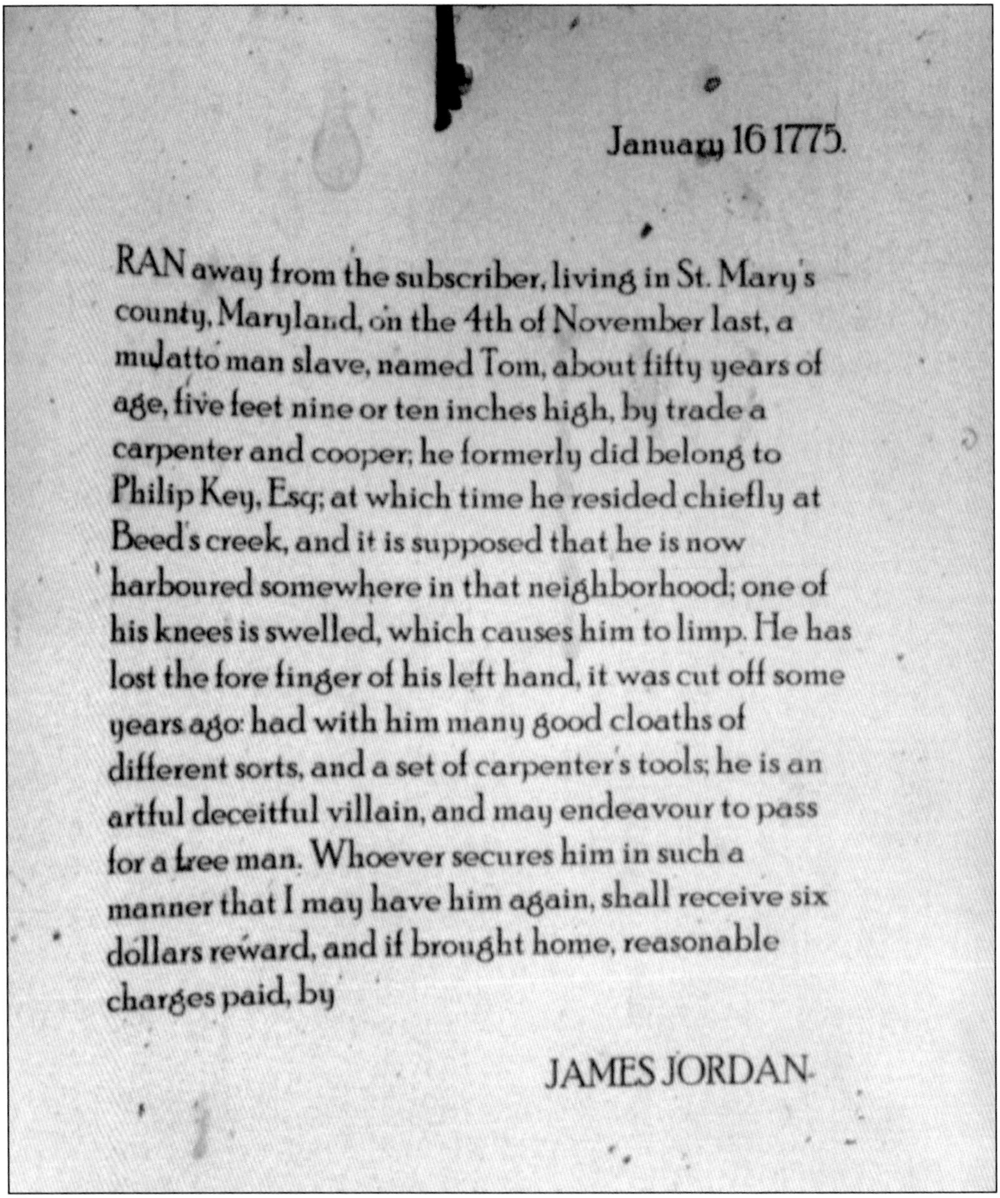

January 16 1775.

RAN away from the subscriber, living in St. Mary's county, Maryland, on the 4th of November last, a mulatto man slave, named Tom, about fifty years of age, five feet nine or ten inches high, by trade a carpenter and cooper; he formerly did belong to Philip Key, Esq; at which time he resided chiefly at Beed's creek, and it is supposed that he is now harboured somewhere in that neighborhood; one of his knees is swelled, which causes him to limp. He has lost the fore finger of his left hand, it was cut off some years ago: had with him many good cloaths of different sorts, and a set of carpenter's tools; he is an artful deceitful villain, and may endeavour to pass for a free man. Whoever secures him in such a manner that I may have him again, shall receive six dollars reward, and if brought home, reasonable charges paid, by

JAMES JORDAN.

RUNAWAY SLAVE. This facsimile of an advertisement seeking the capture and return of a runaway slave is typical of others published before Maryland emancipated its slaves in 1864. Runaway advertisements were placed in newspapers by slave owners or their representatives. Committal notices were announcements of the capture and detainment of persons suspected of being fugitives from slavery. Not being able to prove their free status, persons so detained faced return to their masters if they were fugitives, or sale into slavery at the benefit of the county if no owner claimed the detainee. Only those able to prove their free status, by document or corroboration of status from white persons, were released. Owners seeking fugitives knew that it was to their advantage to give as complete a description of the person being sought as possible. Names and aliases, gender, age, physical features, and distinguishing marks, clothing, and apparel were the most basic components. Often, a biographical sketch was included. This gave highlights about the fugitive's friends and familial connections in other parts of the state or region. (Author's collection.)

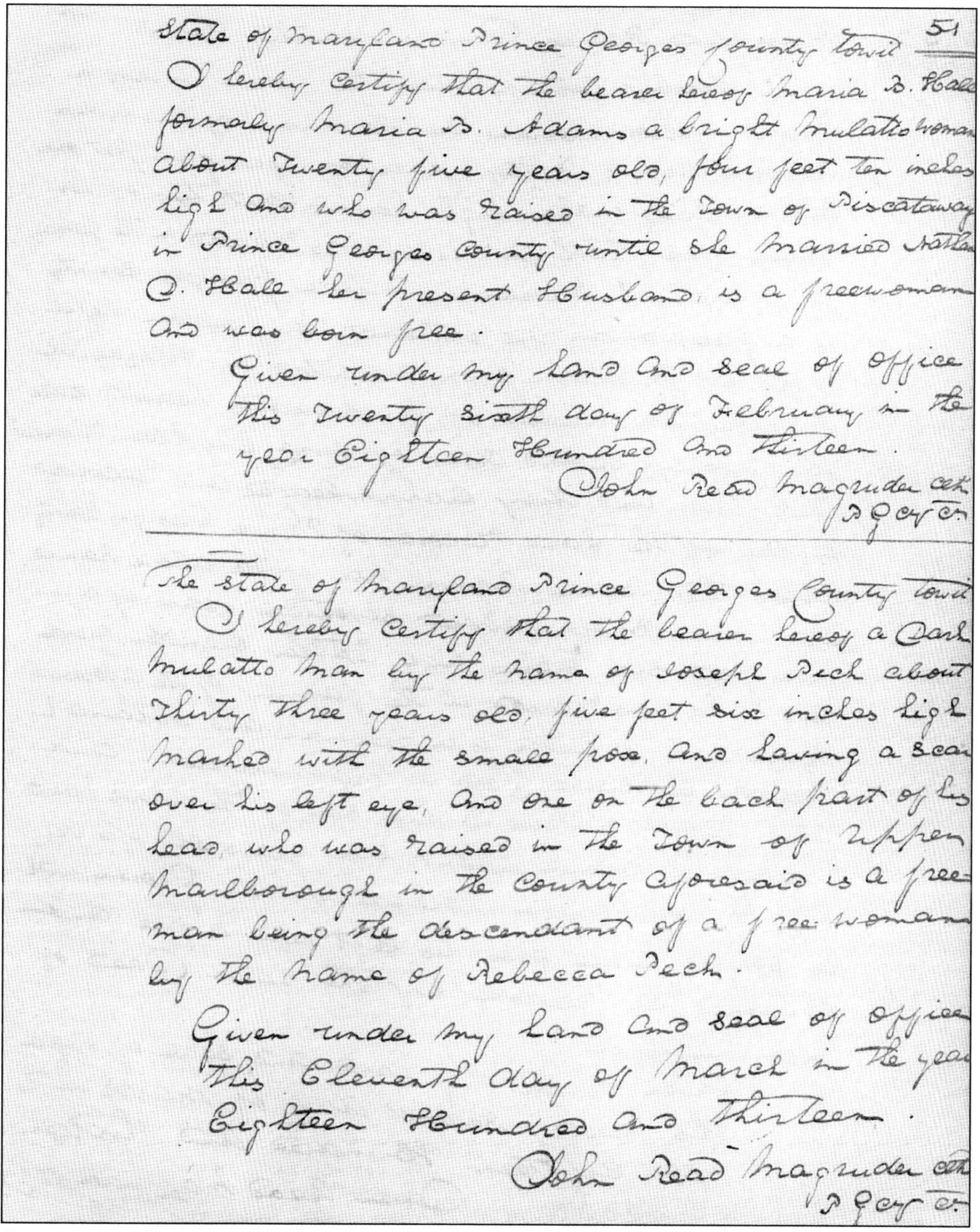

State of Maryland Prince Georges County towit 51

I hereby Certify that the bearer hereof Maria B. Hall formerly Maria B. Adams a bright Mulatto woman about Twenty five years old, four feet ten inches high and who was raised in the Town of Piscataway in Prince Georges County until she married Nathan O. Hall her present Husband is a freewoman and was born free.

Given under my hand and seal of Office this Twenty sixth day of February in the year Eighteen Hundred and Thirteen.

John Read Magruder clk
P G Cy Ct

The state of Maryland Prince Georges County towit

I hereby Certify that the bearer hereof a Dark Mulatto Man by the name of Joseph Peck about Thirty three years old, five feet six inches high marked with the small pox, and having a scar over his left eye, and one on the back part of his head who was raised in the Town of Upper Marlborough in the County aforesaid is a free-man being the descendant of a free woman by the name of Rebecca Peck.

Given under my hand and seal of Office this Eleventh day of March in the year Eighteen Hundred and Thirteen.

John Read Magruder clk
P G Cy Ct

CERTIFICATES OF FREEDOM. Certificates like this were issued according to the following Maryland law: "That from and after the first day of June next [1806], it shall not be lawful for any person or persons, except the clerks of the county courts in the several counties in this state, or register of wills . . . to grant certificates of freedom to any free negro or negroes; and the said clerks and registers are hereby enjoined, when called upon by any negro entitled to freedom, residing in or belonging to, their respective counties, for a certificate thereof, to grant the same under the seal of their respective offices, and to set forth therein the height, age, complexion, the time when such negro became free, the place where he or she, as the case may be, was raised, and such mark or marks as may appear to such clerk or register to be notable in such negro, so applying for his or her certificate of freedom as aforesaid." (Courtesy of the Maryland State Archives.)

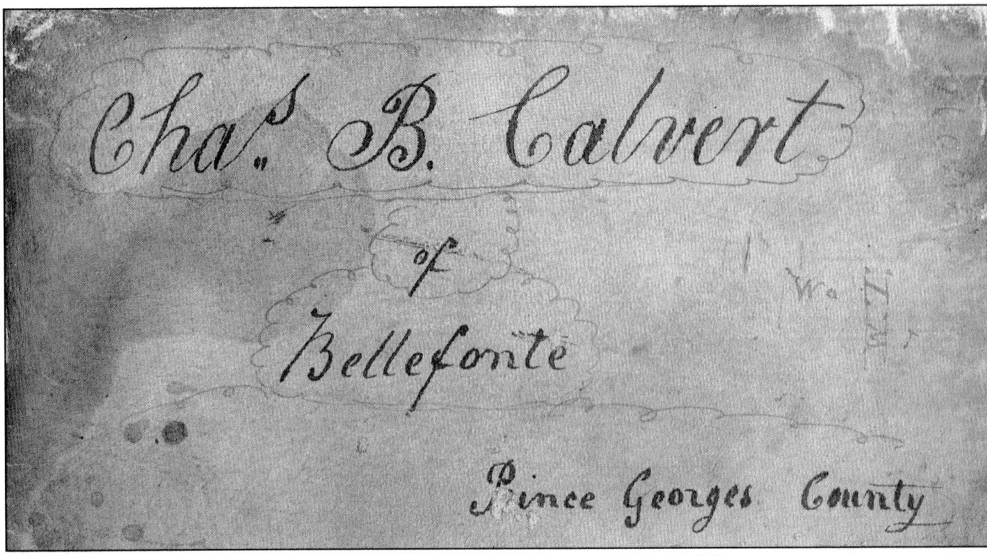

Slaveholder's Account Book. Charles Benedict Calvert (1808–1864) was engaged in agriculture and stock breeding throughout his adult life. He founded the first agricultural research college in America, which later became the Maryland Agricultural College at College Park. He was one of the early advocates for the establishment of the US Department of Agriculture. Calvert was elected as a Unionist to the 37th Congress (1861–1863) to represent all of southern Maryland, including Accokeek. Calvert's account book shows his assessment of the value of 34 of his slaves. The assessments vary according to the slave's age, gender, condition, and skills, from $750 for 40-year-old Isaac to $.01 for 81-year-old Cynthia and 60-year-old Adam. (Both courtesy of University of Maryland Libraries.)

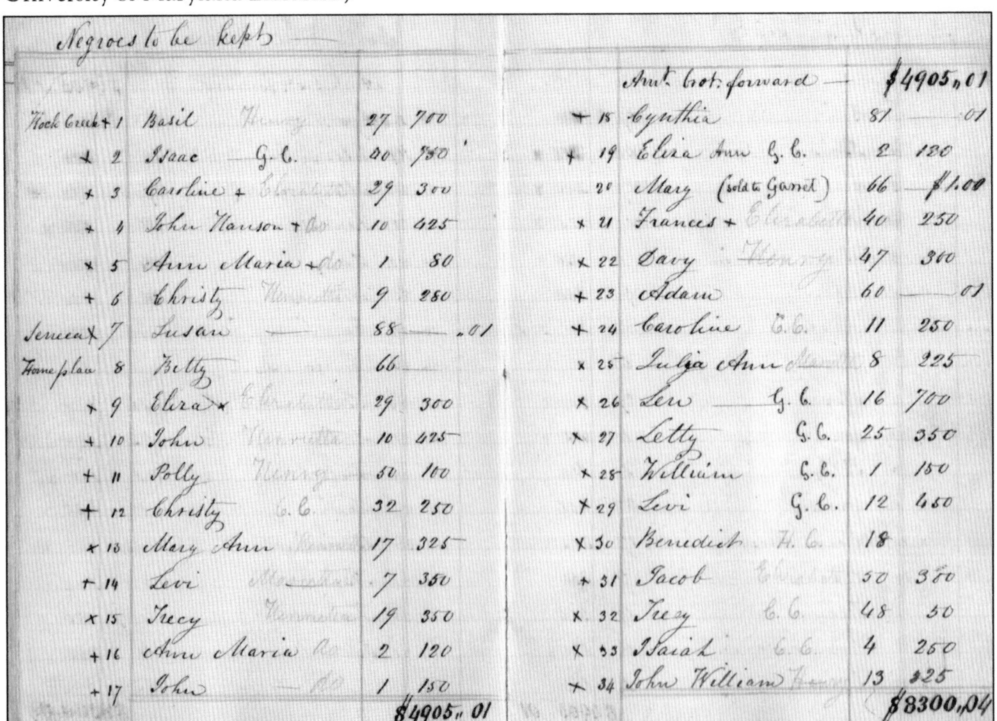

Negroes to be kept

	No.	Name	Age	Value
Hock Creek	+ 1	Basil	27	700
	+ 2	Isaac G. C.	40	750
	+ 3	Caroline +	29	300
	+ 4	John Hanson +	10	425
	+ 5	Ann Maria +	1	80
	+ 6	Christy	9	280
Seneca	+ 7	Susan	88	.01
Home place	8	Betty	66	
	+ 9	Eliza +	29	300
	+ 10	John	10	425
	+ 11	Polly	50	100
	+ 12	Christy	32	250
	+ 13	Mary Ann	17	325
	+ 14	Levi	7	350
	+ 15	Trecy	19	350
	+ 16	Ann Maria	2	120
	+ 17	John	1	150
				$4905.01

No.	Name	Age	Value
	Amt. brot. forward		$4905.01
+ 18	Cynthia	81	.01
+ 19	Eliza Ann G. C.	2	120
20	Mary (sold to Garnet)	66	$1.00
+ 21	Frances +	40	250
+ 22	Davy	47	300
+ 23	Adam	60	.01
+ 24	Caroline C. C.	11	250
+ 25	Julia Ann	8	225
+ 26	Lew G. C.	16	700
+ 27	Letty G. C.	25	350
+ 28	William G. C.	1	150
+ 29	Levi G. C.	12	450
+ 30	Benedict H. C.	18	
+ 31	Jacob	50	350
+ 32	Trecy C. C.	48	50
+ 33	Isaiah C. C.	4	250
+ 34	John William	13	325
			$8300.04

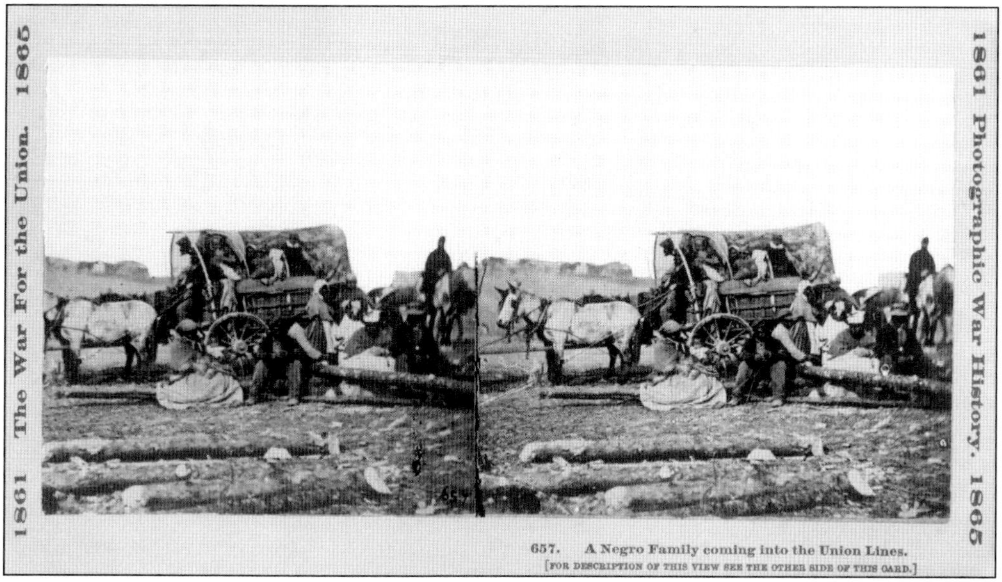

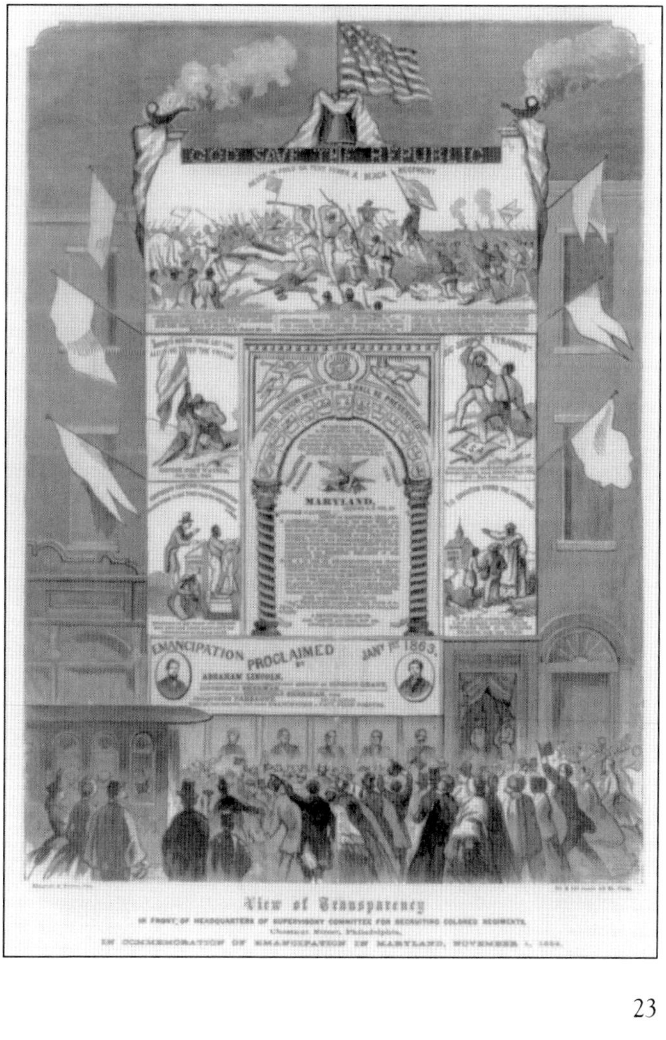

ROUTES TO FREEDOM. The best-known route to freedom from slavery is the Underground Railroad to the north and Canada. Less known is the ability slaves from southern plantations had to gain their freedom by fleeing to Union lines during the Civil War. The Emancipation Proclamation of January 1, 1863, stated that former slaves "of suitable condition will be received into the armed services of the United States to garrison forts, positions, stations, and other places and to man vessels of all sorts." Previously, Pres. Abraham Lincoln had feared offending border states and northern whites and had not allowed blacks to enlist legally in the Union army. Although allowed to fight after January 1, 1863, blacks were placed in their own units, often headed up by white officers. (Both courtesy of the Library of Congress, Prints and Photographs Division.)

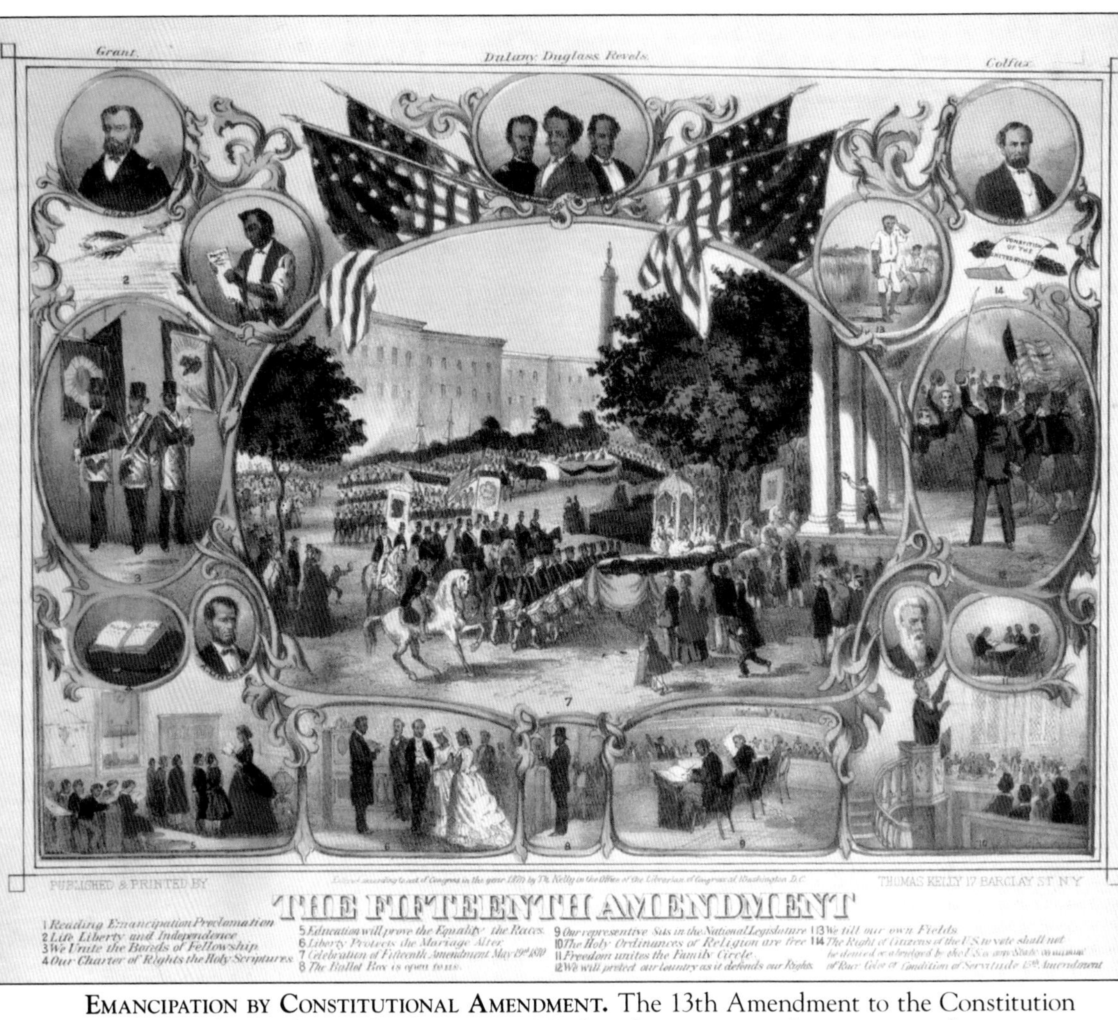

Emancipation by Constitutional Amendment. The 13th Amendment to the Constitution granted freedom to former slaves. It states: "Neither slavery nor involuntary servitude, except as a punishment for crime whereof the party shall have been duly convicted, shall exist within the United States, or any place subject to their jurisdiction." It was passed by the US senate on April 8, 1864, and by the House of Representatives on January 31, 1865, and was adopted on December 6, 1865. The 14th and 15th Amendments granted citizenship and the right to vote to former slaves. In Maryland, slaves were freed by an amendment of the state constitution in October 1864. Maryland governor Augustus Bradford proclaimed the adoption of the new constitution on October 29, and it took effect on November 1, 1864. The vote on the new Maryland constitution on October 12–13, 1864, revealed a division of opinion between citizens of northern Maryland and those on the eastern shore and in southern Maryland. In Prince George's County, 149 voted for and 1,293 voted against. The Charles County vote reflected the opinion of voters in Accokeek and Piscataway, with 13 for and 978 against. (Courtesy of the Library of Congress, Prints and Photographs Division.)

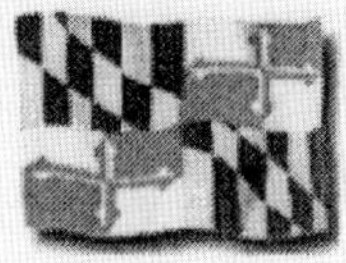

Searching for Ancestors Who Were Slaves:

An Index to the Freedom Records of

Prince George's County Maryland, 1808-1869

by Louise J. Hienton

Maryland State Archives | Summary Description | Help | Search

Huntt, T. I. of the 5th Election District

Declared Charles H. Duckett, age 28, drafted in 1864 at Ellicotts Mills, Md., was not called for, no compensation

Prince George's
Slave Statistics, 1867-1868, p. 189

Edelen, George, a blacksmith, age 40, one leg otherwise good condition

Declared by William H. Gwynn of the 5th Election District

Prince George's
Slave Statistics, 1867-1868, p. 187

SLAVE STATISTICS. Slave Statistics is a register of slaves owned as of November 1, 1864, when the Maryland Constitution of 1864, abolishing slavery, went into effect. The register was compiled in the hope that the federal government would compensate former slaveholders for their "lost property." The Maryland General Assembly of 1867 authorized the compilation of the register. When Democrats gained control of the assembly, they pushed through a new constitution of 1867. This was an effort to rescind part of the "revolution of 1864" by excluding the Negro population in determining legislative apportionment and canceling progressive provisions for education. The new constitution stated that slavery should not be restored but charged the federal government with responsibility for Maryland's emancipation and sought federal compensation. None was forthcoming. (Courtesy of the Maryland State Archives.)

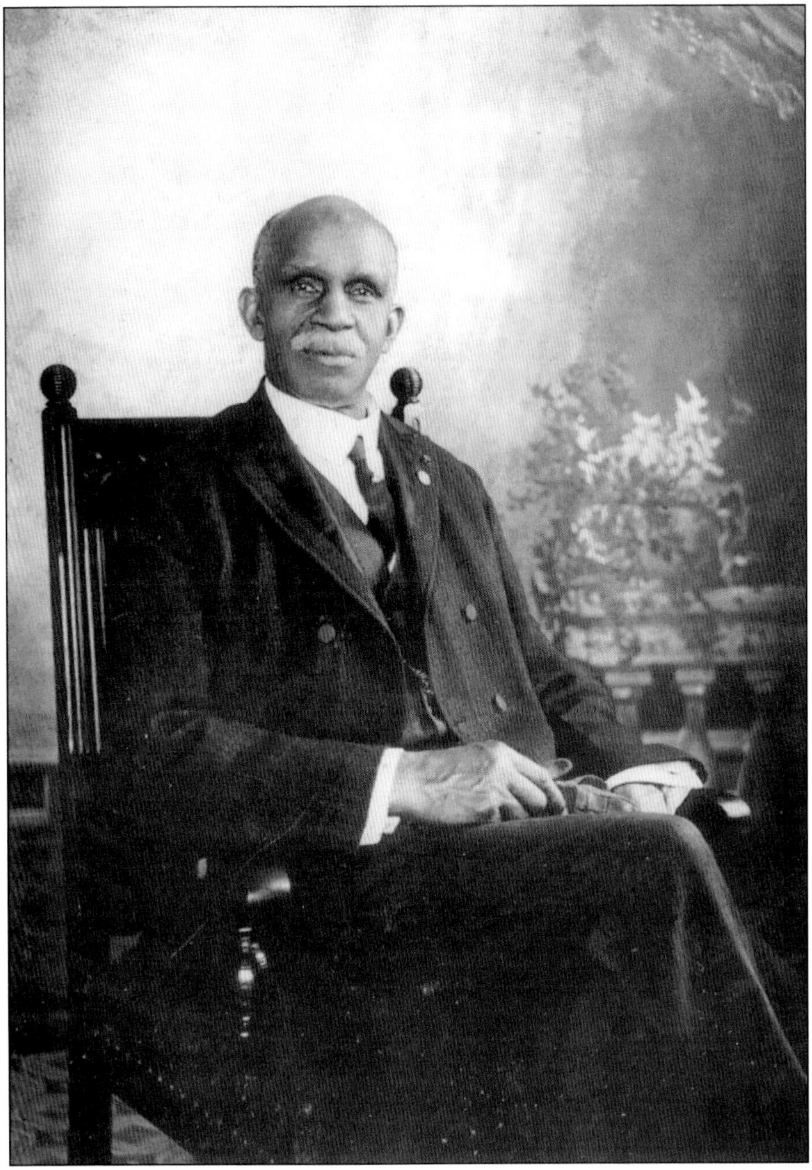

John Edward "Grit" Bruce. John Edward Bruce began life as a slave living along Piscataway Creek. When he was three years old, his father, Robert, was sold and sent to Georgia, never to be heard from again. During the early months of the Civil War, Bruce and his mother, Martha, marched to freedom in the company of Union soldiers to Washington, DC. In Washington, Bruce received both public and private education. Although he enrolled in a three-month course at Howard University, he did not receive much formal education. Nevertheless, he continued to read widely. He was a gifted speaker and writer who attracted the attention of black nationalists such as Marcus Garvey. He wrote columns for 20 black newspapers. Occasionally, his articles appeared in white newspapers, including the *Boston Transcript*, the *Washington Star*, and the *New York Times*. In 1879, Bruce founded his first newspaper, the *Argus*. His writings appeared in publications in Africa, Europe, and the Caribbean. He also wrote two books, as well as hundreds of pamphlets. He died on August 7, 1924. (Courtesy of New York Public Library and the Maryland Historical Society.)

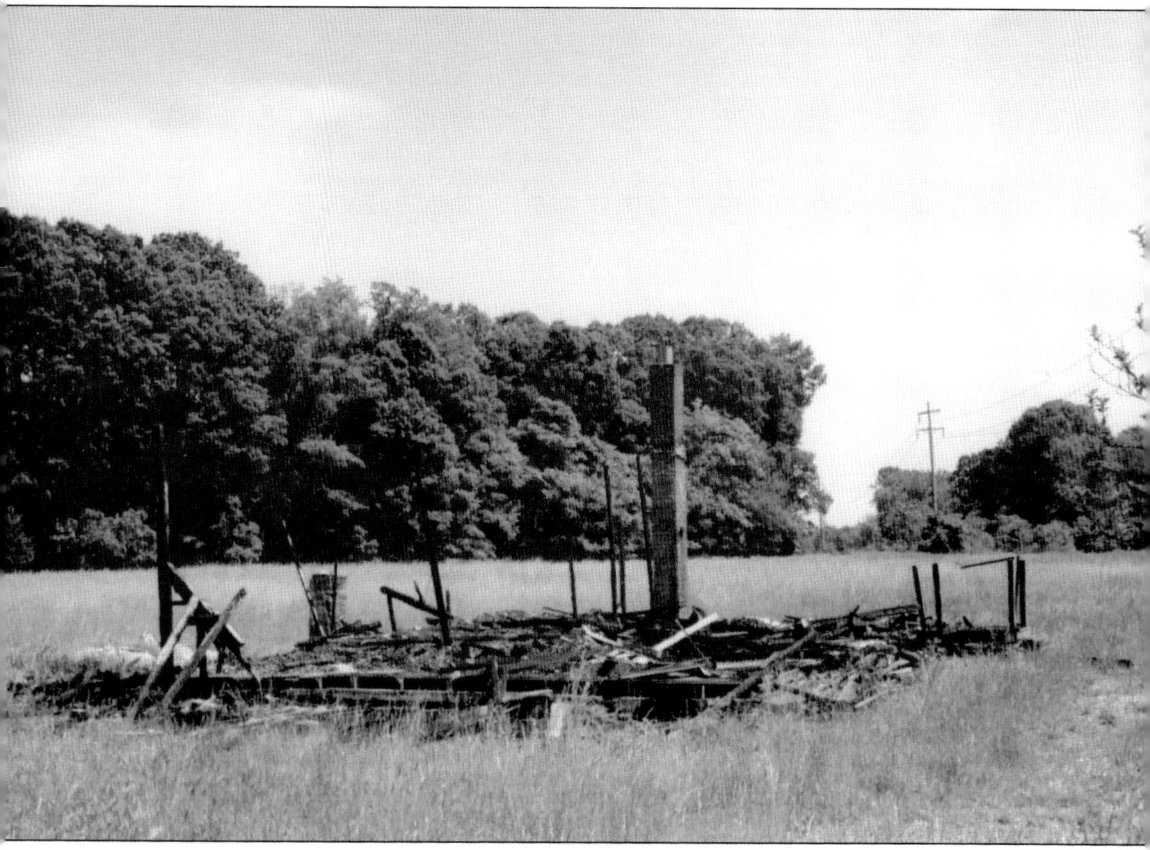

SHARPERSVILLE SCHOOLHOUSE. This was the first schoolhouse built in Accokeek after the period of Freedmen's Bureau schools. A school had been established by the Freedmen's Bureau a short distance to the north in October 1868 with 20 pupils. The Sharpersville schoolhouse is closely associated with Augustus Lancaster (1820–1894). Although he was himself illiterate, his children attended the Freedmen's Bureau school. In 1877, Lancaster purchased 13 acres from William H. Gwynn. Lancaster then offered one acre adjoining his farmhouse to the board of school commissioners for the erection of a new schoolhouse. At times, it served seven grades despite its small size. As other schools were built, students transferred to newer and larger schools, but the Sharpersville school continued to operate until 1940. This landmark of African American heritage was destroyed by fire in 2012. (Author's collection.)

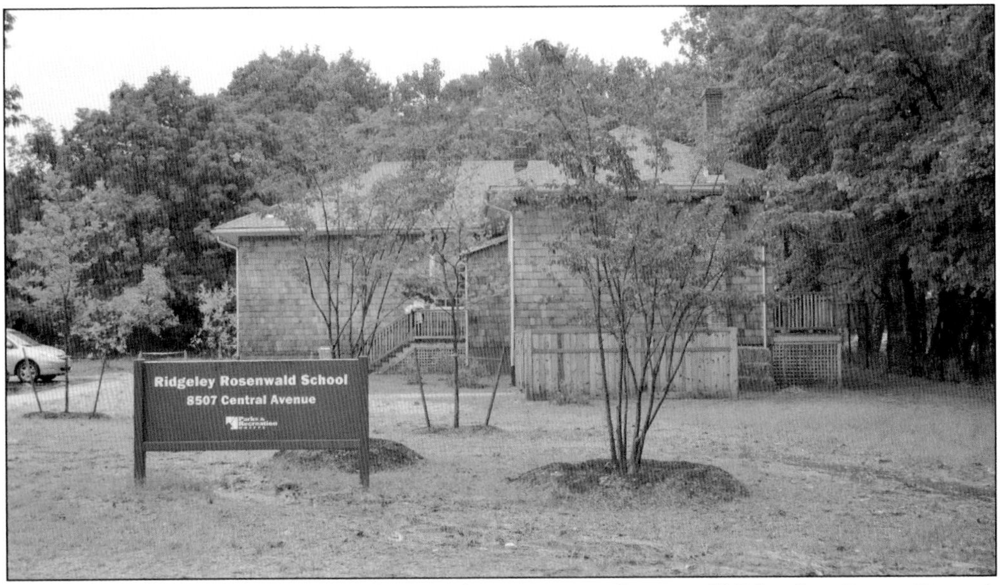

ROSENWALD SCHOOLS. Ridgely School is one of nine surviving Rosenwald Schools in Prince George's County. A total of 5,000 Rosenwald Schools were established throughout the segregated Southern states, including 27 in Prince George's County, by the Rosenwald Fund. The fund's founder, Julius R. Rosenwald (1862–1932), was the president and chairman of the board of Sears, Roebuck & Co. Many Rosenwald Schools were eventually converted to other uses. Ridgely Rosenwald School was established in 1927, and the property was used by the board of education as a bus parking lot for decades. The property was recently restored as a museum and community center by the Maryland–National Capital Park and Planning Commission. The museum, which opened on September 7, 2011, shows how a typical Rosenwald School looked. The film *The Rosenwald Schools*, made by Aviva Kempner, illustrates the legacy of Julius Rosenwald. See www.rosenwaldschoolsfilm.org for more information. (Both photographs by Rachel Lesaar; courtesy of Aviva Kempner.)

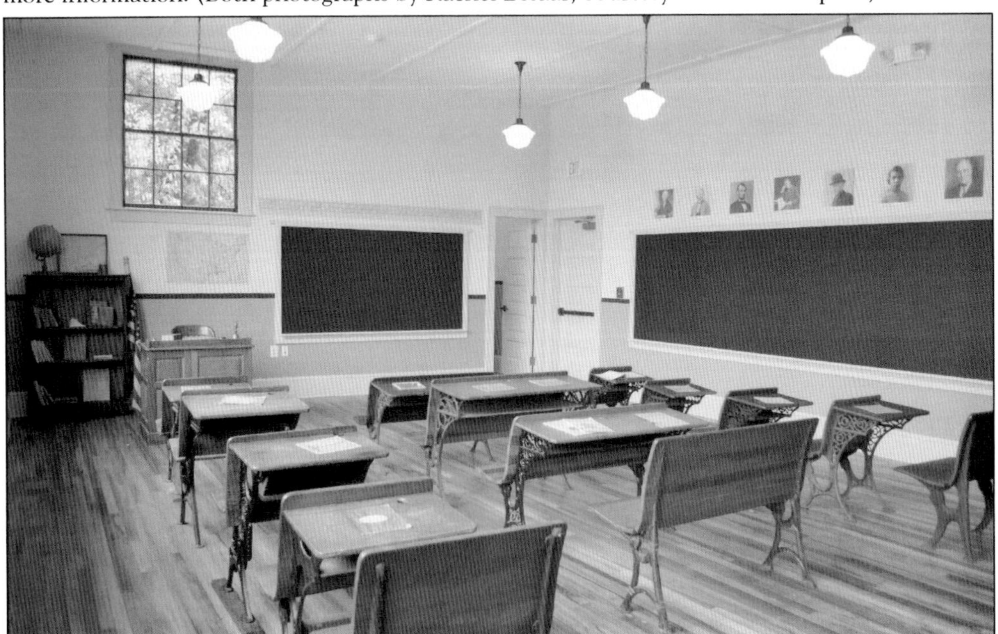

Three

THE CIVIL WAR AND ITS AFTERMATH

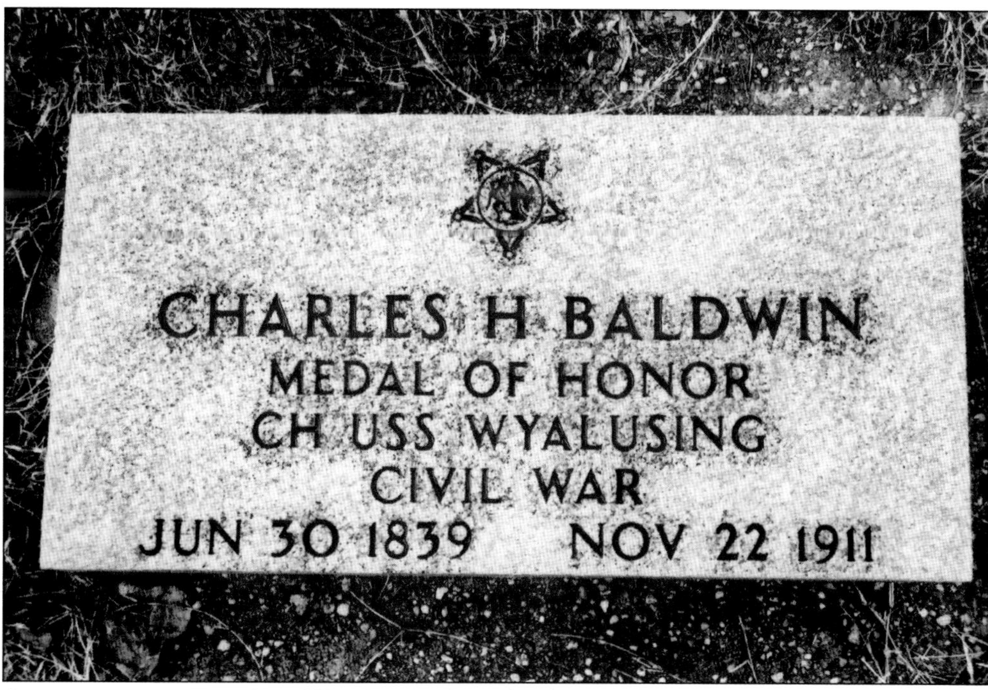

ACOOKEEK DURING THE CIVIL WAR. No Civil War battles were fought in Accokeek, but its residents fought for both the Union and the Confederacy. Graves of two Union and two Confederate soldiers are in the graveyard of St. Mary's Catholic Church in Piscataway Historic Village. The grave of Charles H. Baldwin, an enlisted man in the Navy, is in the graveyard of Christ Episcopal Church in Accokeek. (Author's collection.)

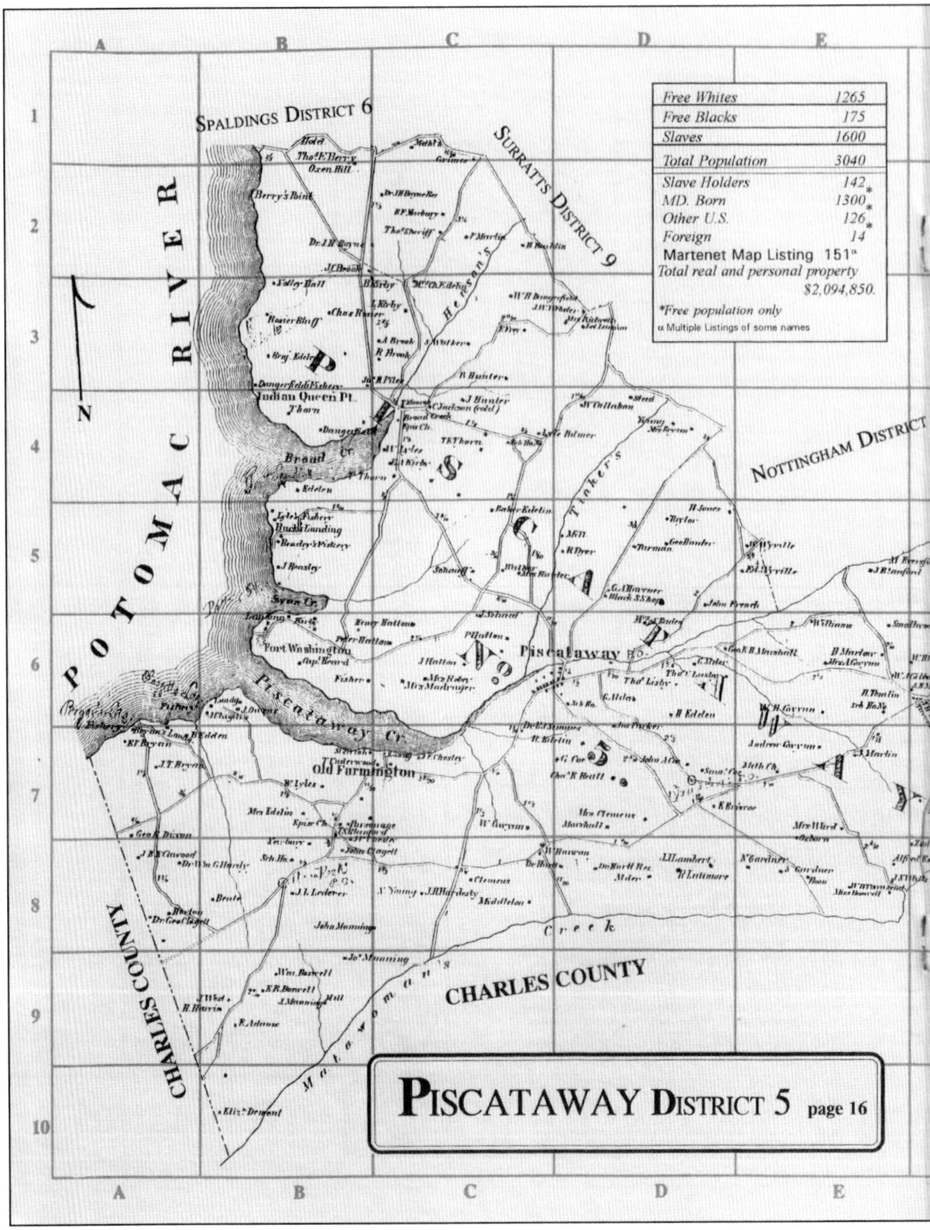

ACCOKEEK, 1861. This map, adapted from Martenet's Map of Prince George's County, Maryland, shows Accokeek and the surrounding area of Election District 5 (Piscataway). The area now known as Accokeek is between Piscataway Creek and Matawoman's Creek on the 1861 map. Names of selected landowners are seen on the map, along with landmarks such as "Epis Ch" (Episcopal church), "Sch Ho." (schoolhouse), "AccoKeek P.O." (Accokeek post office) and some landings and fisheries. The box at the upper right was taken from the 1860 census for the Piscataway district. Out of a total population of 3,040, there were 1,600 slaves and only 175 free blacks. Only 142 of the 1,265 free whites were slaveholders. Of the free population, 90 percent had been born in Maryland. Accokeek in 1861 was a rural area where agriculture dominated the economy. Although tobacco remained predominant, farmers throughout the county began to experiment with new crops on worn-out land. (Courtesy of the Prince George's County Historical Society.)

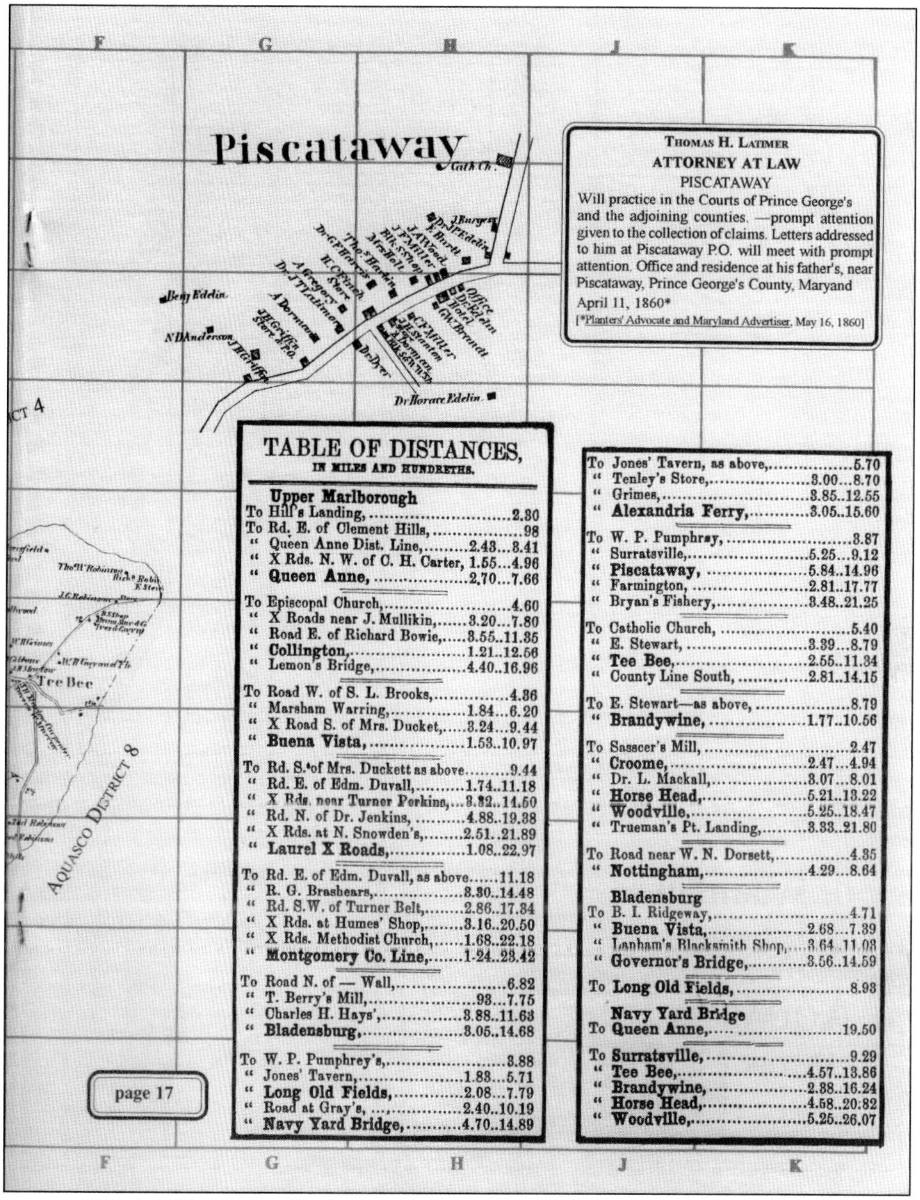

PISCATAWAY, 1861. The area called Piscataway at the top left of this map corresponds to what is now the Piscataway Village Historic District. Then, as now, it consisted of a small number of residences as well as stores, blacksmith shops, a hotel, doctor's offices, and a Catholic church. After the Civil War, the loss of slave labor led to the decline of the plantation system and the creation of a number of small farms, many of which were owned by former slaves. For as long as agriculture prospered, Piscataway continued to provide services to area residents and travelers. By 1890, the population of the village was on the decline. Nearly one-third of the buildings had lost their usefulness and had fallen into states of deterioration. In 1900, the occupations of heads of households in Piscataway included four farmers, four merchant farmers, two merchants, two government employees, two gardeners, one physician, one mail carrier, one blacksmith, one tobacco buyer, one domestic, and one laborer. (Courtesy of the Prince George's County Historical Society.)

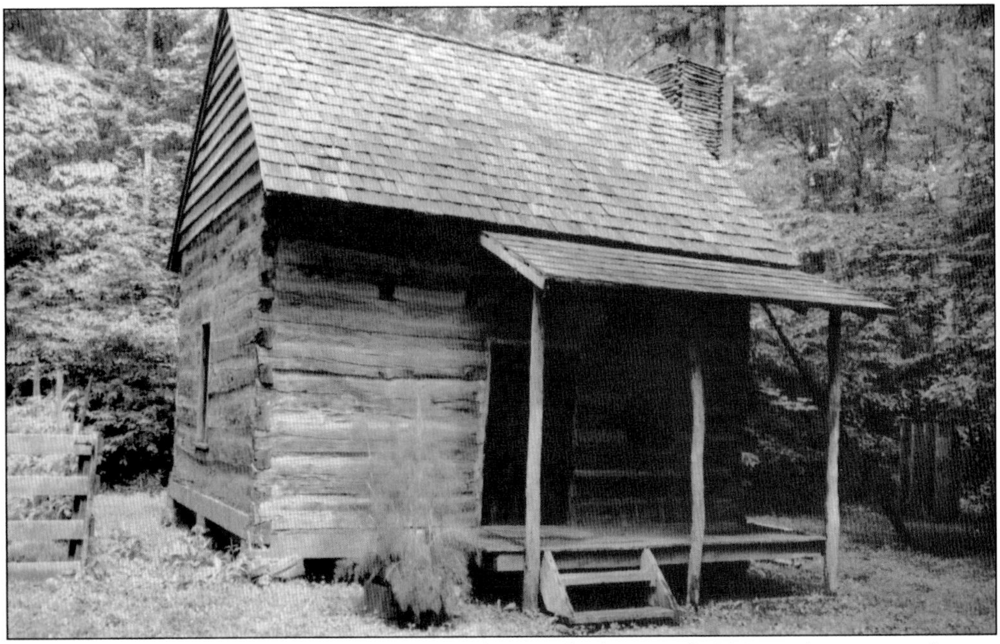

Farm Tenant House. This hand-hewn log cabin was built around 1880 as a farm tenant house. It represents the standard style for most low-income households of the late 1800s. The Trueman family's oral history attributes the construction of this cabin to former slave Charles Duckett. In 1864, Duckett enlisted in the Union army, joining the 19th Regiment of Colored Troops, Company I. When he was discharged in 1866, Duckett worked as a farmhand on the Trueman property in Aquasco. He built this cabin around 1880, when he married Judith Blake Cross, also a former slave. The cabin was occupied until the 1920s. In the 1970s, the Trueman family donated the abandoned cabin to the Maryland–National Capital Park and Planning Commission. The restored cabin is now part of the Rural Life Museum. (Both, author's collection.)

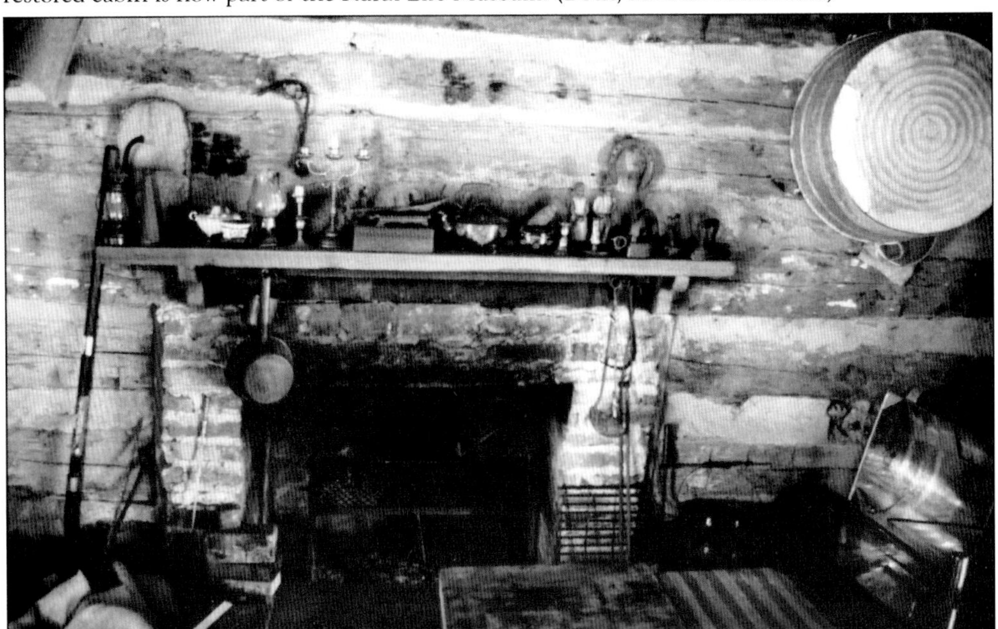

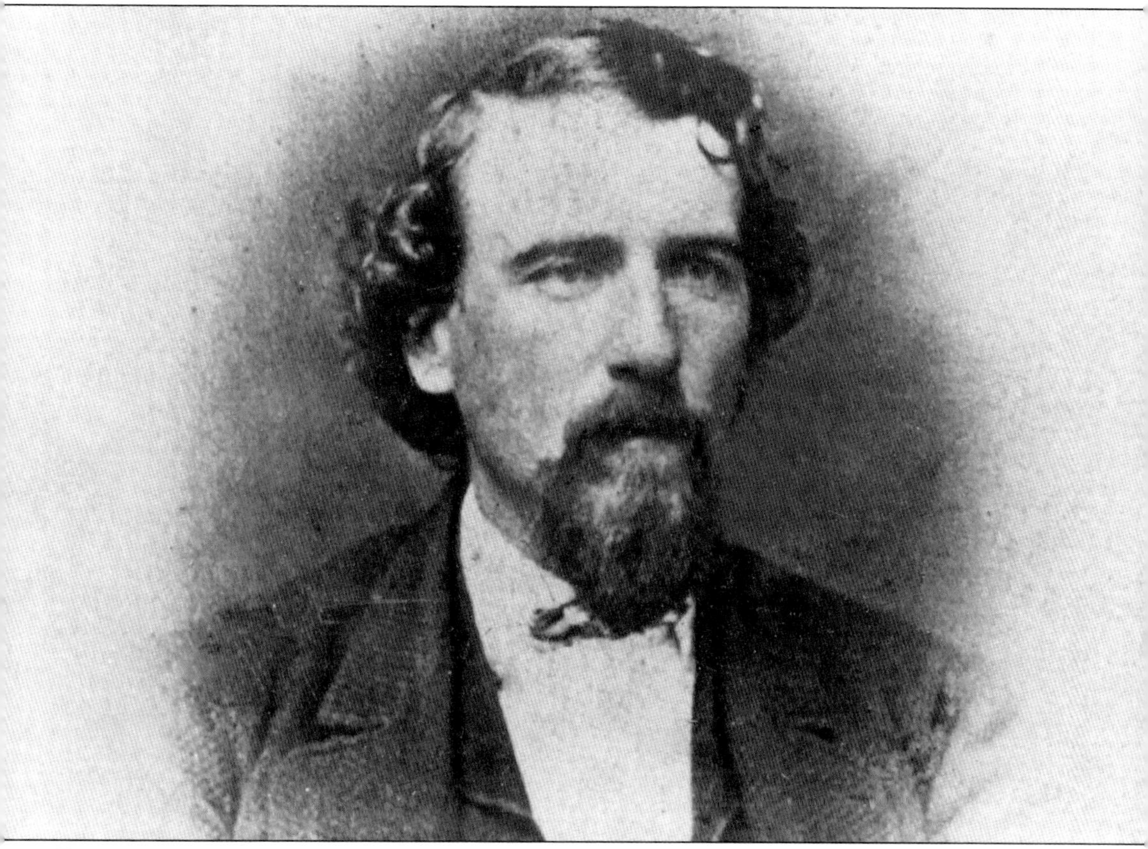

Thomas H. Harbin. Thomas Harbin (1833–1885) lived in Piscataway Village, where he was the proprietor of a hotel, Harbin House, which later became the Piscataway Tavern. He was a Confederate spy who was involved in a plot to kidnap President Lincoln. Harbin reported directly to Jefferson Davis using the alias Thomas Wilson during his time as a spy. On July 9, 1865, the *Baltimore American* published a confession of George Atzerodt admitting Harbin's involvement in the conspiracy to kidnap the president. Harbin was never charged with the crime. He returned to Washington in the late 1860s, where he worked as a desk clerk at the National Hotel. In an 1885 interview, he admitted involvement in the Lincoln assassination plot and told how he came to meet John Wilkes Booth. On November 18, 1885, Harbin died of cirrhosis of the liver at the age of 52. He is buried at Mount Olivet Cemetery in Washington, DC. (Courtesy of Joan Chaconas, Surratt House Museum.)

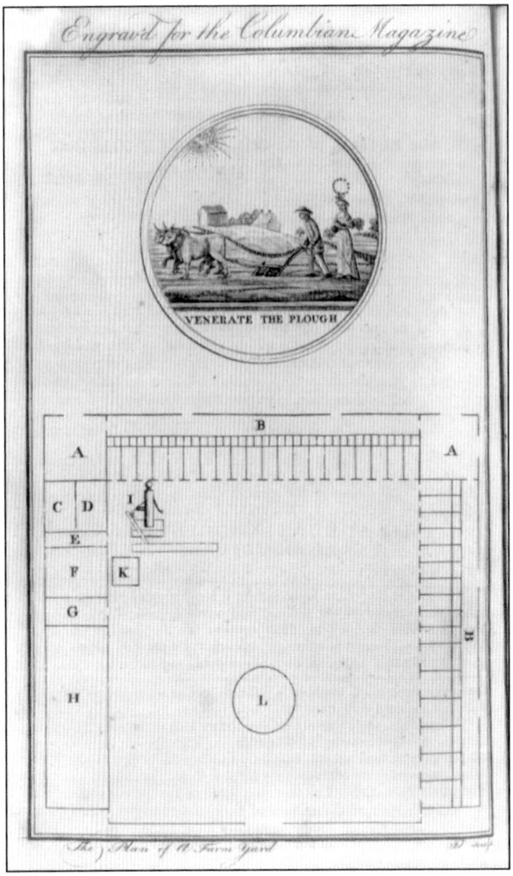

Venerate the Plough. This 18th-century engraving for *Columbian* magazine touts the virtue of farming. In Accokeek, widespread use of the plough transformed the landscape. Silt filled Piscataway Creek, making it impossible for boats to pass. Other areas became swampy. Ecological damage continued in the 19th century with the introduction of chemical fertilizers and pesticides. (Courtesy of the Library of Congress, Prints and Photographs Division.)

Bunting the Seine. This photograph shows the abundance of fish in the Potomac River. The noticeable decrease in the fish population after the Civil War led to the creation of the US Commission of Fish and Fisheries in 1871. The commission was established to protect, study, manage, and restore the fish population. (Courtesy of NOAA, Historic Fisheries Collection; archival photographer Stefan Claesson.)

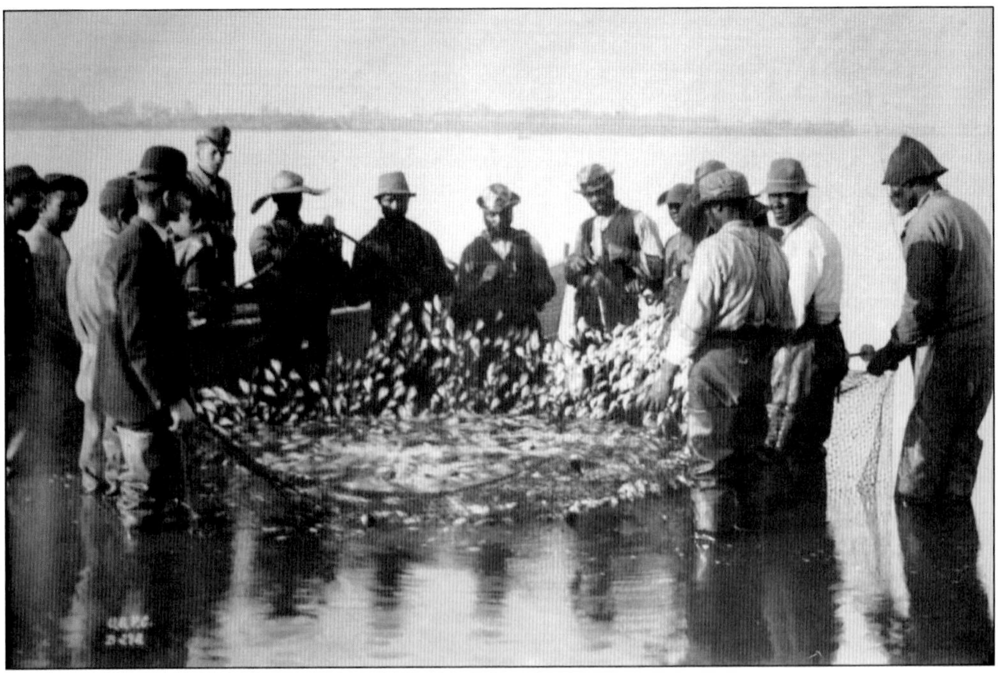

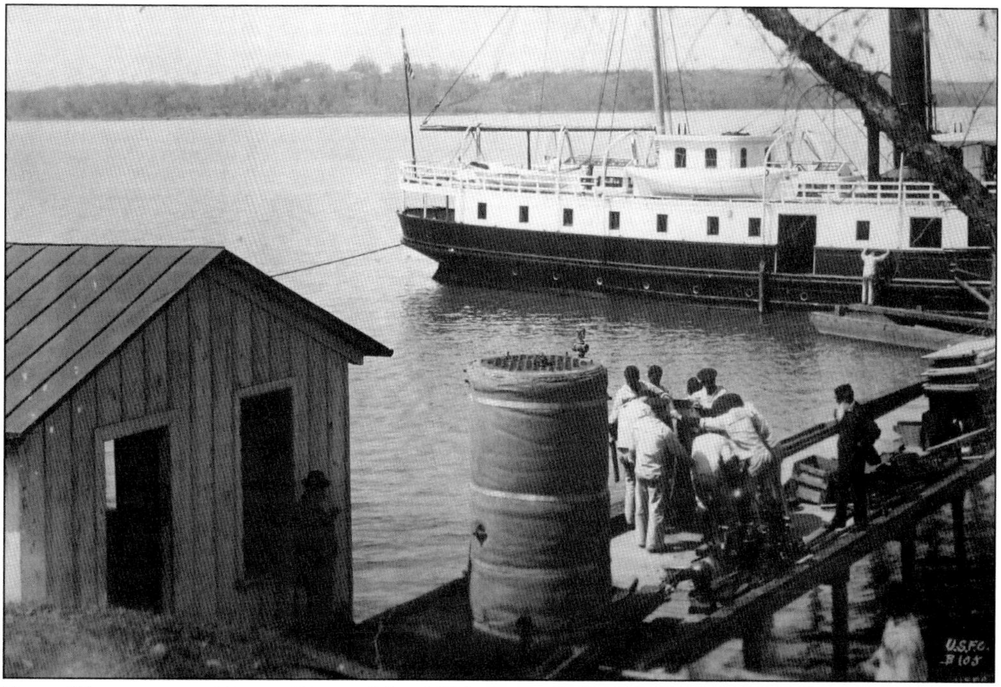

SHAD HATCHERY AT BRYAN POINT. The 1897 report of the US Commission of Fish and Fisheries describes the establishment of the shad hatchery at Bryan Point. During the summer and fall, a hatchery with a capacity for 40 million shad eggs was erected. The laying of submarine mines at Fort Washington during the Spanish-American War made it impossible to go up and down the river at the proper times. Nonetheless, the work was pushed so vigorously that, by May 26, the total collection amounted to 68,724,000. The number of shad fry hatched was 47,306,000. These were then planted in the Potomac River between Broad Run and Occoquan Creek. (Both courtesy of NOAA, Historic Fisheries Collection; archival photographer Stefan Claesson.)

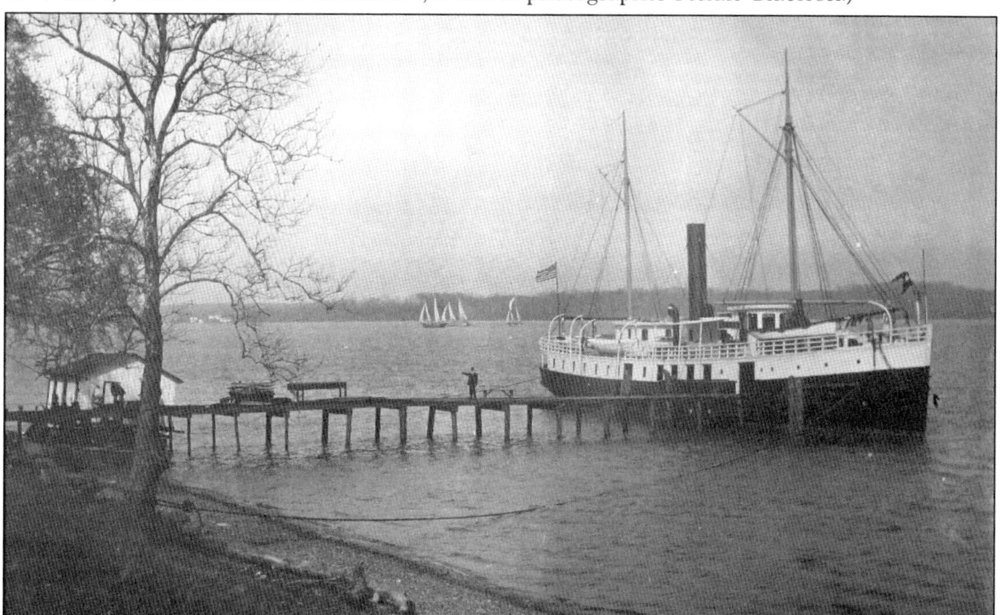

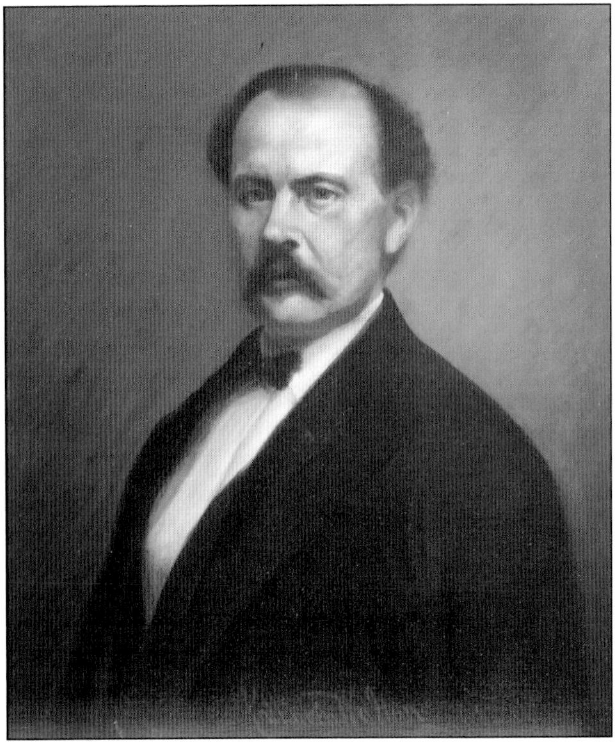

Oden Bowie, Maryland Governor 1869–1872. Bowie was born in 1826 at his family's 1,000-acre estate, Fairview, in Prince George's County. Although he was an ardent Democrat and a warm sympathizer of the South, he opposed secession. In the election of November 5, 1867, Bowie received 63,694 of the 85,744 votes cast. He carried with him into office a legislature with no Republican members. This portrait was painted by Katherine Walton in 1912. (Courtesy of the Maryland State Archives.)

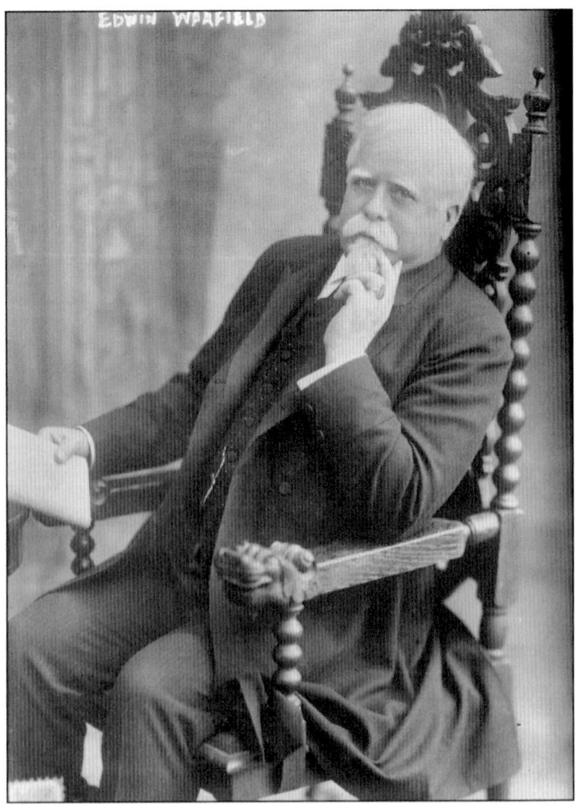

Edwin Warfield, Maryland Governor 1904–1908. Warfield was born in 1848 at Oakdale plantation in Howard County. During his tenure, he opposed the Gorman Amendment to the Maryland Constitution, which would have effectively disenfranchised all black voters in the state. The bill easily passed in the Democrat-controlled legislature, but Warfield refused to sign it into law. When it was put to the public, it was defeated. (Courtesy of the Library of Congress, Prints and Photographs Division.)

Four

ALICE FERGUSON AND "FERGIE'S GANG"

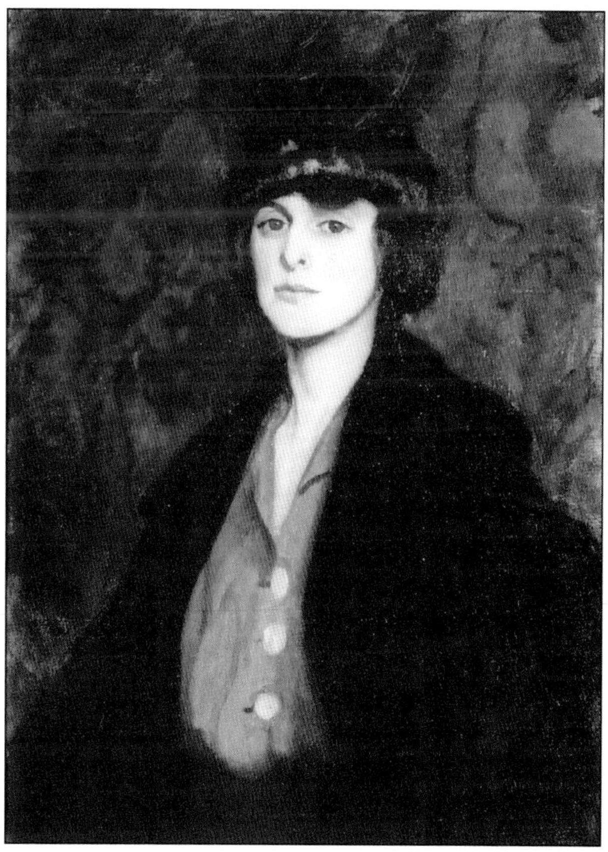

ALICE FERGUSON. Alice Lescinzka Lowe Ferguson (1880–1951), the wife of Henry G. Ferguson, was a dynamic, creative artist who trained as a painter at the Corcoran School of Art in Washington, DC. This portrait of her was painted by Burdis Baker, her teacher at Corcoran. (Photograph by Alexandra Tice, courtesy of the Alice Ferguson Foundation.)

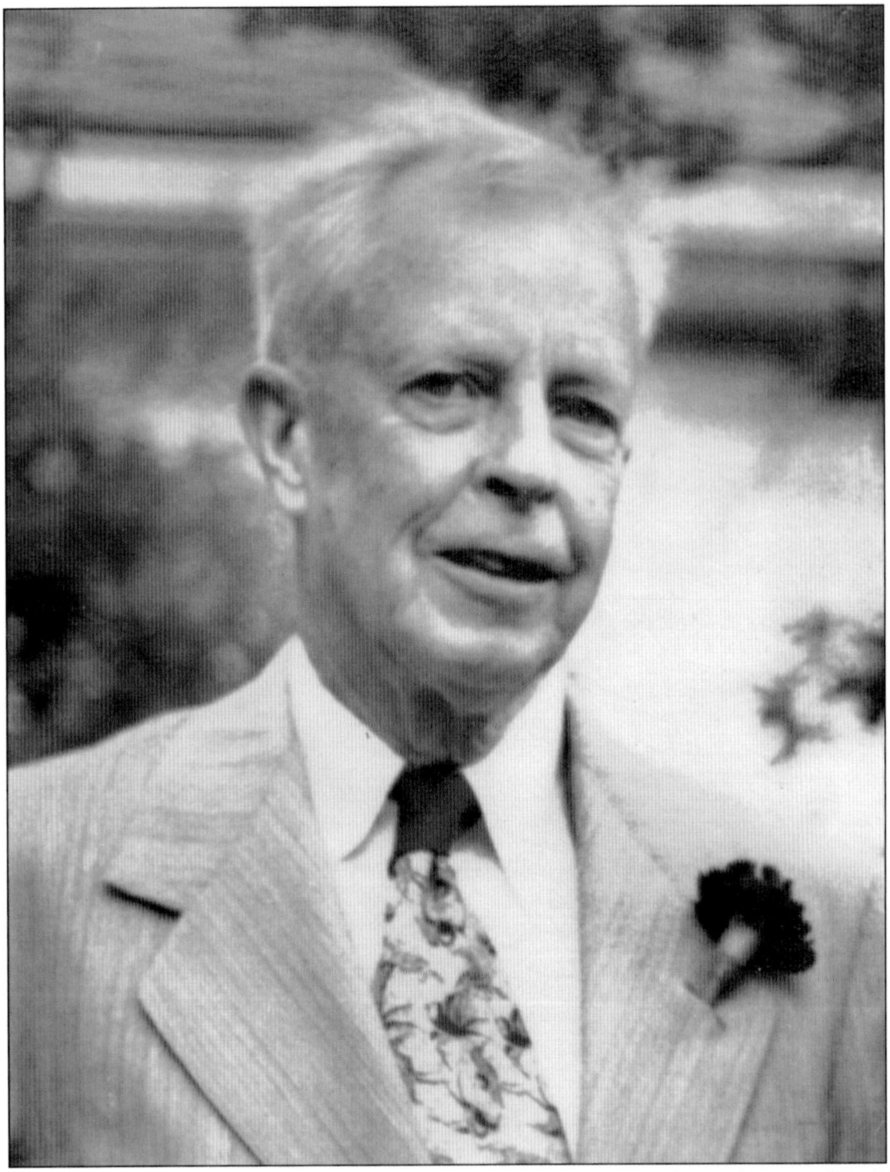

HENRY G. "FERGIE" FERGUSON. Henry Gardiner Ferguson (1882–1966) was the son of Dr. Henry Ferguson, an Episcopalian minister. The younger Ferguson was a well-known US Geological Survey geologist. He married Alice in September 1914 at St. Paul's Episcopal Church in Washington. The groom's father conducted the ceremony. After their wedding, the couple lived on California Street in northwest Washington, DC. In 1922, the Fergusons acquired a 139-acre farm in Accokeek with breathtaking views of the Potomac River and George Washington's estate, Mount Vernon. The property had been named Hard Bargain by a previous owner and the land and buildings were in poor condition. The farm became a place where the couple would bring their friends and entertain them on weekends. The farm was Alice's passion, where she developed her creative forces as a painter, architect, garden planner, writer, amateur archeologist, environmental conservationist, and philanthropist. After her death, Henry established the Alice Ferguson Foundation in her memory. Regarding this photograph, Nancy Wagner noted, "Fergie didn't always look this good." (Courtesy of Nancy and Holly Wagner.)

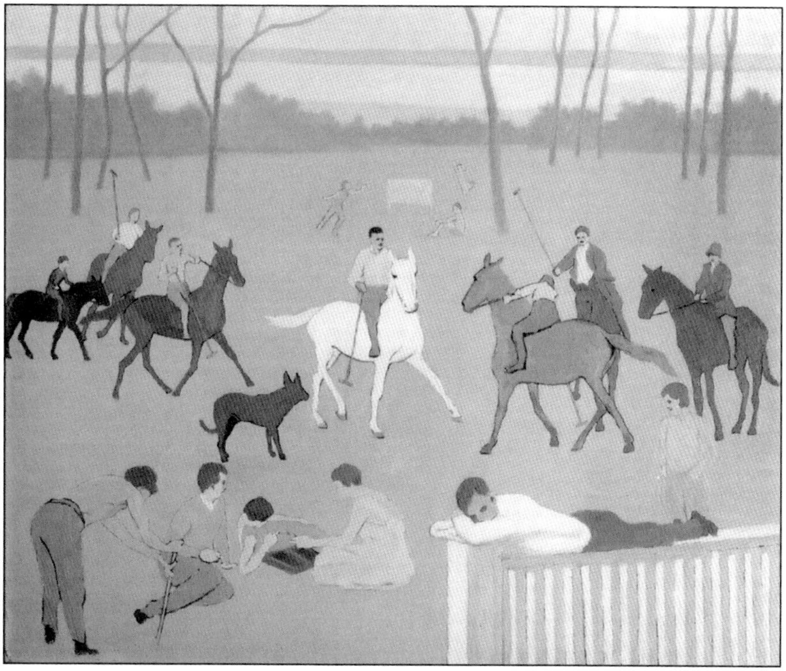

Paintings by Alice. These are two of the many paintings by Alice Ferguson. *A Day at the Farm* (above) shows a polo game. Below, bathers are seen at *The Frog Pond*, a swimming area in a small stream on Hard Bargain Farm that was often enjoyed by "Fergie's gang" and guests. The water was very cold, but they apparently enjoyed it. On weekends during the pre–World War II years, a fascinating assortment of guests came to Hard Bargain, including geologists, archeologists, artists, architects, a few professors, and an occasional priest or nun. Elizabeth Kenah recalls a volleyball game in 1940: "The game was played all over the field. There was no need for a net. It was an intriguing afternoon." (Both photographs by Alexandra Tice, courtesy of the Alice Ferguson Foundation.)

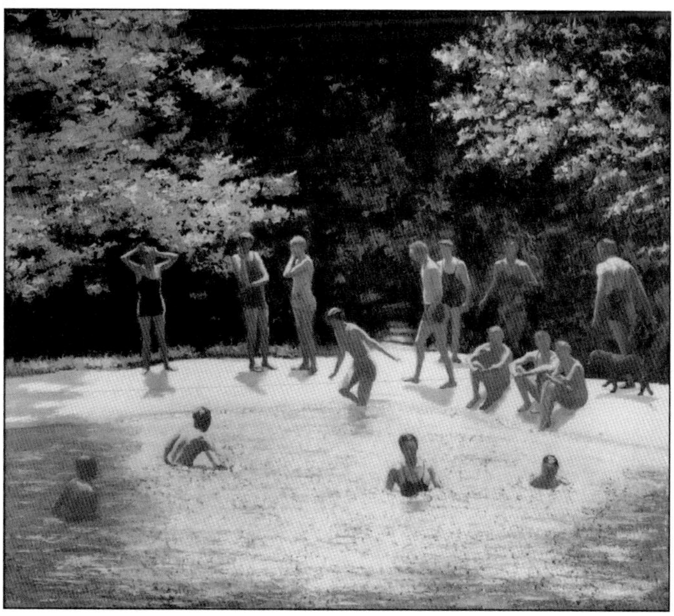

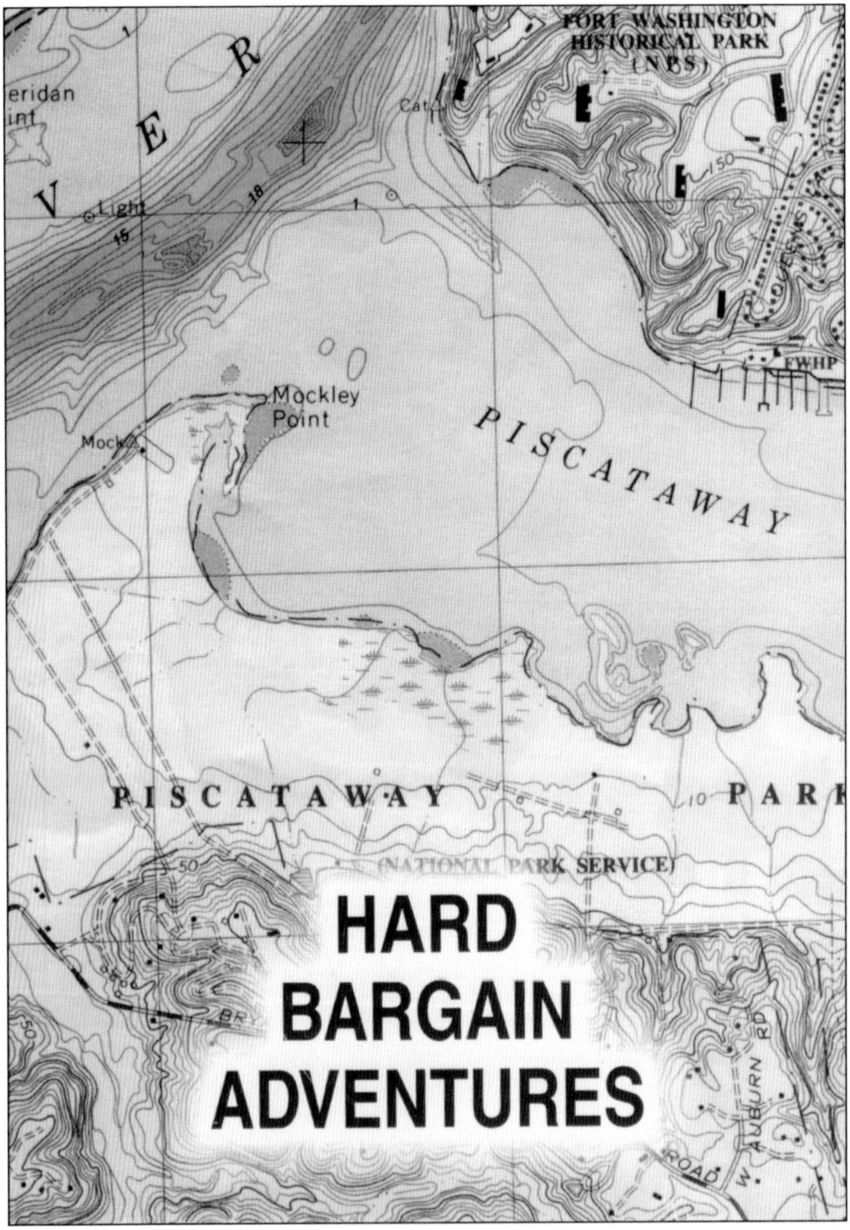

The End of the Gang and the War Years. According to Henry G. Ferguson's *Hard Bargain Adventures*, "One sunny afternoon on Sunday in December the gang was out in full force. Alice gave them a particularly delicious lunch and then they had a grand game of volleyball. Alice didn't play, staying indoors to listen to the radio. The game was well advanced. She came out and interrupted with the news of Pearl Harbor. We got on with the game but the spunk was out of it. The gang never really got together again. Bobby [Straus] lived on his yacht in Newport News where he took control of the storage depot belonging to the Navy. Charlie [Wagner] and Jack [Kennedy] had Navy commissions and both had distinguished records largely in the Pacific. Jack at one time was in command of an experimental boat and after the war there was a very amusing article in the *New Yorker* that was afterwards made into a movie." (Courtesy of the Alice Ferguson Foundation.)

The Farmhouse at Hard Bargain. Alice Ferguson designed and built the farmhouse at Hard Bargain Farm. It replaced the original farmhouse, which was in poor condition when the property was purchased from the original owner in 1922. The view at right of the front of the house was taken in the 1930s. The photograph below, from the back of the house, shows some of the breathtaking view of the then-unpolluted Potomac River. The woman seated on the stone bench is Alice Ferguson. The woman standing is probably her sister Edith Lowe. Alice managed the working farm, which is still operating today, and created a Country Place Era–style formal garden. (Both courtesy of the Alice Ferguson Foundation.)

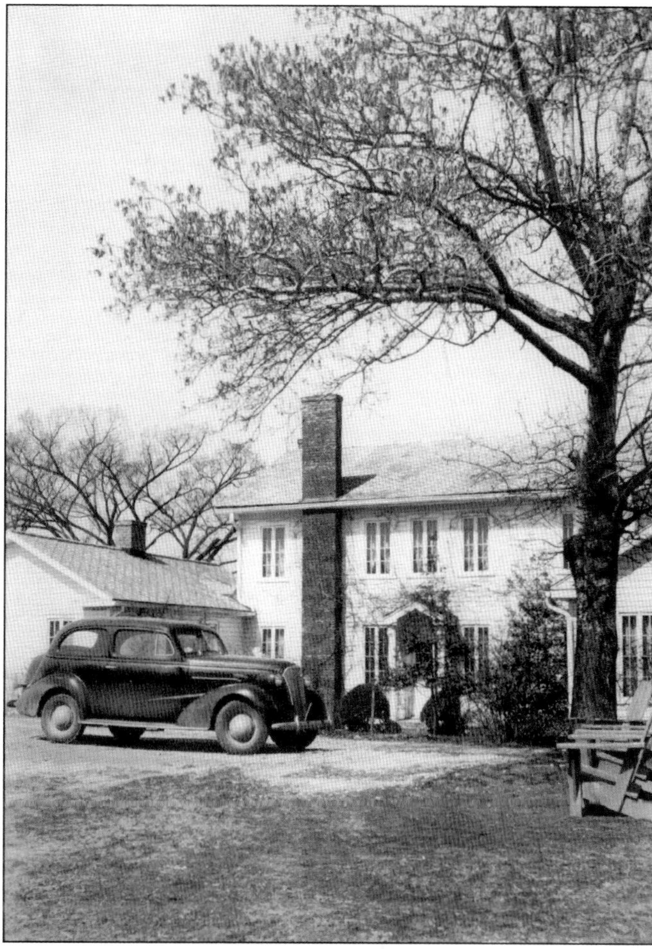

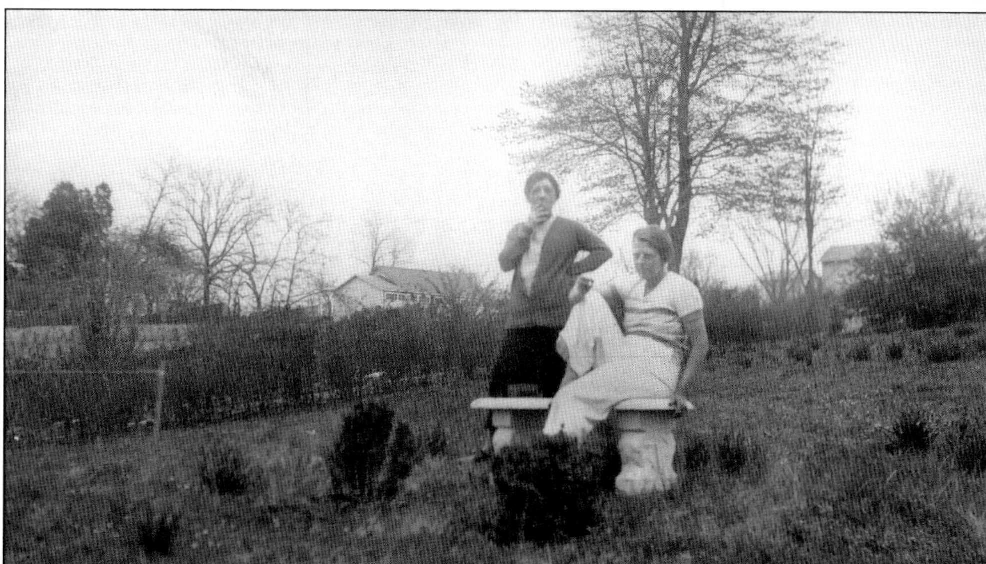

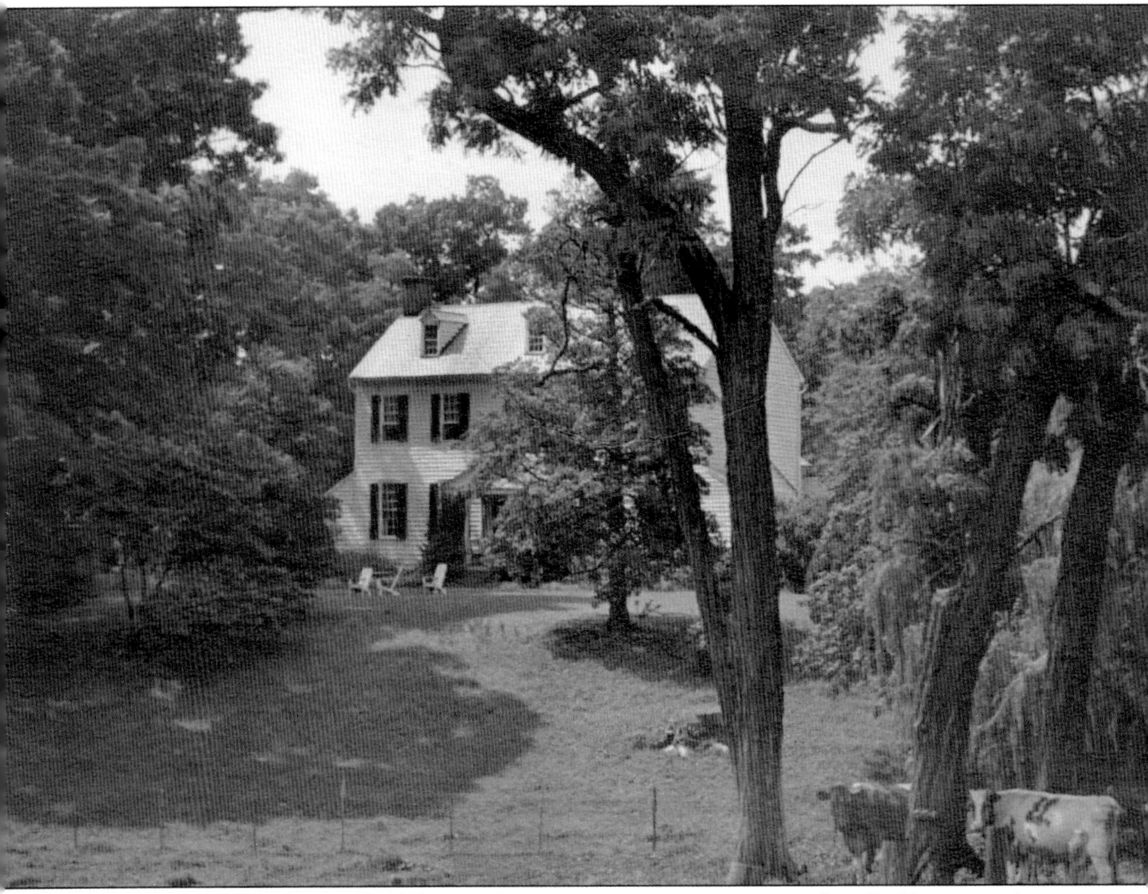

Longview. Next door to Hard Bargain Farm was a property appropriately called Longview because of the magnificent view up the river to Washington. Alice Ferguson had built a house there and offered the property for sale. Her intent was to attract a "gentleman farmer" with a point of view similar to hers to help with community needs. Failing that, she was looking for tenants. The young group living there in 1935 included Sally Ringe, Lenore Thomas, Charles Wagner, and a revolving number of young visitors. From 1935 to 1942, Sally Ringe had belonged to a Communist Party study group. After her marriage to Jonathon Goldmark, a Harvard Law School graduate and distinguished Navy veteran, the couple moved to Washington State. Jonathan Goldmark became involved in politics and was elected to the Washington State Legislature. Two decades later, Sally would speak of her activism as a youthful indiscretion. "I think I made a mistake," she would insist, adding that, in any case, she was never "fully committed" to the party. (Courtesy of Juli Whyte; caption based on material in *The Moyaone Reserve* by G.L. Hanssen.)

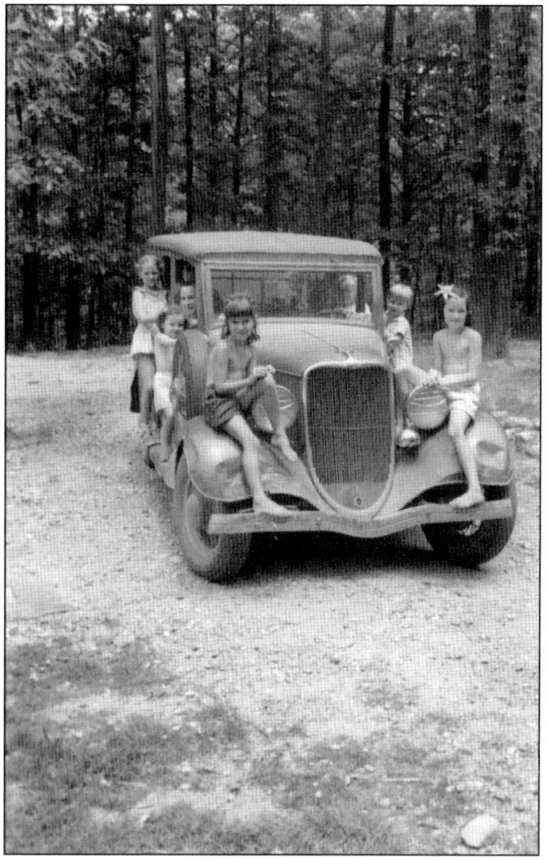

The Egg Route. Hard Bargain was, and continues to be, a working farm. Elizabeth Kenah recalled: "Another thing which interested me was the egg route. The children were allowed to hang on the running board, the fenders, and sit on the tailgate. And then they would go to the river to cool off." The children in the 1953 photograph at right are, from left to right, Karen Kenah (standing), Jo Ann Fowler (standing), Mary Alice Fowler (sitting on the fender), Carla Kenah (visible through the windshield), Chris Fowler (the boy standing) and Cathy Hughes (sitting). The adults are Henry "Fergie" Ferguson (driving) and Mrs. Mary B. Fowler (passenger). The photograph below shows Nancy Wagner, the new owner, with unidentified students from the Canterbury School. (Both courtesy of the Alice Ferguson Foundation.)

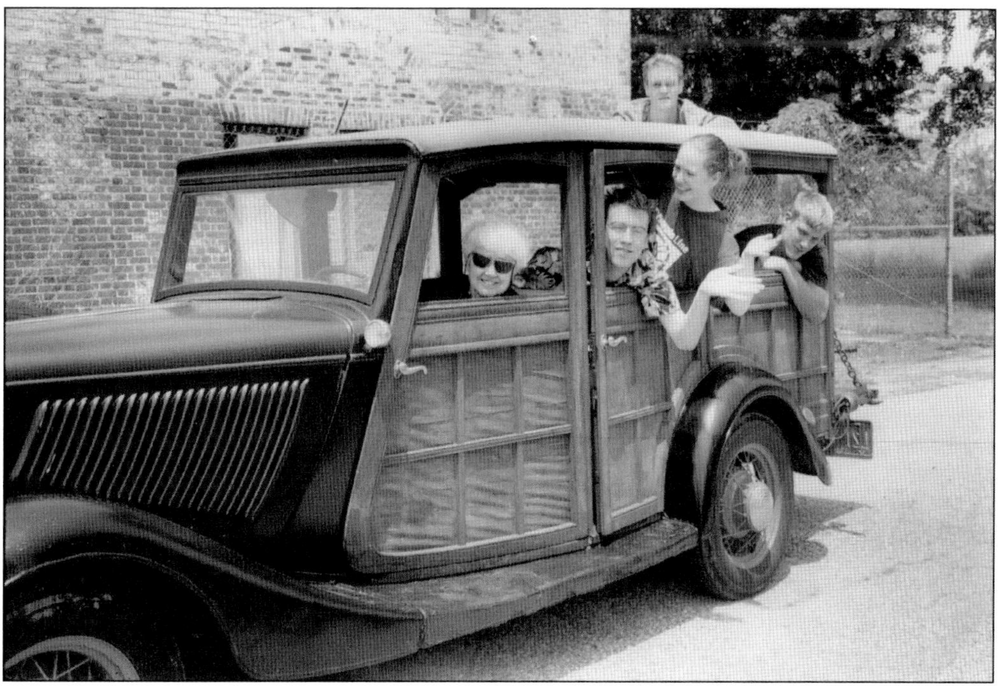

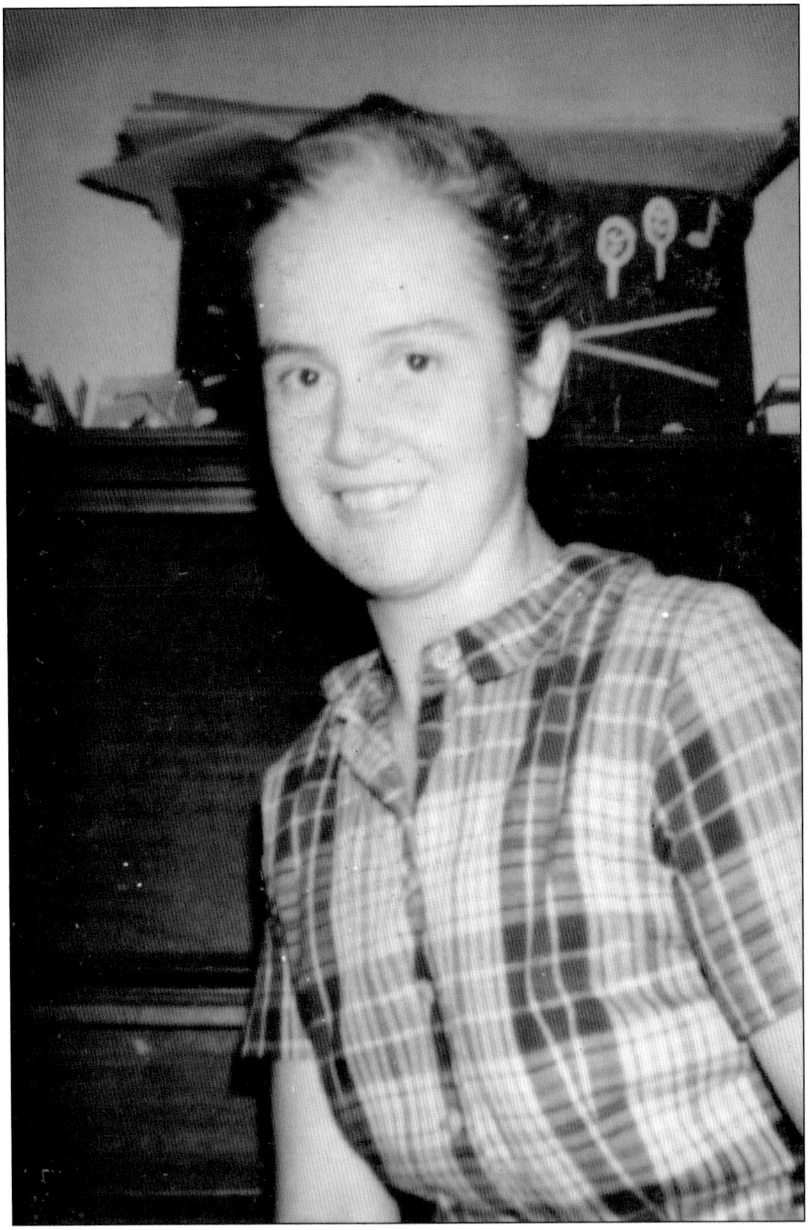

Nancy Wagner. This 1954 photograph shows Nancy Wagner when she was a teacher at the Accokeek Cooperative Nursery School, which was founded in 1951. During the first two years, it met at Christ Episcopal Church and at Accokeek Elementary School. In 1953, it moved to one of the Fergusons' tenant houses near the present Moyaone Swimming Pool. Robert Straus commented about the school: "Although the new, highly educated, upper middle-class owners were happy with the life in the woods, their need for amenities quickly became apparent. A preschool was launched and my children were a substantial part of the first graduating class." The *Washington Star* wrote about the school in 1954: "Accokeek is especially proud of its cooperative nursery school. . . . Two teachers guide the 3-to-5 year-olds from 9:30 to noon on Tuesdays, Wednesdays, and Thursdays." (Courtesy of Nancy and Holly Wagner; caption based on material in *The Moyaone Reserve* by G.L. Hanssen.)

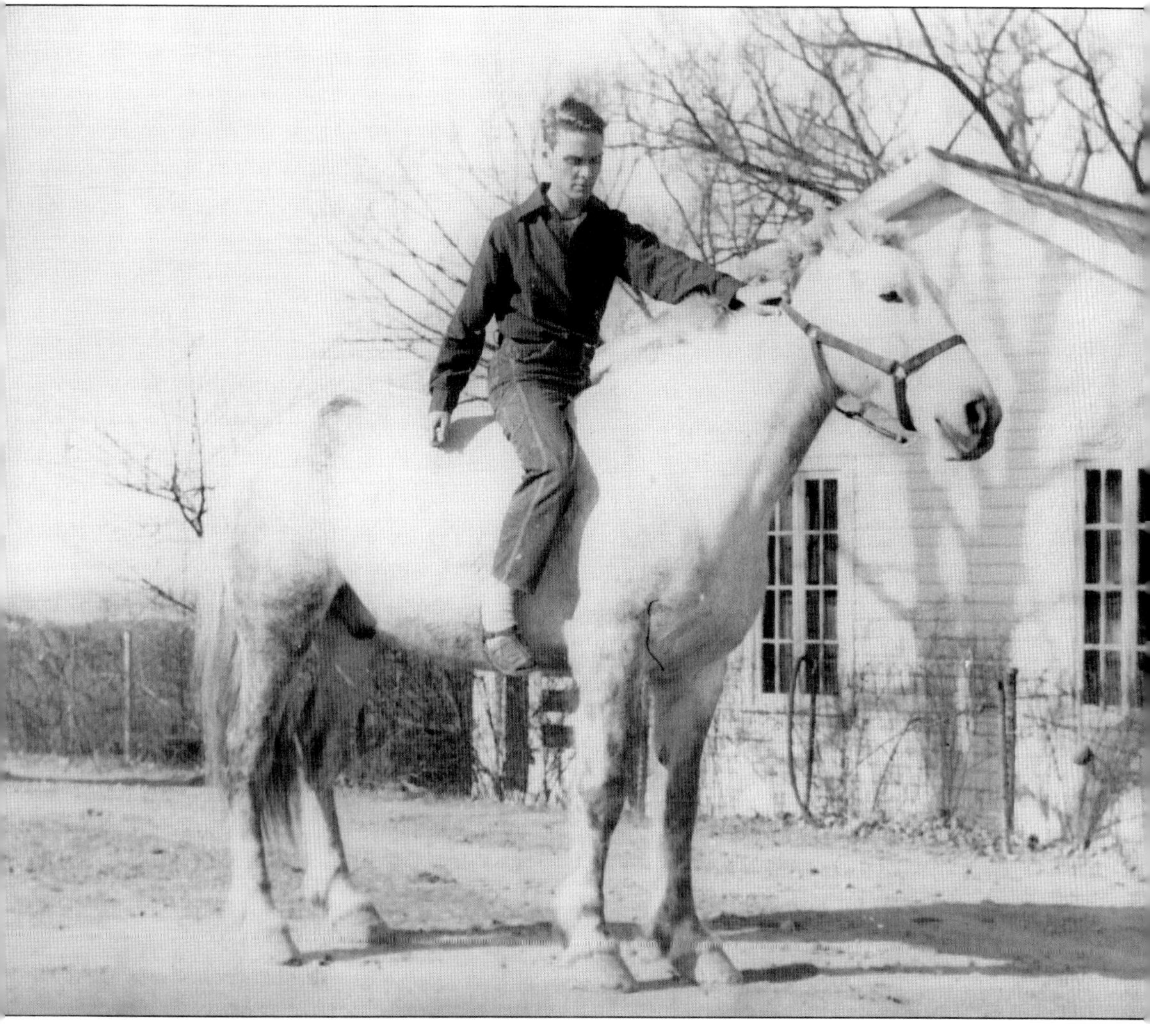

CHARLES WAGNER ON BONEY. Nancy Wagner recalls, "Alice Ferguson would invite [Charles Wagner] over for volley ball games and dinner. At one point Charles had a bad cough and Alice bundled him up and took him to her house in town and gave him hot buttered rum until he was better." Prior to his settling in Accokeek in 1935, Charles Wagner (1909–1998) earned a degree in architecture from the Georgia Institute of Technology. Frank Lloyd Wright's work impressed him, and his architectural style reflected Wright's concepts. He was a member of the original "Fergie's gang" and lived with other likeminded individuals at the Fergusons' Longview farmhouse in the late 1930s. After a tour in the Navy during World War II, he returned to the area and joined the Office of Health Education and Welfare, where he traveled worldwide designing public facilities. He designed and built his own home in 1947 and designed more than 15 houses for his neighbors over the next 30 years. (Courtesy of Nancy and Holly Wagner; caption based on material in *The Moyaone Reserve* by G.L. Hanssen.)

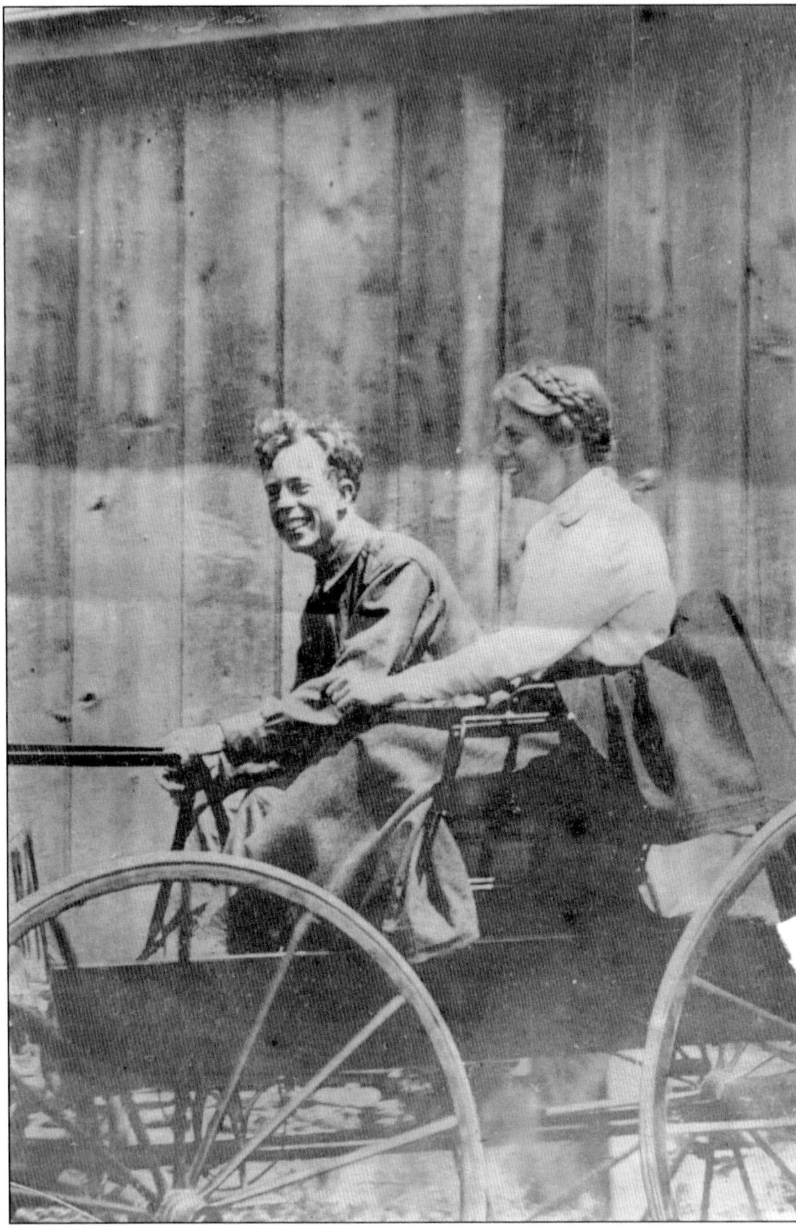

ALICE AND FERGIE IN THE BUGGY, C. 1922. Alice and Henry "Fergie" Ferguson knew from the minute they met that they would have good times together. Late in life, he reflected on what he and Alice had built at Hard Bargain Farm, saying, "I wish I was a little surer about immortality and could see what my successors would make of things. I rather hope they would not try anything too useful or uplifting. The place has always been a symbol of good times, but I suppose the two viewpoints are not necessarily incompatible." In 1943, a poem written by him was discovered, in which he wrote, "Nine and twenty years ago, two little gutter cats started out to see the world in their best shoes and hats. Later we cruised the Indes, afterward went to Spain; maybe the war will quit next year, then we can start again. My choice would be Atlantis—Hesprides would be swell—but if you'd rather see Sangri-La, twould suit me just as well." (Courtesy of the Alice Ferguson Foundation.)

Five

The Moyaone and Greater Accokeek

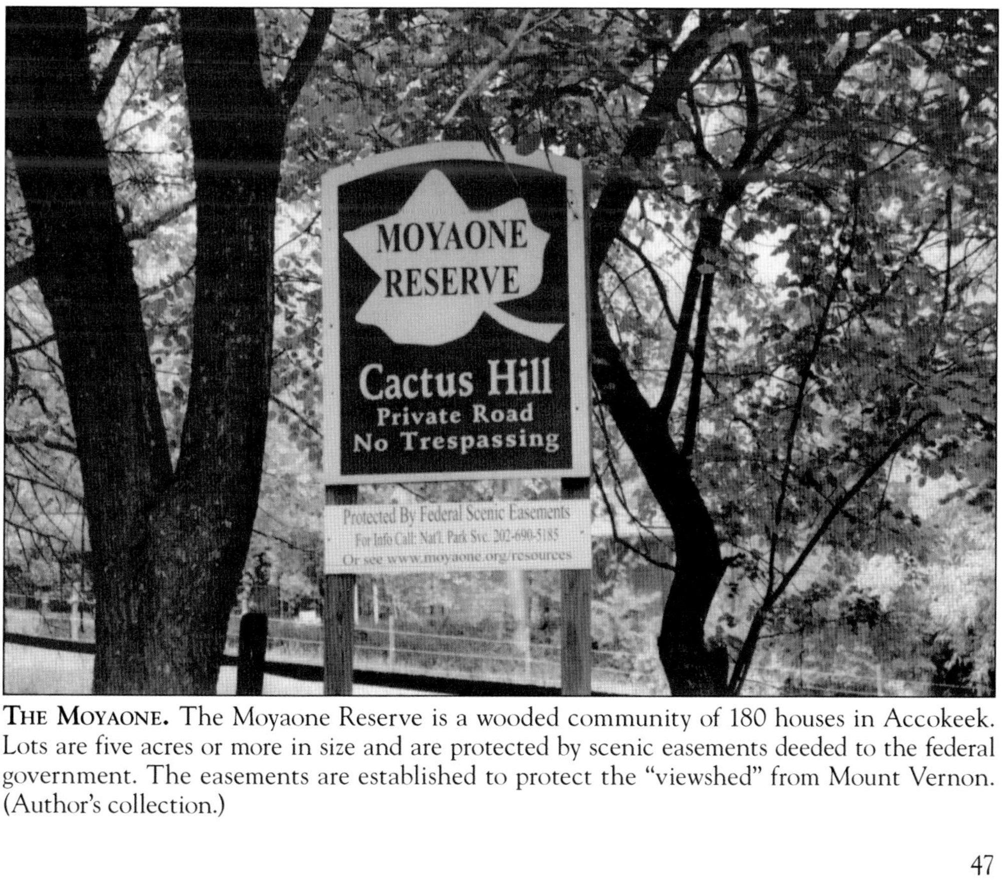

The Moyaone. The Moyaone Reserve is a wooded community of 180 houses in Accokeek. Lots are five acres or more in size and are protected by scenic easements deeded to the federal government. The easements are established to protect the "viewshed" from Mount Vernon. (Author's collection.)

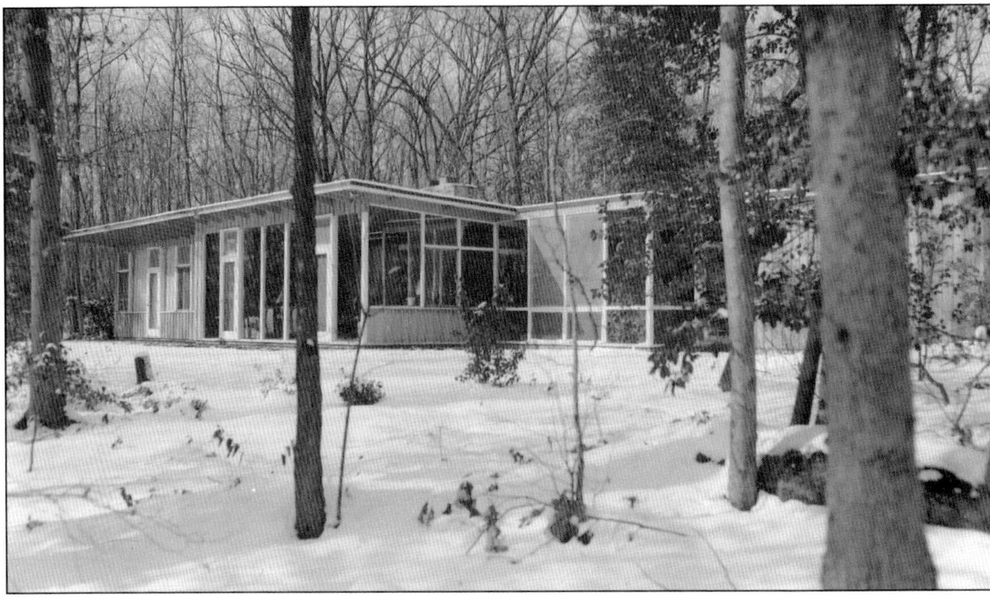

The Wagner Home. Nancy Wagner recalls, "My husband [Charles Wagner] loved this area. When he went overseas in World War II he wrote and said he would like to buy a piece. He was offered 200 acres at $50 per acre but he said he couldn't afford it. Mrs. Ferguson purchased Bond's Retreat and we purchased a lot there. Fergie surveyed it. We have a lot of ravines and undergrowth." Like all of the houses designed by Charles Wagner, his house is sited to take advantage of south-facing windows, with sun-flooded tile or slate floors. Once, a four-year-old visiting the Wagner home for the first time said, "I just love that house. You could go indoors and outdoors and indoors and outdoors." (Both courtesy of Nancy and Holly Wagner; caption based on material in *The Moyaone Reserve* by G.L. Hanssen.)

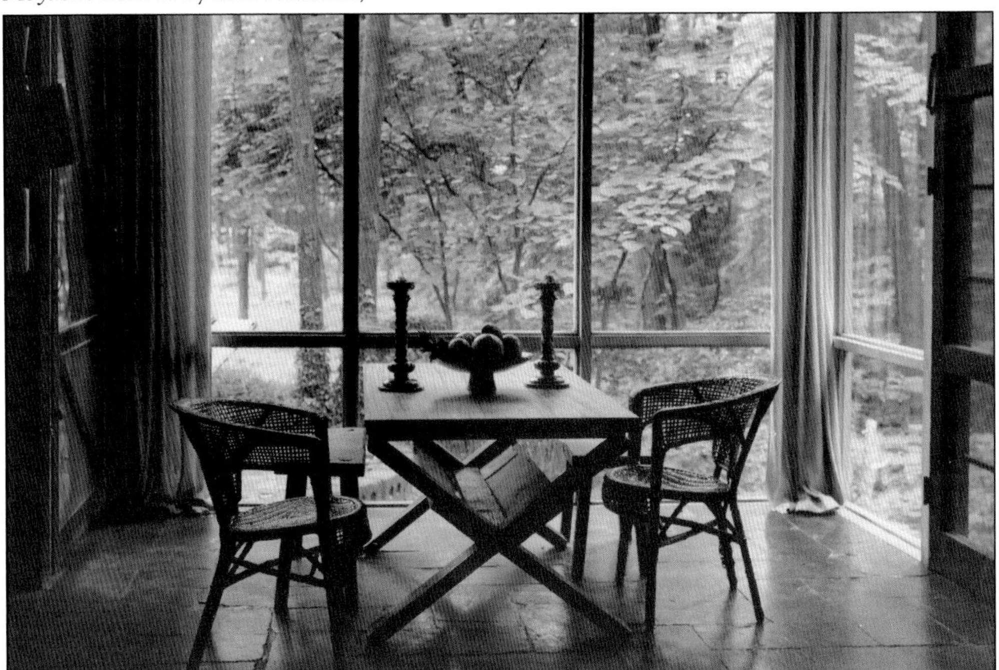

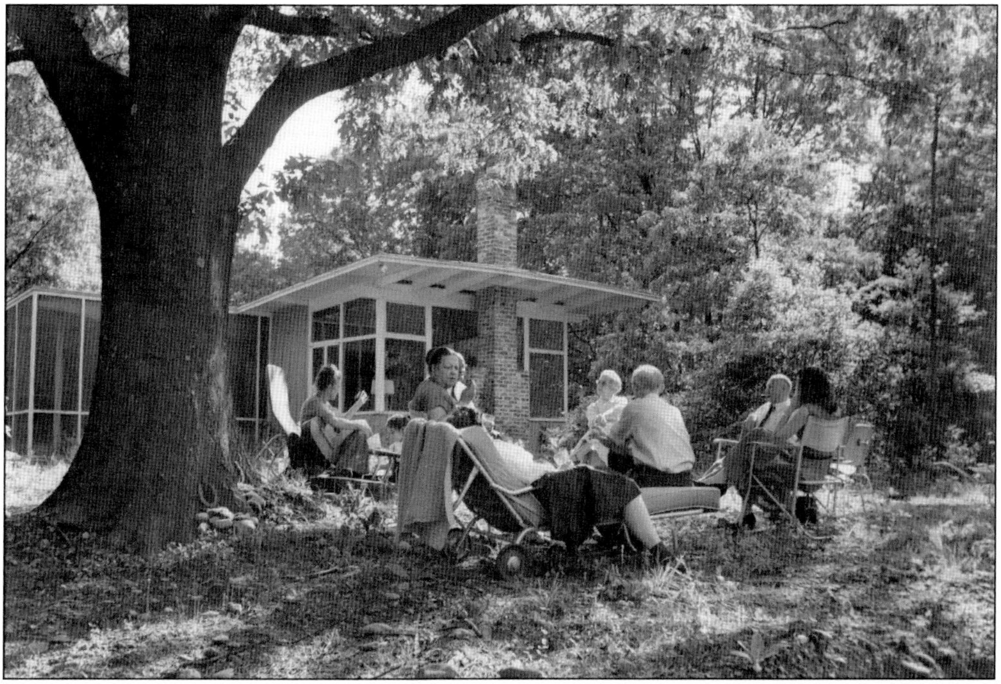

Avalon. The home of James and Polly Whyte was named Avalon. According to Juli Whyte, the view from Avalon is the second-best of all the houses in the Moyaone. Early buyers of homes in the Moyaone found many difficulties in building. The postwar building boom caused a shortage of building materials, contractors were few, and lending institutions were reluctant to grant building loans in such a remote area. A few of the more enterprising residents managed to build their homes on weekends and during their vacations. These photographs of Avalon show the Whytes and their guests combining work with play. Note the guitarist in both images. (Both courtesy of Juli Whyte; caption based on material in *The Moyaone Reserve* by G.L. Hanssen.)

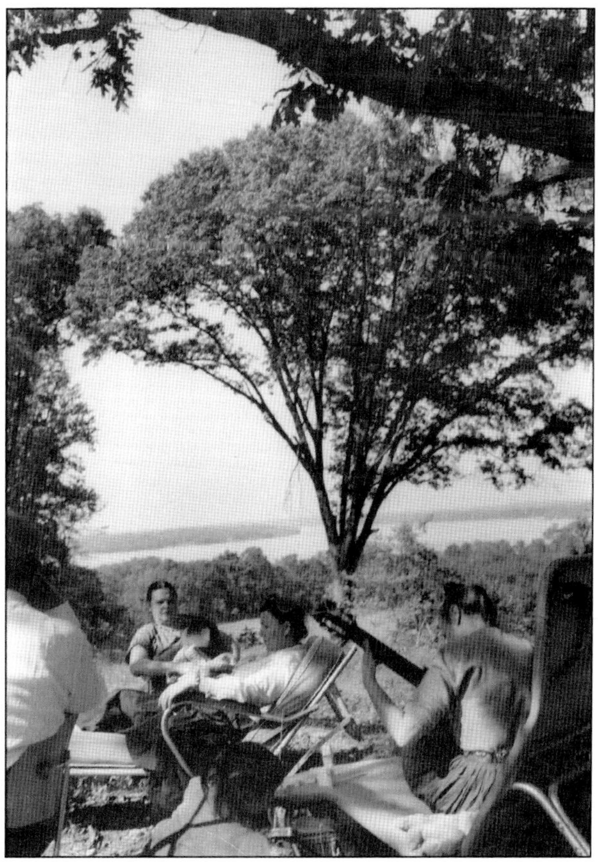

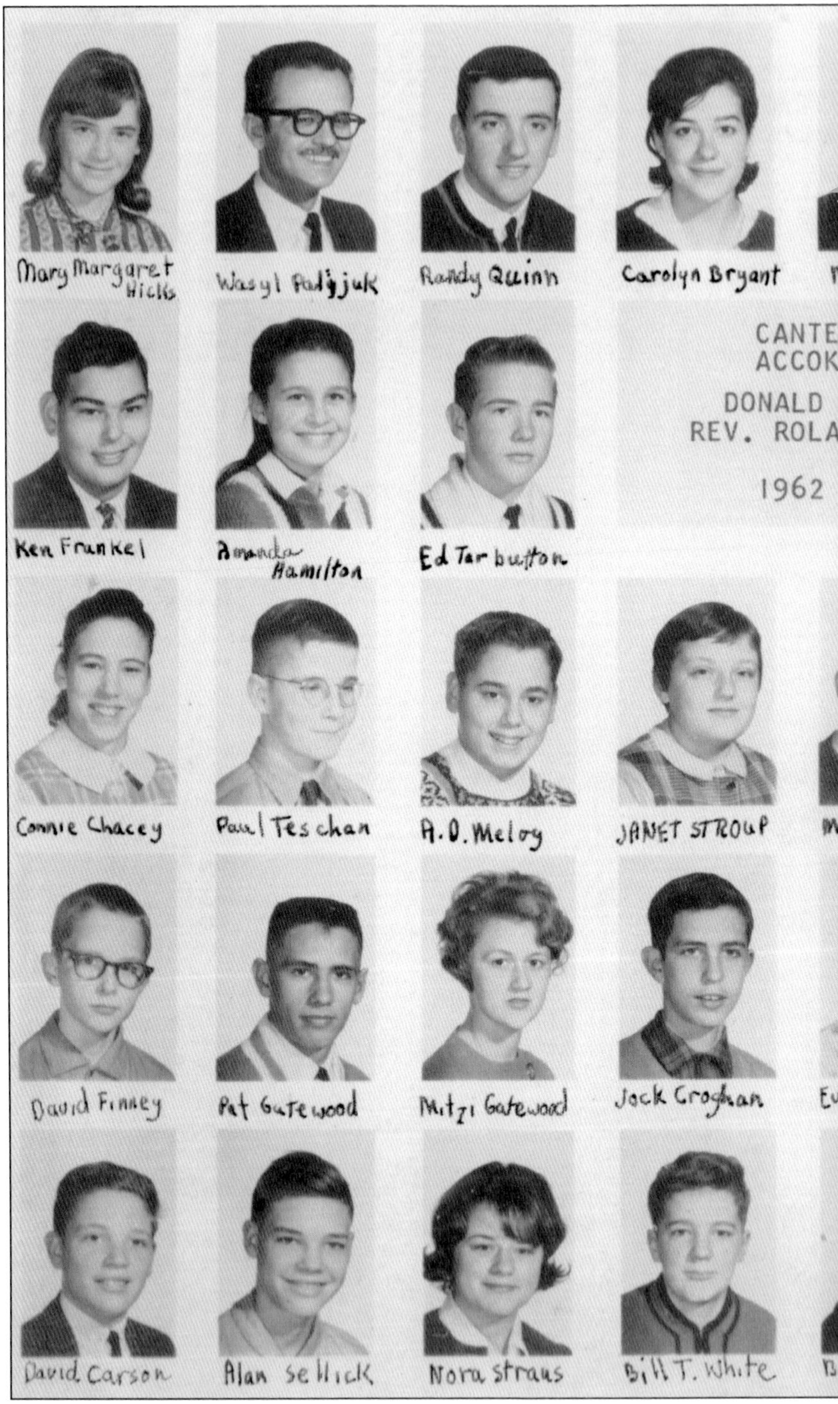

Canterbury School at Christ Church. According to John H. Clagett IV in his book *Christ Church Accokeek, Maryland 1698–1998*, "In addition to the Sunday School, a parochial school, Canterbury School, would hold classes in the new parish hall beginning in 1961. The vestry hired Donald Mills as its headmaster. Mills had taught at the University of Kentucky and had been principal of Tayac School on Allentown Road in Prince George's County, Maryland. Bishop

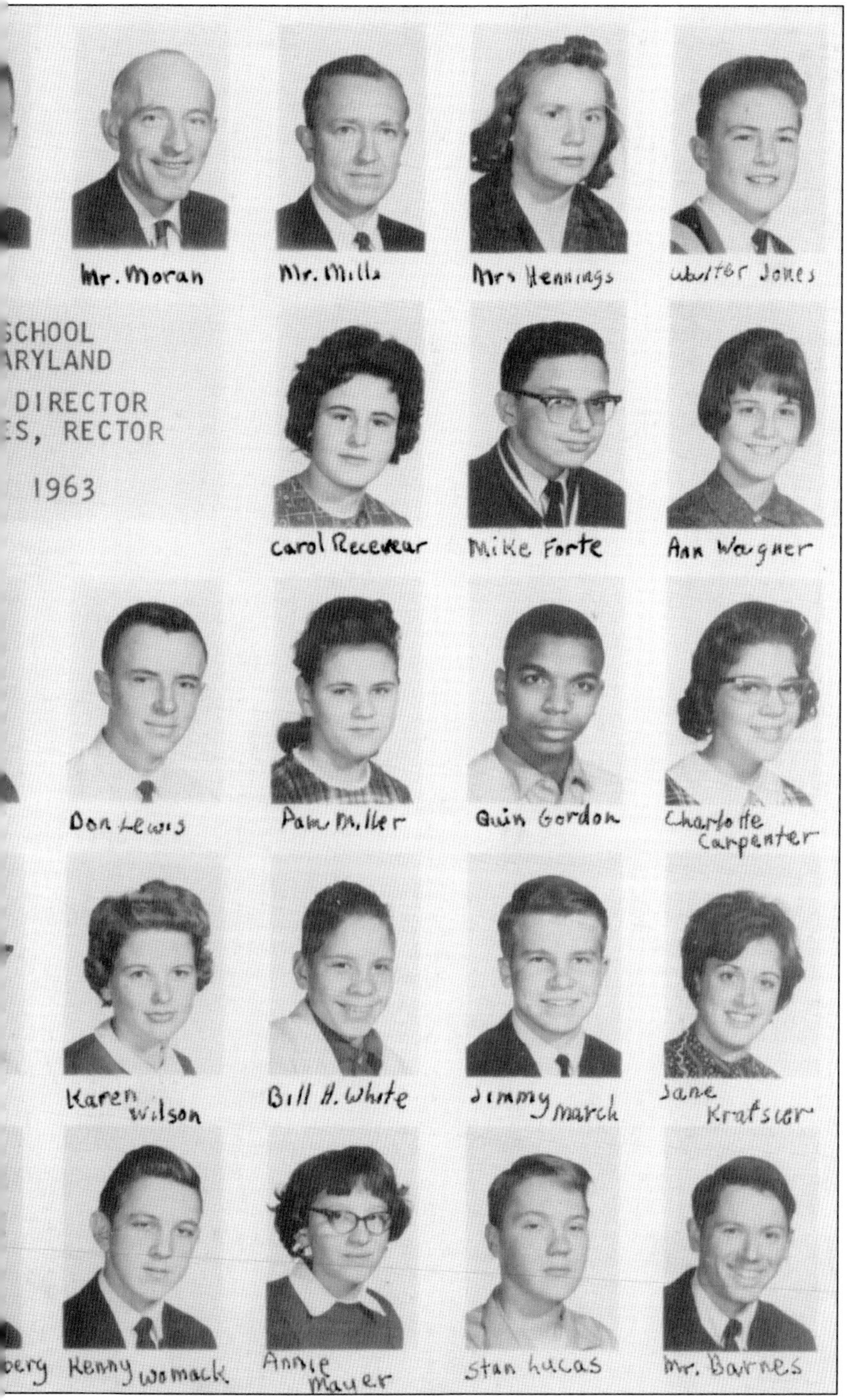

William Creighton was the school's president and Reverend Jones its executive secretary. The vestry chose Charles Dillon, William Penn Jameson, Jennie DeWilde Clagett, and T. Grady Hicks as board members. The school taught grades seven through twelve and promised a class size of no more than fifteen students per instructor." (Courtesy of Nancy and Holly Wagner.)

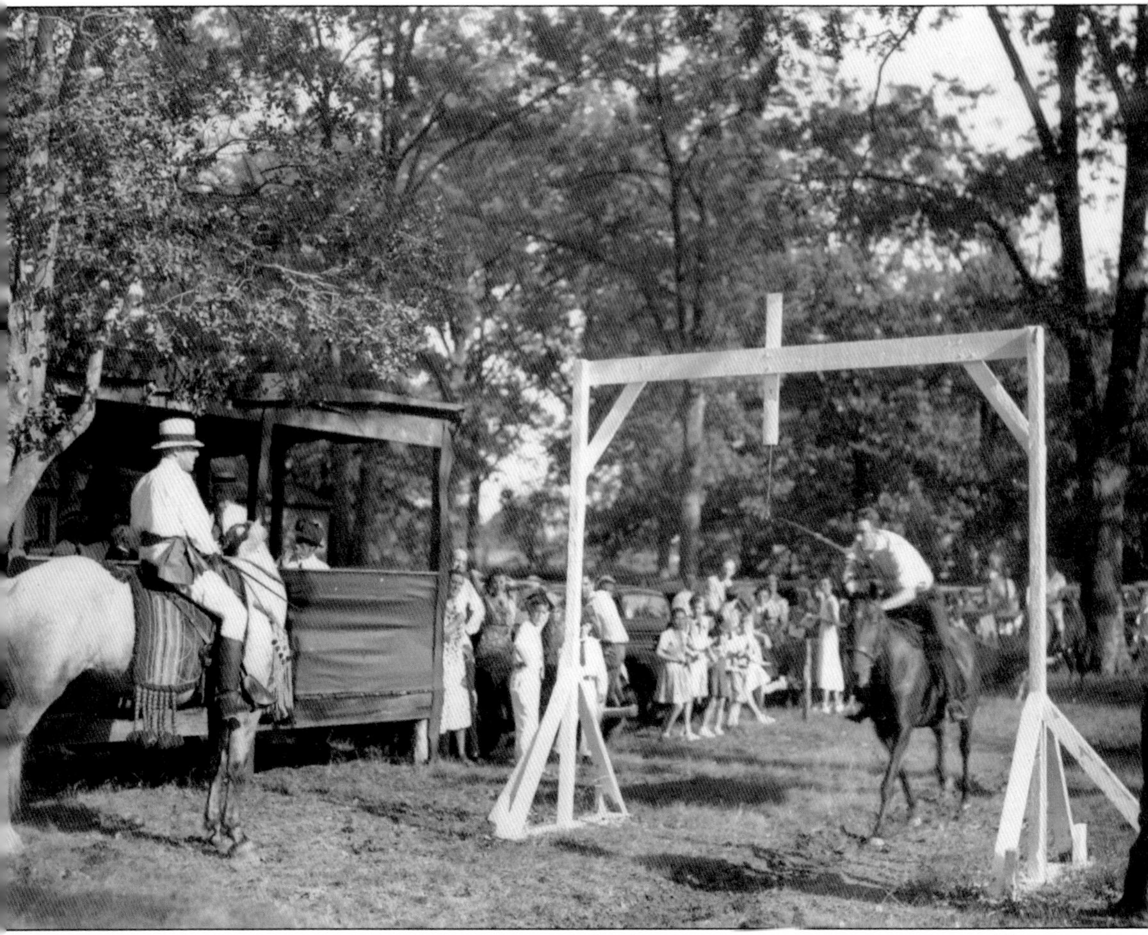

JOUSTING AT CHRIST CHURCH. Jousting, the Maryland state sport, was a popular and lucrative means of raising money at Christ Church. The sixteenth annual tournament took place on Saturday, August 28, 1937. The *Enquirer Gazette* reported, "Arches erected in the grove of large oak trees at the beautiful Christ Church and its rectory formed a pleasant setting." According to John H. Clagett IV in *A History of Christ Church, Accokeek, Maryland 1698–1998*, the winning knight, Adelbert Hungerford, had to leave before the coronation ceremony, so he presented the crown to William Coleman, who chose Jane Page as queen. Hyattsville attorney Walter Green gave the coronation address and Henry Xander was the chief marshal. Karl Berryman's orchestra provided entertainment in the parish hall. Admission to the grounds was 25¢, and a "good old southern Maryland supper" was 75¢. The top prize was $15 for professional knights and $5 for successful amateurs. (Courtesy of the Alice Ferguson Foundation.)

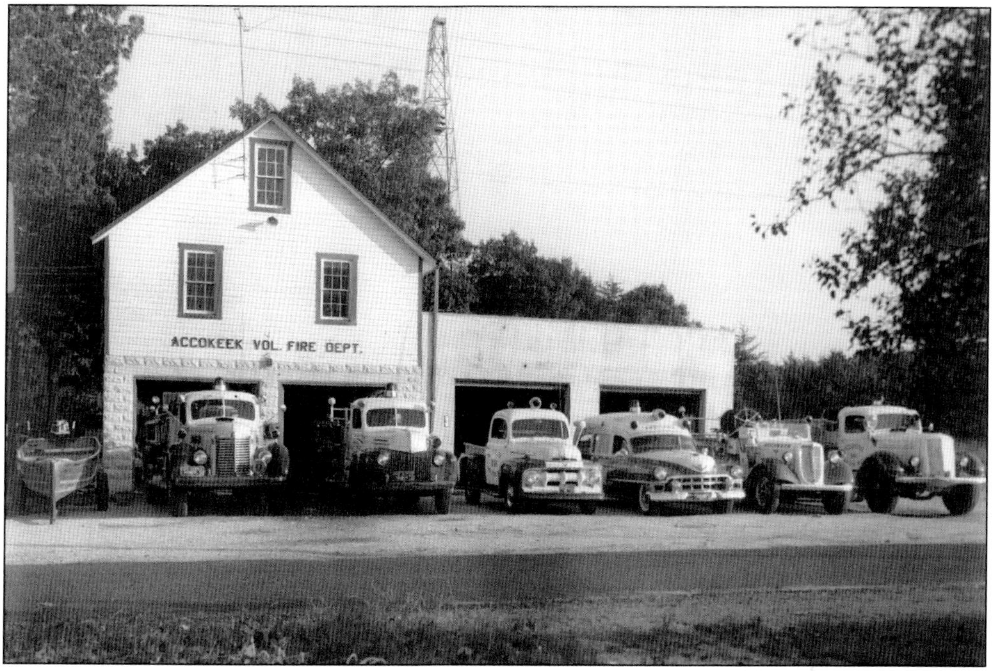

Accokeek Fire Department. The formation of the fire department, in 1932, was another civic venture of Alice and Henry Ferguson. The first fire engine was a Cadillac automobile that was converted into a truck by members of the department. The original firehouse was enlarged in 1949. In the ensuing years, better and additional equipment was purchased, including ambulances and watercraft to assist in rescues on the Potomac River. To properly house the equipment, a new, larger building was needed, and the new fire station was dedicated on July 4, 1962. (Above, courtesy of Betty Dillon; below, courtesy of Eric Straus.)

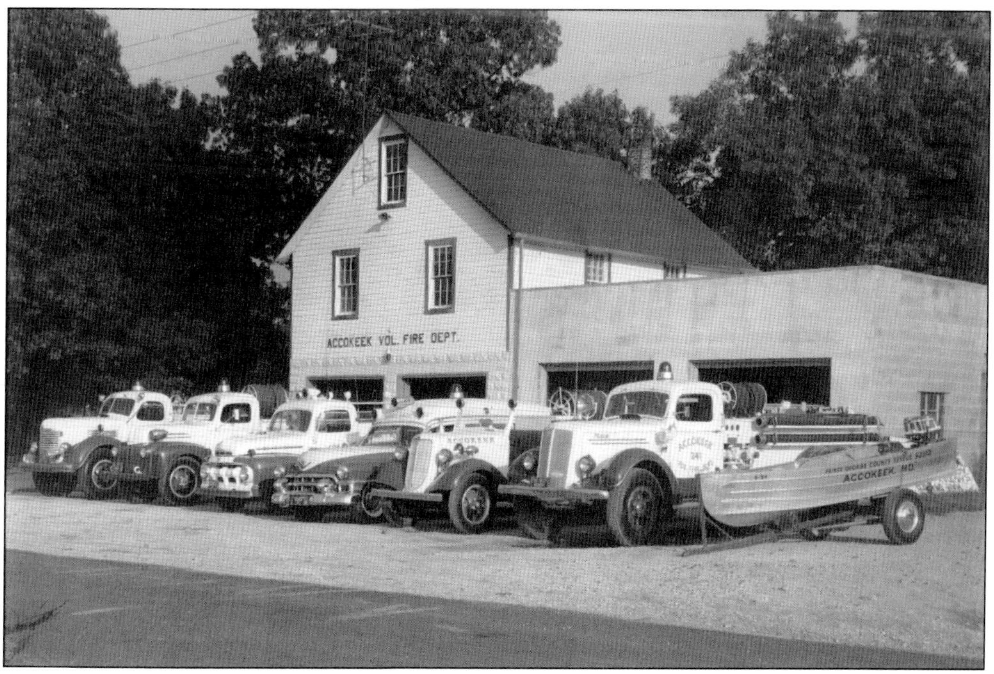

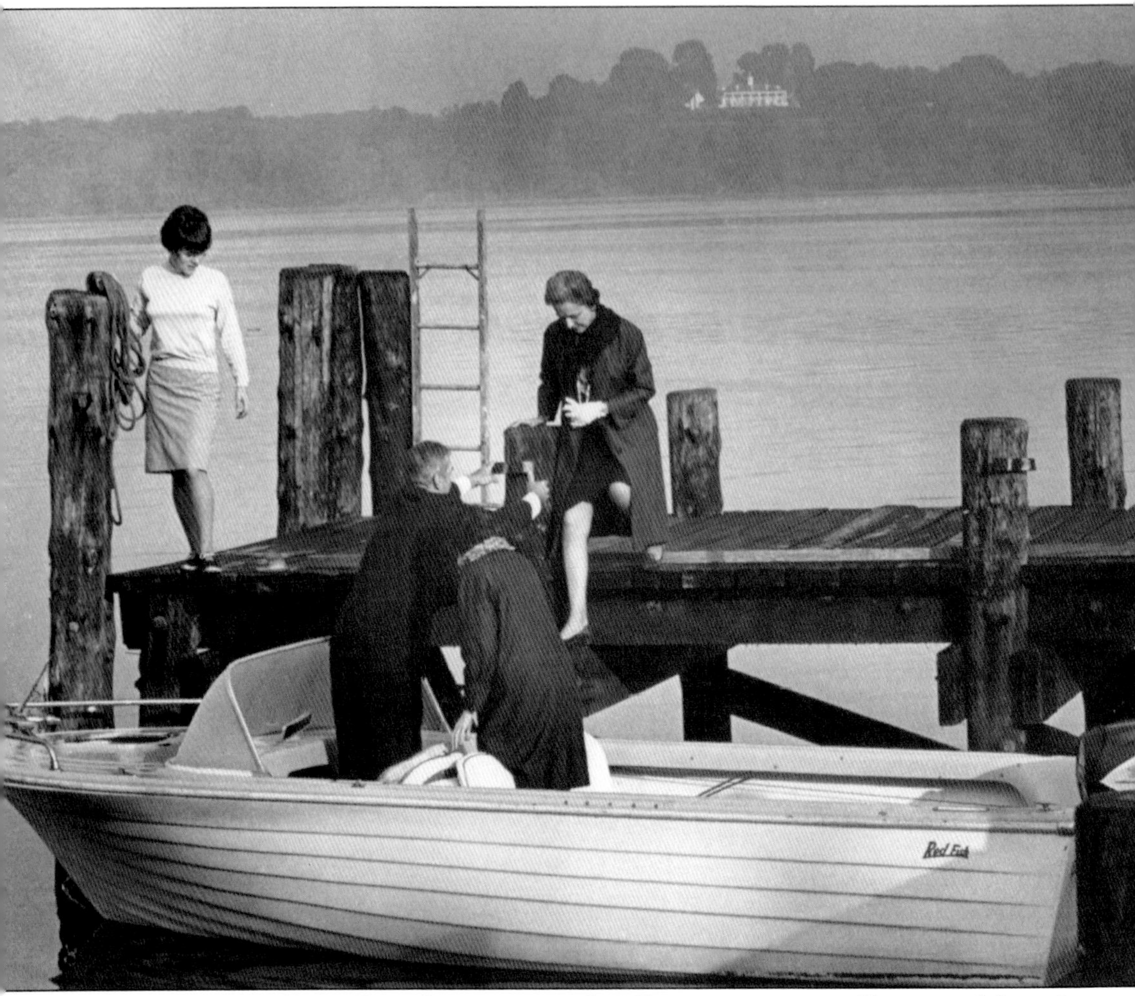

The Commuter Boat. For a few years around 1965, commuters were able to travel from the dock at the end of Bryan Point Road to the Washington Marina. This was operated by Bob Straus. Some Accokeek residents used this method of travel every day to reach their offices in downtown Washington. Others used the commuter boat occasionally to travel to Washington for appointments. Pictured here are, from left to right, (on the dock) Nora Straus and Clara Moran; (in the boat) Bob Straus and Martha Mills. Note Mount Vernon in the background, across the Potomac River in Virginia. In recent years, as automobile traffic on Indian Head Highway has become more and more congested, whether or not this is "progress" is doubtful, but the commuter boat has not made a comeback. (Courtesy of Eric Straus.)

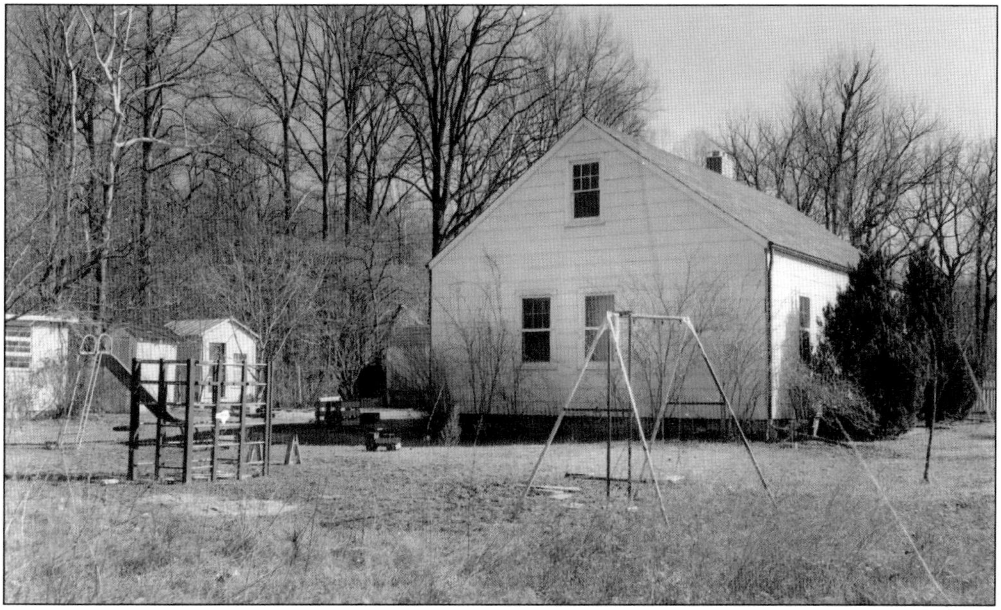

Cooperative Nursery School. The Accokeek Cooperative Nursery School was founded in 1951 by Nancy Wagner, Louise North, and Elizabeth Kenah. During its first two years it met at Christ Episcopal Church and at Accokeek Elementary School. In 1953, it moved to one of the Fergusons' tenant houses near the present Moyaone swimming pool. The children in the June 1961 graduation photograph below are, from left to right, Nancy Hack, Cathy Jones, Peter Finney, Candy Wagner, Peggy Jo Smith, Jo Ann Copeland, Debbie Chandler, Ralph Swick, Jimmy Clagett, Bill Grimes, and the Hicks twins, Dwight and Douglas. (Above, courtesy of Nancy and Holly Wagner; below, courtesy of Adelaide Copeland.)

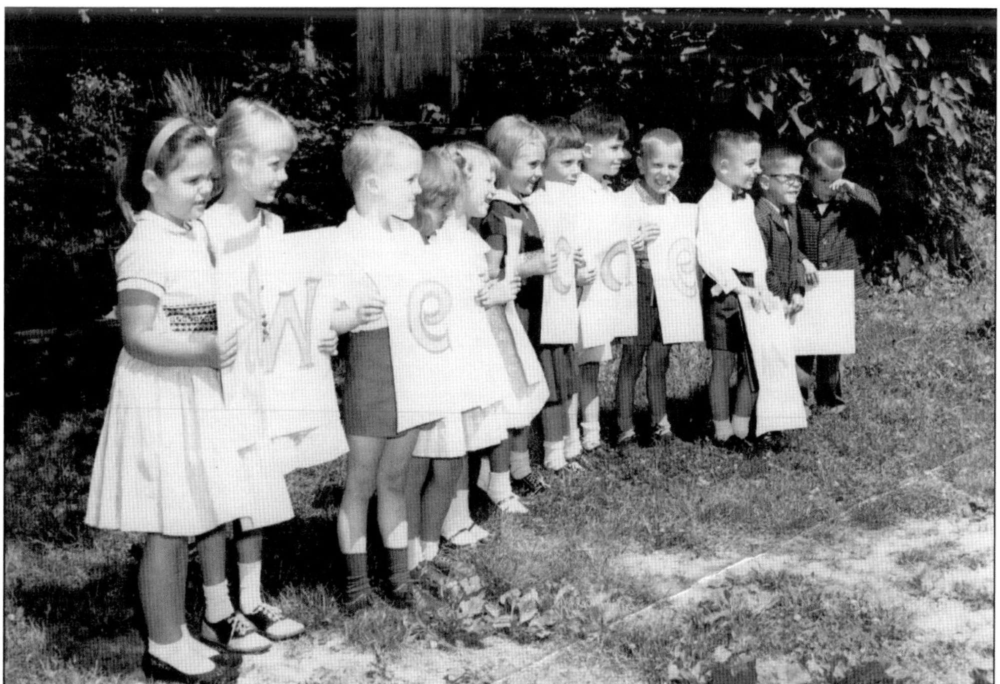

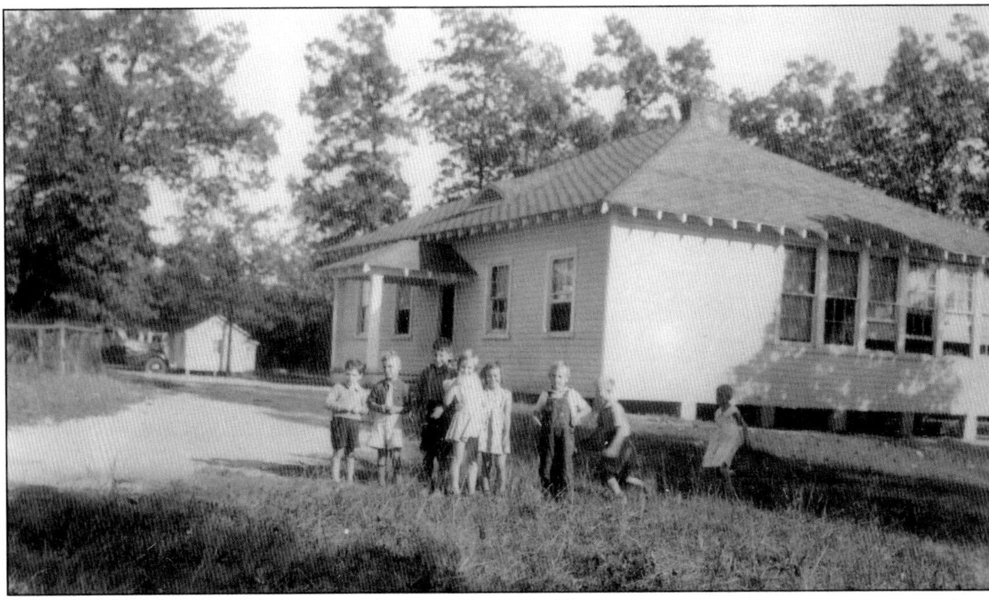

Accokeek Elementary School. The old Accokeek Elementary School was a two-room school that had been in operation since shortly after the Civil War. Above, in 1939–1940, the students in front of the school are, from left to right, Floyd Allen, Billy Combes, Billy Gosnell, Minnie Xander, Lottie Pickeral, Claude Oliver, Ray Johnson, and Maybelle Willett. Alice Ferguson took the photograph. The new brick Accokeek Elementary School (below) replaced the two-room school in 1953. Gilbert E. Wilson, the father of Lucille Hennings, officiated at the ground-breaking for the new school in 1952. Owing to the consolidation of schools, Accokeek Elementary School was closed in the early 1980s. (Above, courtesy of Nancy and Holly Wagner; below, courtesy of Dorothy Showalter.)

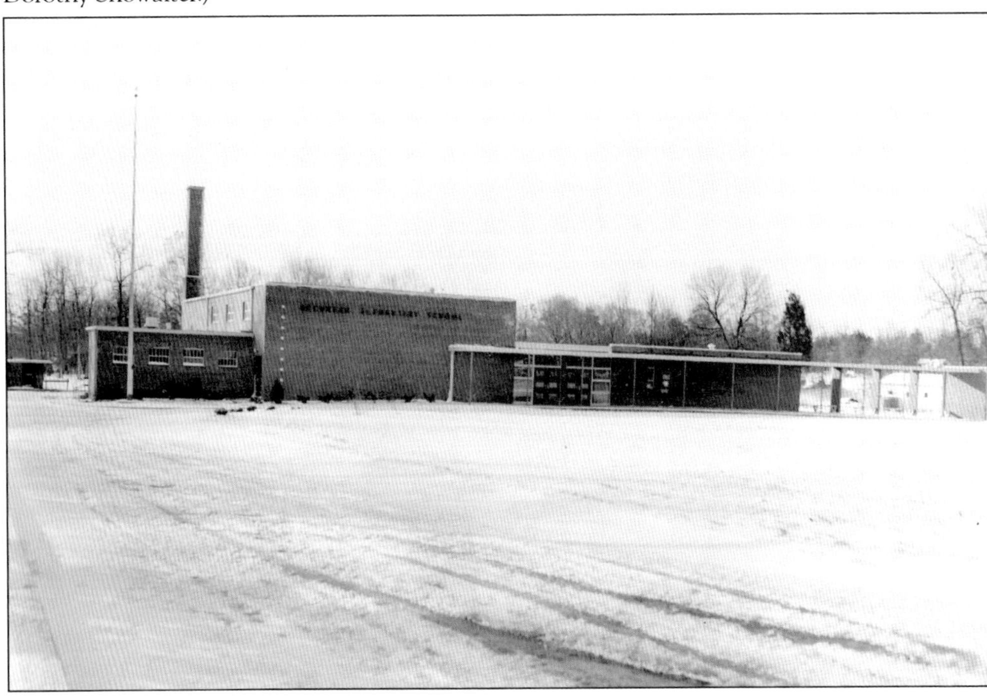

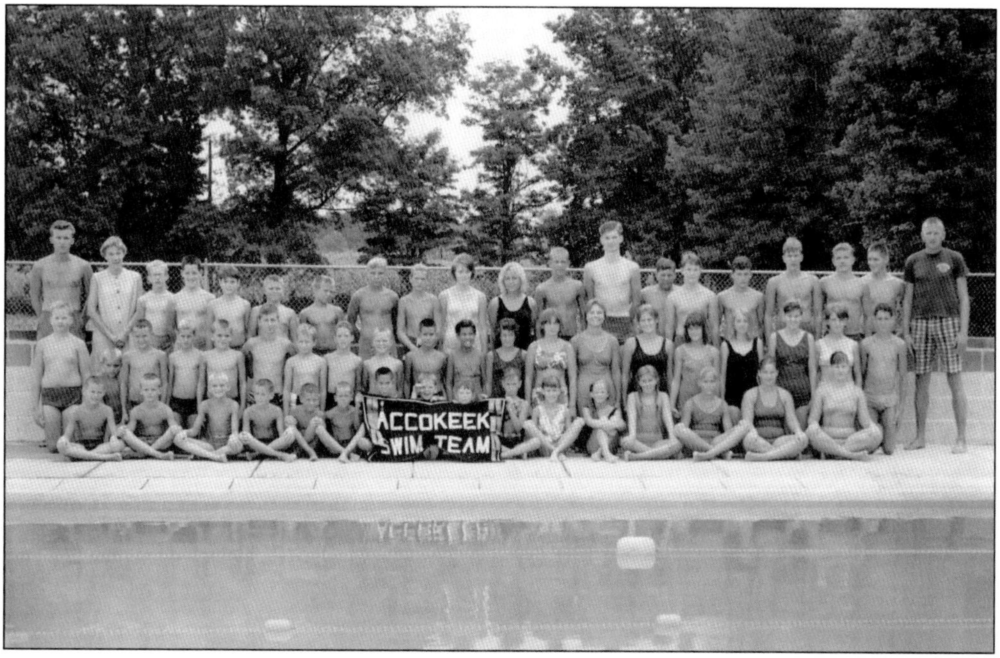

ACCOKEEK SWIM AND BASEBALL TEAMS. The Accokeek swim team is shown above in full glory in 1964 at the Moyaone community pool. Holly Wagner recalls: "We were a huge, powerful team!" The 1954 photograph of the baseball team below includes, from left to right, (front row) Jebby Wells, Bobby Martin, and Billy Brock (bat boy); (second row) Bobby Wells, Russell Cool, Doyle Funkhauser, Jack Dent, and Kenny Waugh; (third row) Jim Martin (assistant manager), Elmo Willett (assistant manager), Billy "Squeaky" Carson, Johnny Reese, and Bruce Martin (manager); (fourth row) Bobby Blanford, Bobby Moreland, and Gene Foster. (Above, courtesy of Nancy and Holly Wagner; below, courtesy of Adelaide Copeland.)

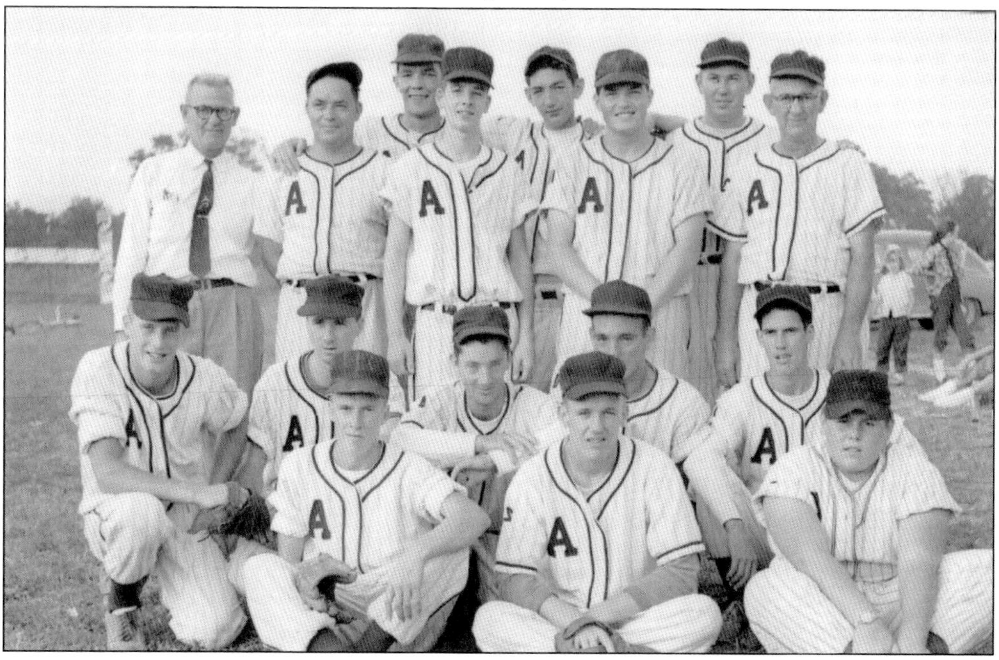

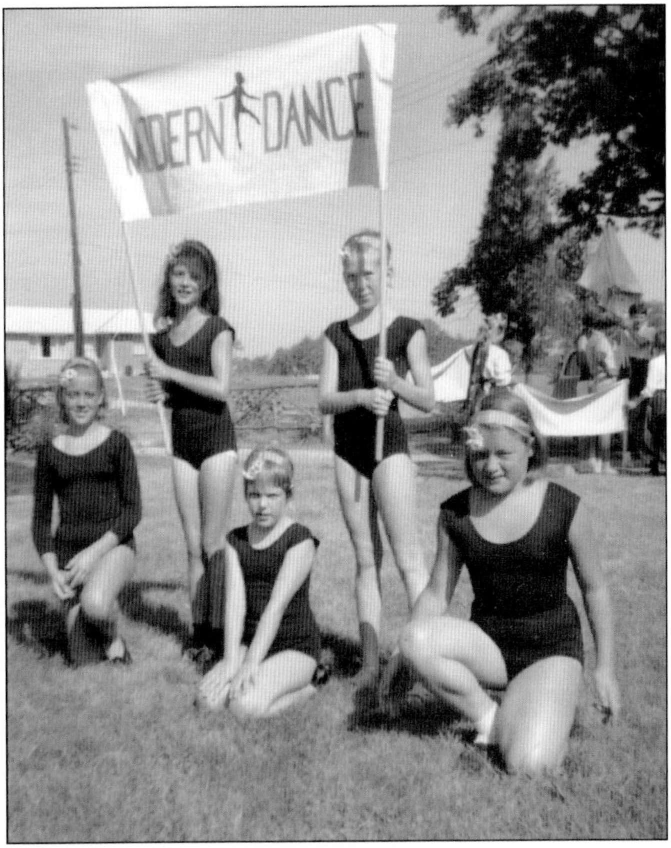

Fourth of July Parade. At left, the modern dance troupe prepares for their place in the Fourth of July parade. The troupe members are, from left to right, Carla Kenah, Ann Wagner, Lisa Startup, Lynn North, and Nora Straus. Other groups in that parade included the Scouts, the Young Naturalists, Group Piano, and many more. Below, Miss Accokeek rides on the back of Sophie Zadoretsy's convertible. The Calvert Manor Garden Club float was decorated by Nancy Hock. This was the Calvert Manor Garden Club's first entry in the parade. Ginny Chandler was the chairwoman of the garden club. (Left, courtesy of Rhonda Hanson, Lisa Startup, and Nancy and Holly Wagner; below, courtesy of Frank Kahan.)

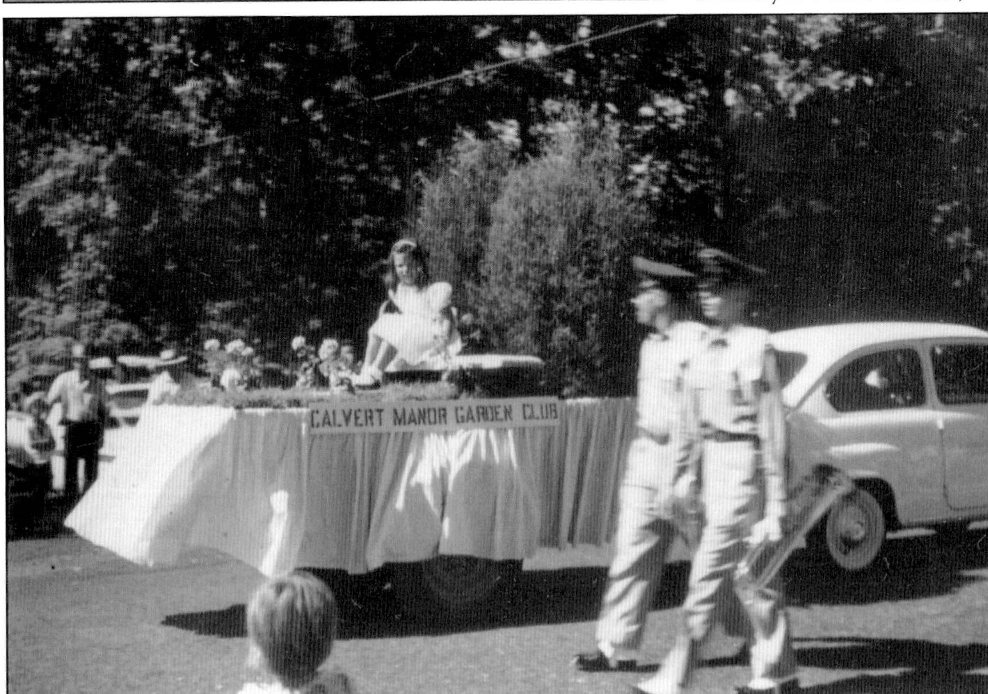

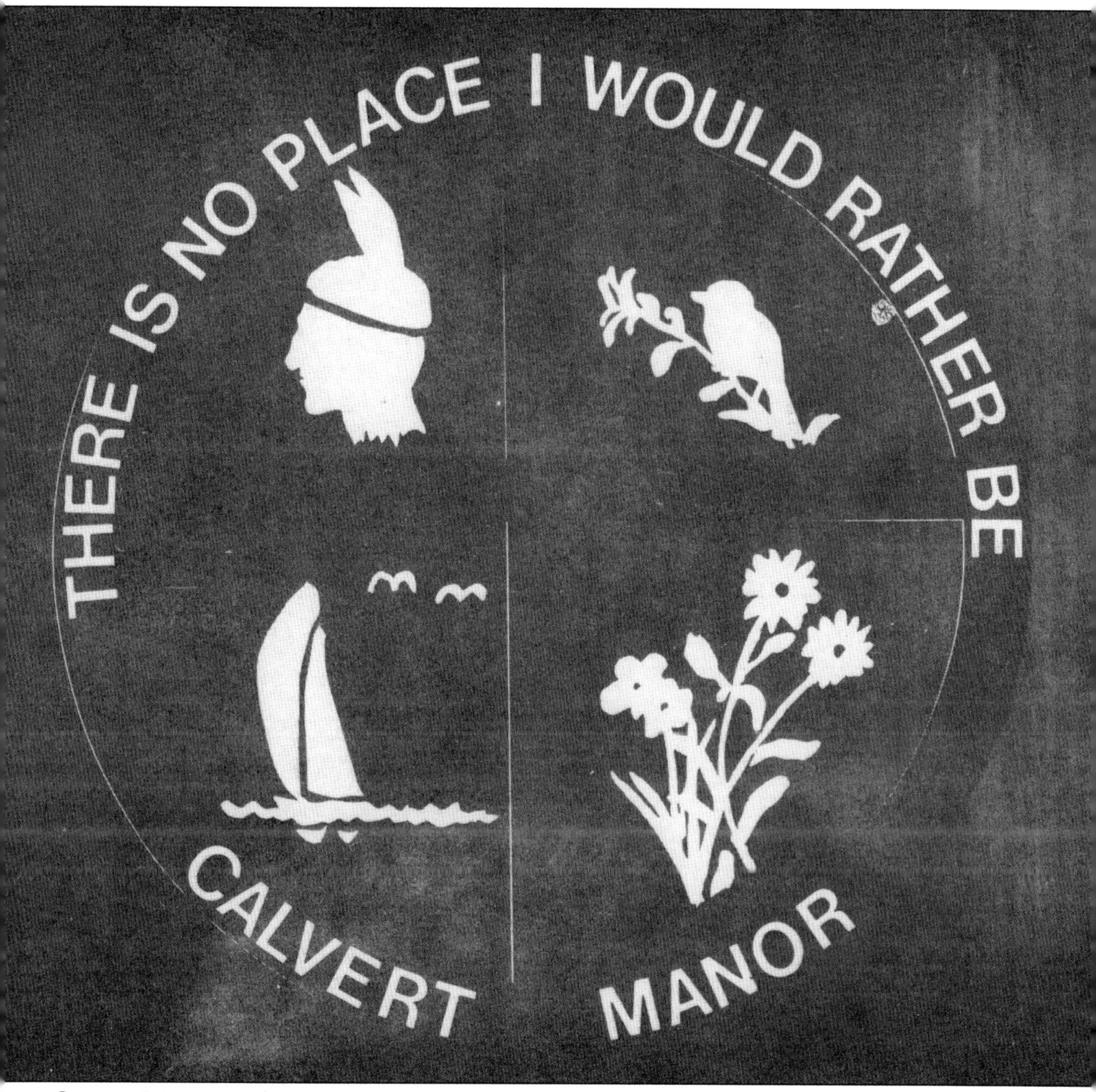

CALVERT MANOR. Calvert Manor is a small community of 96 homes located in a wooded portion of the Piscataway Creek valley near the Moyaone. In 1662, Cecil Calvert, the second Lord Baltimore, granted a tract of land to his nephew William Calvert. Known originally as Piscataway Manor, the name of the 3,000-acre tract was later changed to Calvert Manor. In 1946, the developer, Theodore F. Menk, and the owner, Gustav A. Bonnnet, collaborated on developing part of the waterfront property of the former Smoot Sand & Gravel Company. A promotional brochure described Calvert Manor thusly: "A year round place to live where you can occupy the long weekends by improving your property. Protective covenants and restrictions are in force to assure stable values and conditions. Many of the one-half acre or more building sites command the beautiful marine and land views for which this tributary of the Potomac is noted." (Courtesy of the Calvert Manor Civic Association.)

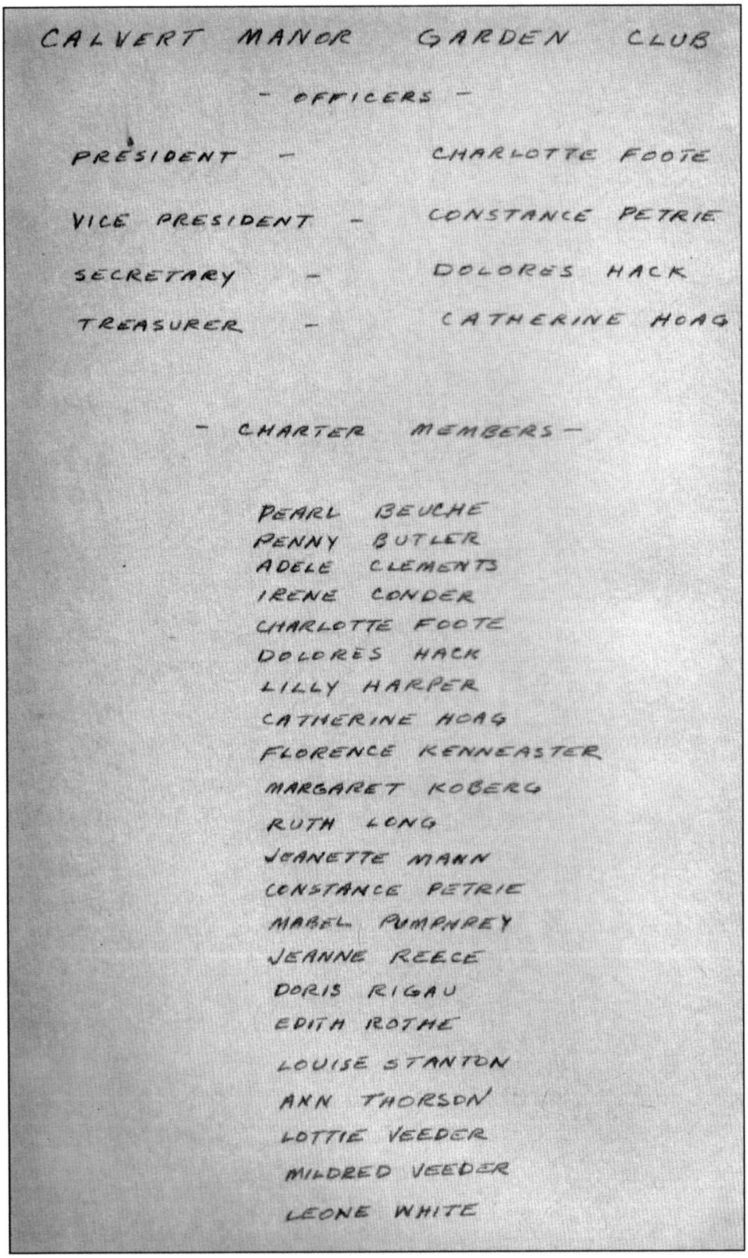
CALVERT MANOR GARDEN CLUB

- OFFICERS -

PRÉSIDENT - CHARLOTTE FOOTE

VICE PRESIDENT - CONSTANCE PETRIE

SECRETARY - DOLORES HACK

TREASURER - CATHERINE HOAG

- CHARTER MEMBERS -

PEARL BEUCHE
PENNY BUTLER
ADELE CLEMENTS
IRENE CONDER
CHARLOTTE FOOTE
DOLORES HACK
LILLY HARPER
CATHERINE HOAG
FLORENCE KENNEASTER
MARGARET KOBERG
RUTH LONG
JEANETTE MANN
CONSTANCE PETRIE
MABEL PUMPHREY
JEANNE REECE
DORIS RIGAU
EDITH ROTHE
LOUISE STANTON
ANN THORSON
LOTTIE VEEDER
MILDRED VEEDER
LEONE WHITE

CALVERT MANOR GARDEN CLUB. In May 1953, the Calvert Manor Garden Club was founded with 22 charter members. The original bylaws described the purpose of the club thusly: "To stimulate the interest in the historical and civic improvements throughout the community; to aid in the protection of trees, shrubs, wild flowers and birds; and actively to support the Federated Garden Clubs of Maryland, Inc., in their state-wide programs." Early standing committees included Bird Preservation and Conservation (Penny Butler and Leone White), Horticulture (Lottie Veeder and Mabel Pumphrey), Waterfront and Civic (Louise Stanton), Flower Show (Louise Stanton, fall 1953; Lilly Harper, spring 1954; and Ann Thorson, spring 1955), Program (Margaret Koberg and Mildred Veeder), Publicity and Historian (Constance Petrie), and Parliamentarian (Pearl Beuche). (Courtesy of Frank Kahan, Calvert Manor Garden Club.)

Arrangement Classes

"While Summers Pass"

For further information and reservation in the Arrangement Classes, call Mrs. Lawrence M. Harper, Fairview 2-4461, not later than Saturday, September 15.

A. "Autumn Glow" - A composition to be shown in a black shadow box 23 in. high, 18 in. wide, and 10 in. deep. Limited to 8 entries.

B. "Cream of the Crop" - An arrangement of colorful autumn flowers in a pitcher, to be shown in a light grey niche 12 x 8 x 6. Limited to 12 entries.

C. "Fall in Line" - A line arrangement using your favorite fall colors to be shown in a light grey niche 30 x 26 x 18. Limited to 8 entries.

D. "Drifting Along" - A composition using colorful dried material and driftwood, to be shown in a light grey niche 28 x 24 x 18. Limited to 8 entries.

E. "Tea Time" - Arrangement for an informal tea to be shown on a tea or hostess cart (to be provided by exhibitor). No flatwear or food.

F. "September's Reward" - For those who have never won a blue ribbon. An arrangement in a pottery container. Not to exceed 15 in. overall.

G. "The Gardener" - For men only. An arrangement using local fruit and vegetables. Plant material permitted.

H. Junior Classes

a) "Merry Marigolds" - A flower arrangement using small marigolds. For ages 5 - 10.

b) "School Daze" - A flower arrangement using your school colors in a suitable container. Limited to 12 in. overall. For ages 11 - 17.

FLOWER SHOW. The first annual spring flower show, featuring iris, was held on May 15, 1954, at the Accokeek School. The public was invited to make entries in both the specimen and arrangement classes. The specimen classes included 16 different iris varieties. In addition to iris specimens, other specimen classes include peonies, roses, bulbs, perennials, biennials, annuals, flowering shrubs, and houseplants. The nine arrangement classes included Bob-White, for men only; Dinkey Bird Song, for ages 5–10; and The Hummingbird, for ages 11–15. The program for the 1956 Fall Flower Show included the arrangement classes described here. The flower show was held at the Accokeek School on Saturday, September 22. Every other year, Federated Garden Clubs of Maryland, District II, held a flower show, with the best of all the state's garden clubs participating. (Courtesy of Frank Kahan, Calvert Manor Garden Club.)

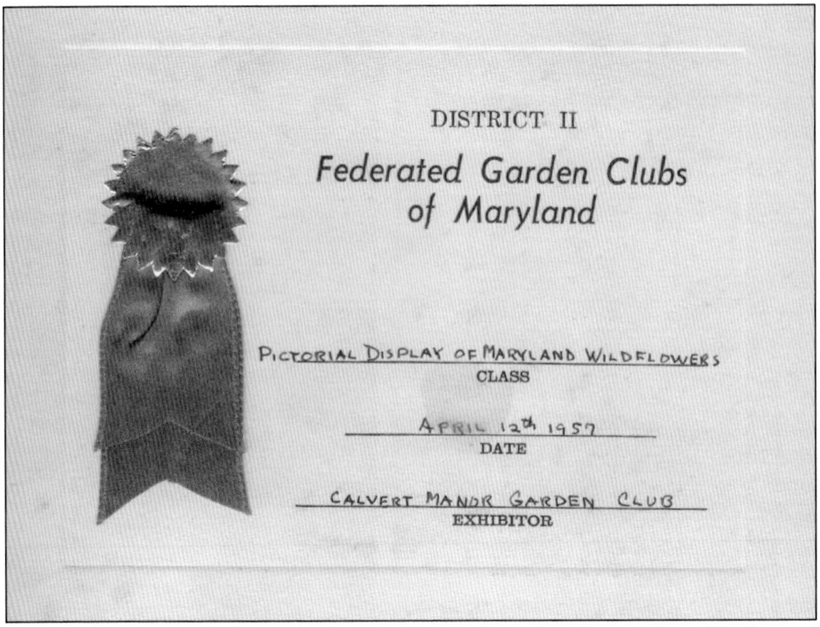

FEDERATED GARDEN CLUBS OF MARYLAND AWARDS. In 1960, District II of Federated Garden Clubs of Maryland included 14 garden clubs in southern Maryland. Awards given at the Calvert Manor Garden Club flower shows included a purple ribbon for outstanding horticulture exhibit and a green ribbon for outstanding arrangement. Two green ribbons awarded to the Calvert Manor Garden Club in 1957 are seen here. In 1959, the Calvert Manor Garden Club hosted the iris show at Gwynn Park High School. A portion of the school grounds were landscaped and planted with many types of shrubs and trees, which were donated to the school at the end of the show as a permanent example of planning and planting. At the same show, members of Calvert Manor Garden Club were presented with the silver bowl, awarded to the club with the most blue ribbons for horticultural specimens. (Courtesy of Frank Kahan, Calvert Manor Garden Club.)

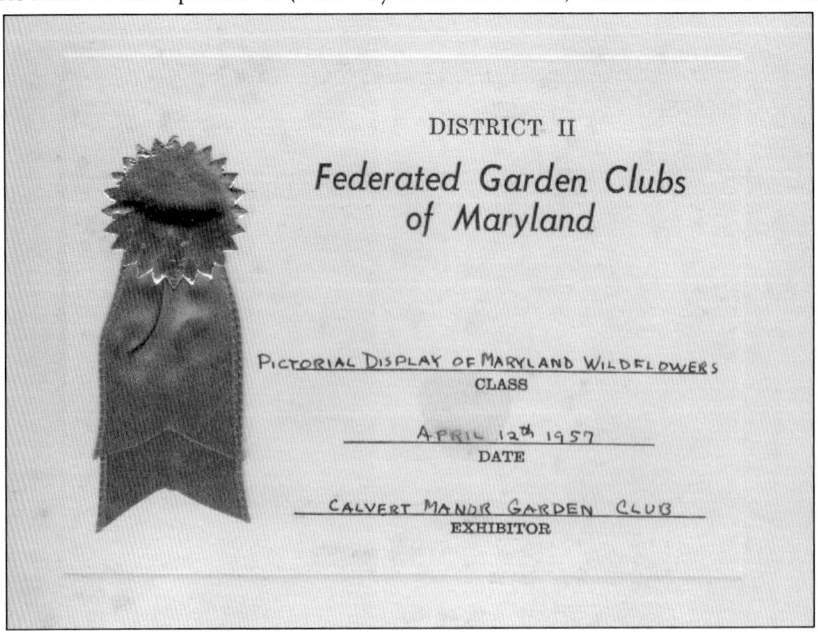

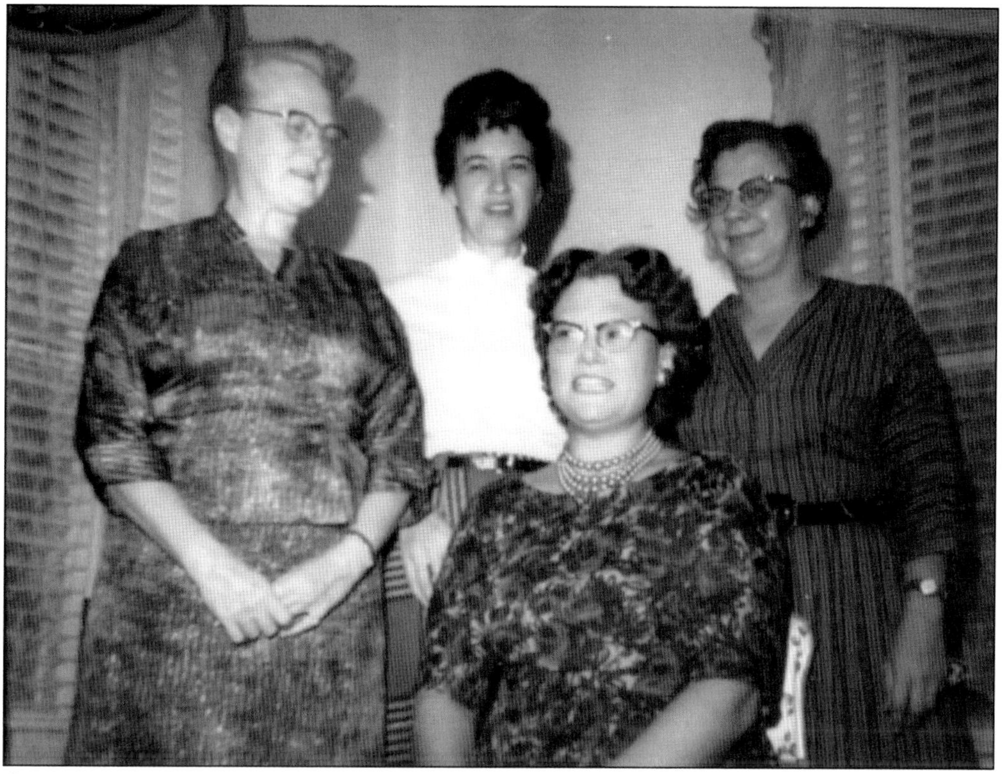

Calvert Manor Garden Club in the 1960s. The June 1962 photograph above shows four members of the Calvert Manor Garden Club. Lillian Gardiner (far left), who died in 1965, had a distinguished career. She joined the faculty of the Catholic University of America in 1934 and became a member of the US Public Health Service in 1946. She helped establish a nursing school in Bangkok, Thailand, in 1951. The cover of the 1969–1970 calendar of activities (right) shows both the serious and fun aspects of the Calvert Manor Garden Club. In 1960, Alison Koberg noted, "To help forget the stiff knees and sore backs brought on by their favorite hobby, club members relax once a year at a family picnic." (Both courtesy of Frank Kahan, Calvert Manor Garden Club.)

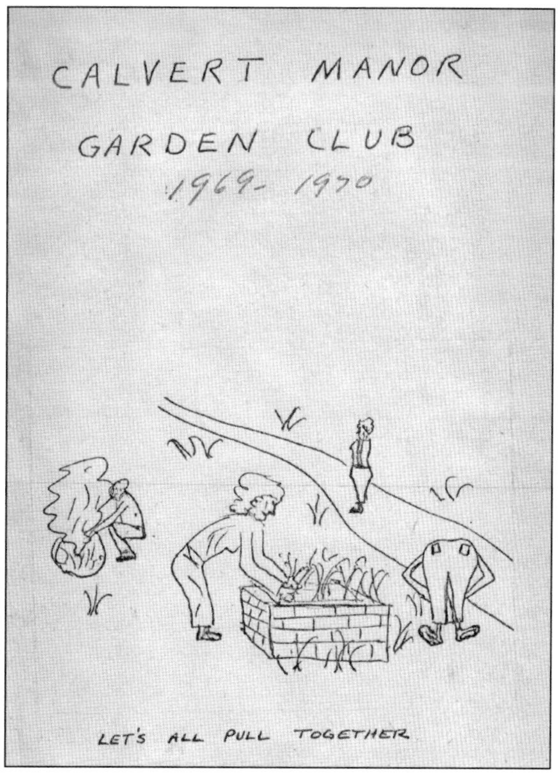

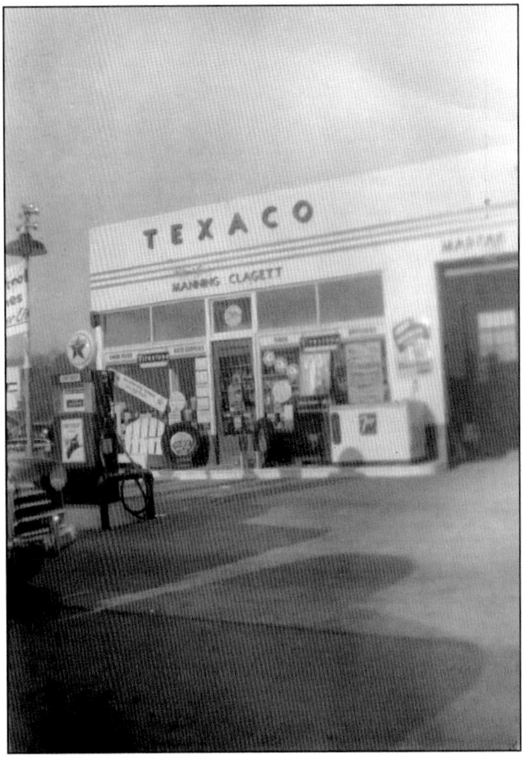

Manning Clagett Texaco. The building of Indian Head Highway, linking Accokeek with Washington and the Indian Head Naval Reservation, opened up new business opportunities in greater Accokeek. These 1953 photographs show the Manning Clagett Texaco station near the northern boundary of Accokeek. According to current residents, Manning Clagett Texaco provided employment for many residents of the area. The site is now occupied by Ted's Towing. Today, at the age of 88, Manning Clagett continues to be a prominent member of the Accokeek business community. He is a real estate broker for Clagett Realty, located at the intersection of Indian Head Highway and Livingston Road. (Both courtesy of Manning Clagett.)

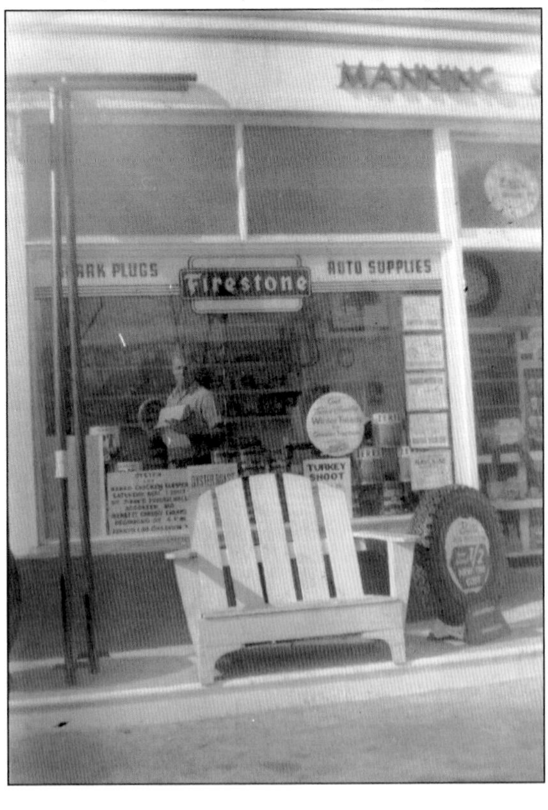

Six

Silesia

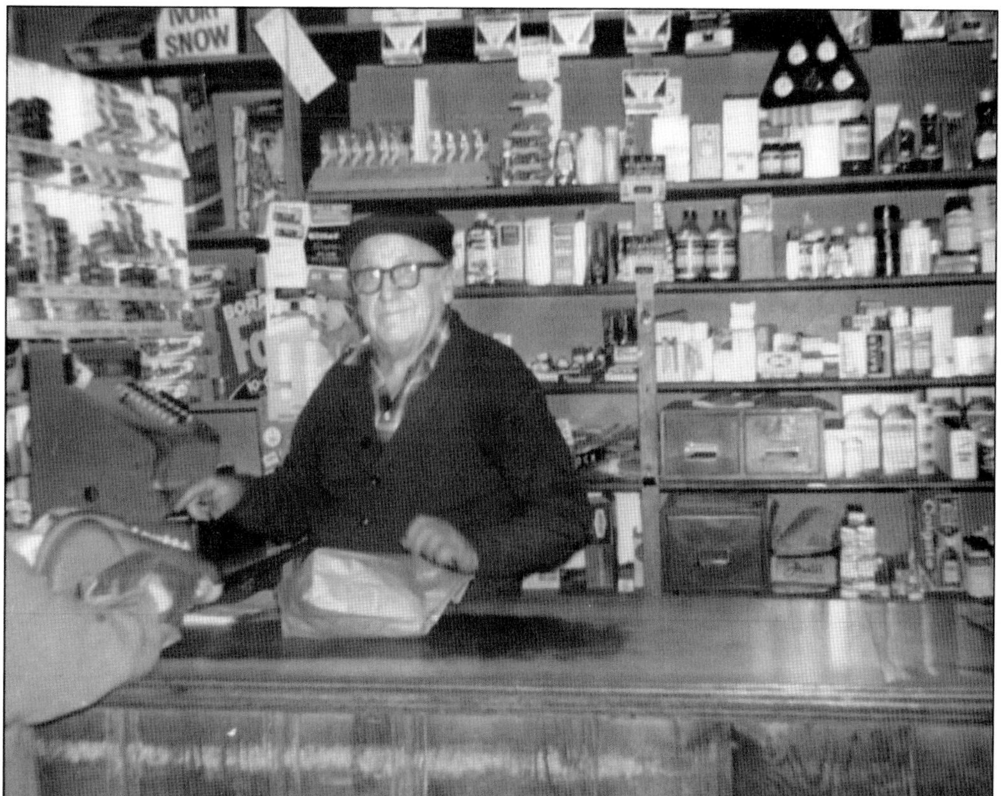

Silesia. The local area of Silesia is named for a region of Prussia that was once part of the German Empire and is now part of Poland. Robert "Papa" Tilch is seen in 1933 or 1934 in his store just north of Accokeek. Tilch came to America in 1895. (Courtesy of Carol and Karen Tilch.)

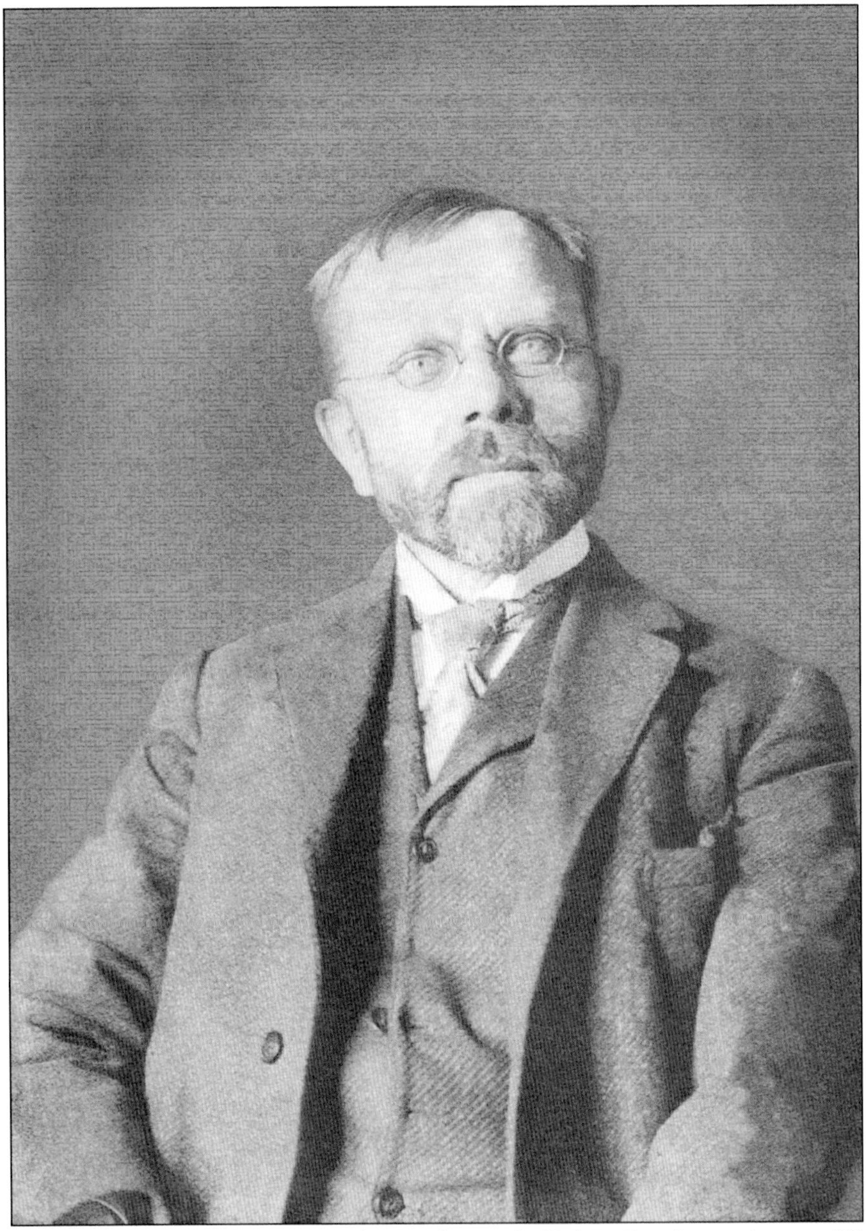

Robert Stein, Arctic Explorer. According to the article "Robert Stein's expedition to Ellesmere Island 1899–1901," written by William Barr in the *Polar Record* in September 1982, "Robert Stein was born in Glatz, in the Silesia region of Prussia, in 1857. He was educated at Heidelberg and studied for the priesthood for three years. After emigrating to the United States he continued his studies receiving an MD from Georgetown College in 1886. In addition to medicine his studies included linguistics. He joined the U.S. Geological Survey where he translated scientific papers into English from German, Swedish, Danish, Dutch, French, Italian, Portuguese, and Russian. Stein also had some knowledge of Eskimo languages. During the summer of 1897 he accompanied the Peary expedition to Greenland aboard the *Hope*. Landing on August 10, 1897, he made observations of geomorphology and biology on islands of Hubbard Bay. He was picked up by the *Hope* on September 1 and returned to New York." (Courtesy of Carol and Karen Tilch.)

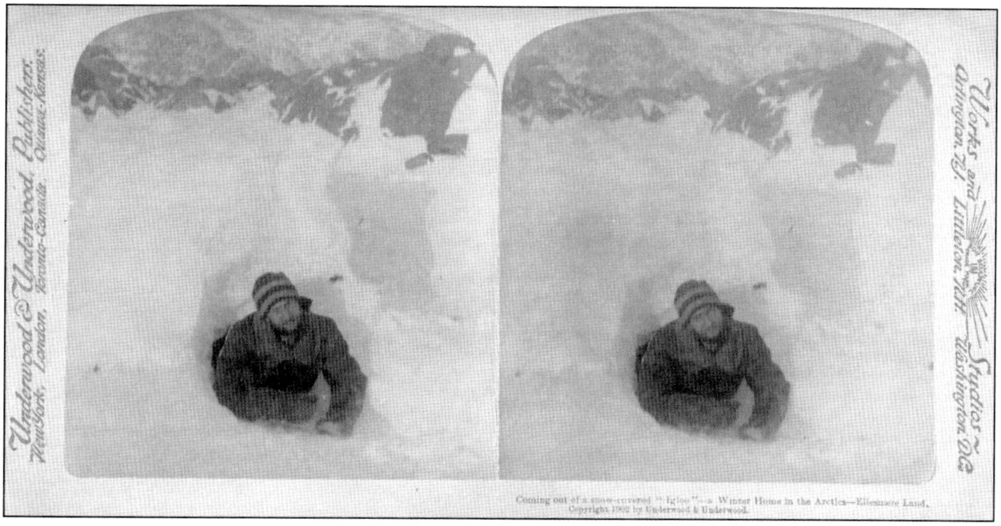

Robert Stein's 1899–1901 Expedition. Barr's article in the *Polar Record* continued, "Stein's interest in Arctic exploration was heightened by his experiences in 1897. He recruited two others to accompany him. One was Dr. Leopold Kahn, a 25-year-old Austrian, who had a degree in mathematics, physics, and philosophy from the University of Vienna. The other was Julian S. Warmbath, a Boston taxidermist, who had been born of German parents in Poland. Kahn was to be in charge of the meteorological program. Warmbath was a photographer to whom we are indebted for these stereo photographs. In the summer of 1899 the sealing steamer *Diana* sailed north from Sydney, Nova Scotia, on July 21, 1899, with the Stein party on board." (Courtesy of the Library of Congress, Prints and Photographs Division.)

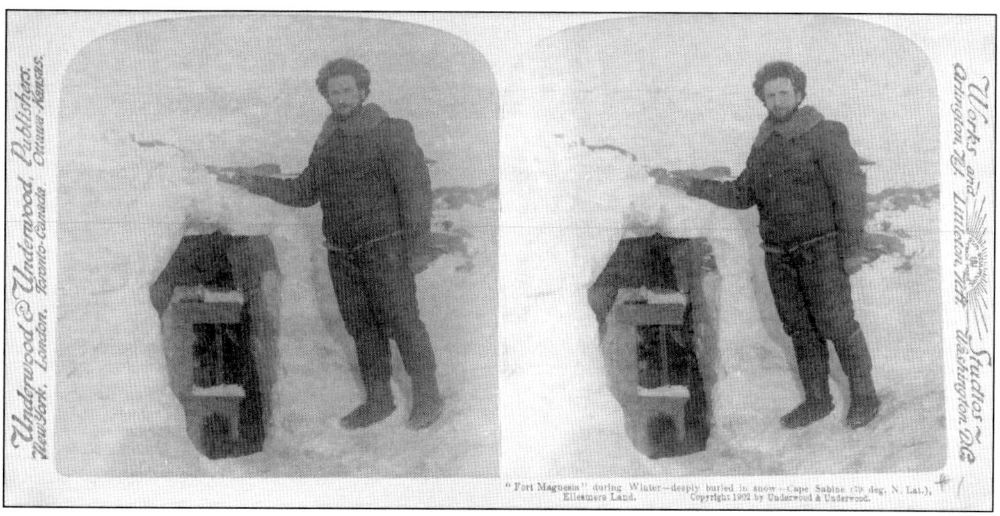

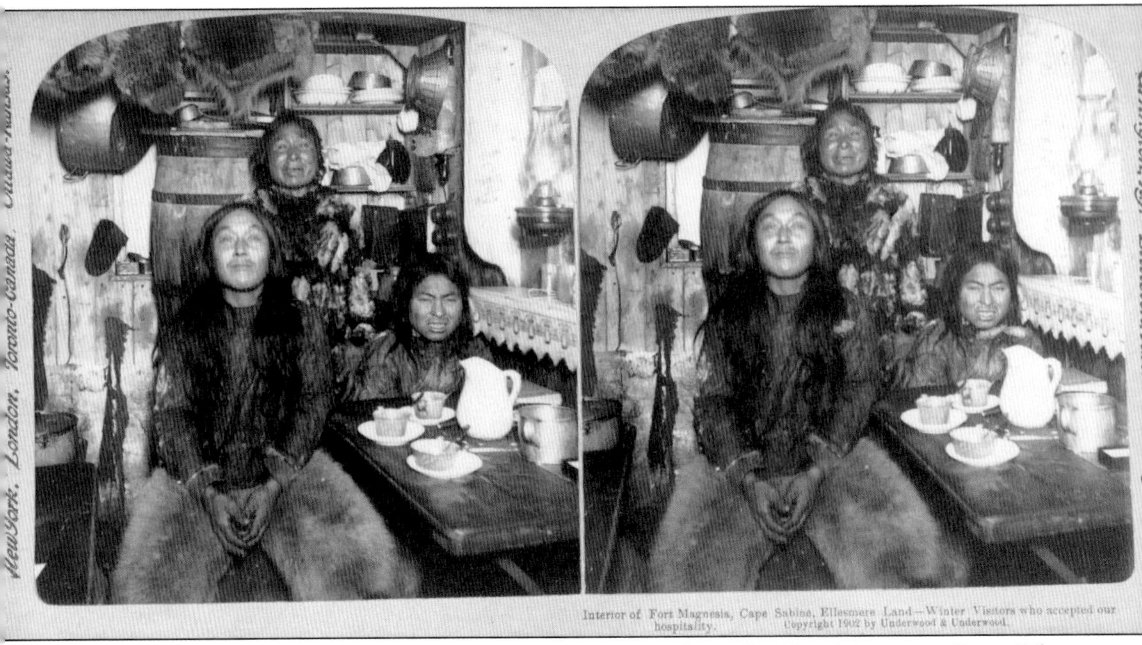

ESKIMO VISITORS. The caption of this stereo photograph reads, "Fort Magnesia, Cape Sabine, Ellesmere Land—Winter Visitors who accepted our hospitality." According to William Barr's September 1982 *Polar Record* article, "Fort Magnesia was a hut 5 meters long, 4 meters wide, and 2.8 meters high. 'Magnesia board,' normally used to insulate boilers and steam pipes, was put between the two layers of tar paper attached to the timber frame. The hut was named Fort Magnesia in honor of the Keasbey and Mattison Magnesia Company of Ambler, Pennsylvania, which had contributed the insulating material. The Eskimo visitors were Otuniahsoah, Aseyo and Pinatto. Initially the arrival of the Eskimos with three dog teams had frightened the men inside the hut who had heard stories of fierce and even cannibalistic Eskimos of Ellesmere Island. Kann, as an army lieutenant, was elected to throw open the door and step outside with a revolver in each hand. He must have been embarrassed to be met by this friendly, laughing group." (Courtesy of the Library of Congress, Prints and Photographs Division.)

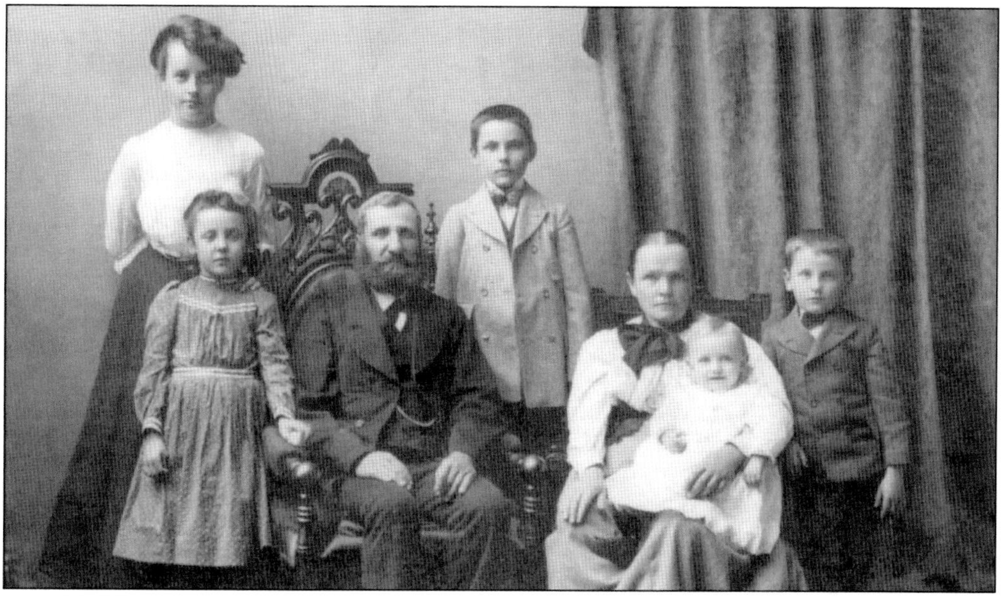

Anna Stein Tilch. Anna Stein, Robert Stein's sister, was born in 1861. She and her husband, Joseph Tilch, immigrated to America in 1895. They moved into Harmony Hall. Pictured are their children, from left to right, (first row) Martha, Bernard (on Anna's lap), and Robert; (second row) Anselma (Minkel) and Richard. John and Elfrieda (Freida) were born sometime after this photograph. (Courtesy of Carol and Karen Tilch.)

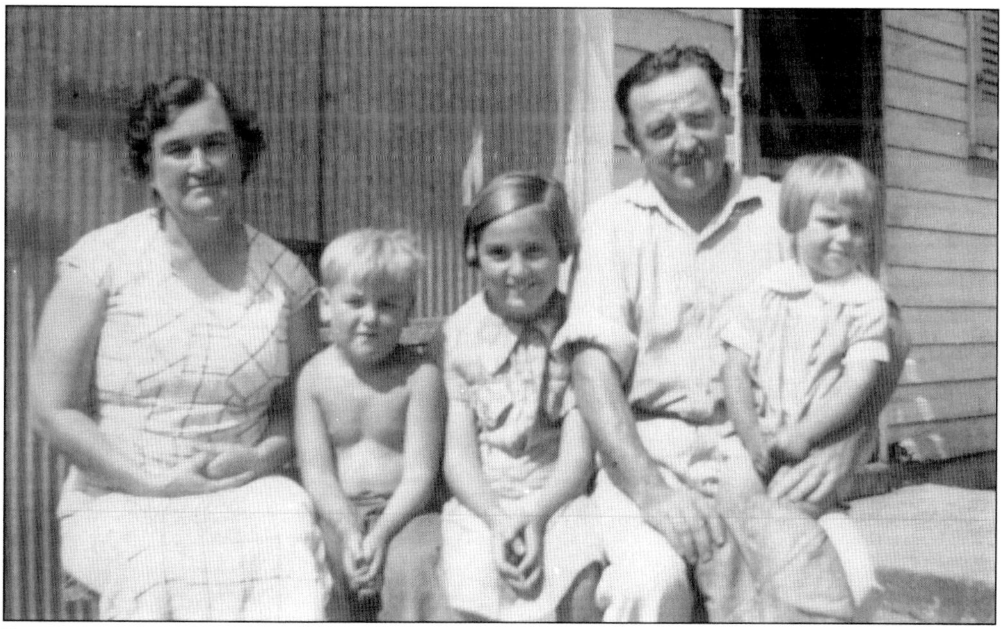

Robert "Papa" Tilch. Robert Tilch was one year old when Joseph and Anna Tilch moved into Harmony Hall with their other children at the time, Richard and Martha. Robert and his wife, Marie, had seven children. The couple is seen here with (from left to right) Edwin Francis, Anna Marie, and Mary Catherine. Robert "Papa" operated Tilch's General Store. People who had fallen on hard times were carried on his books until things got better. He never let anyone go hungry. (Courtesy of Carol and Karen Tilch.)

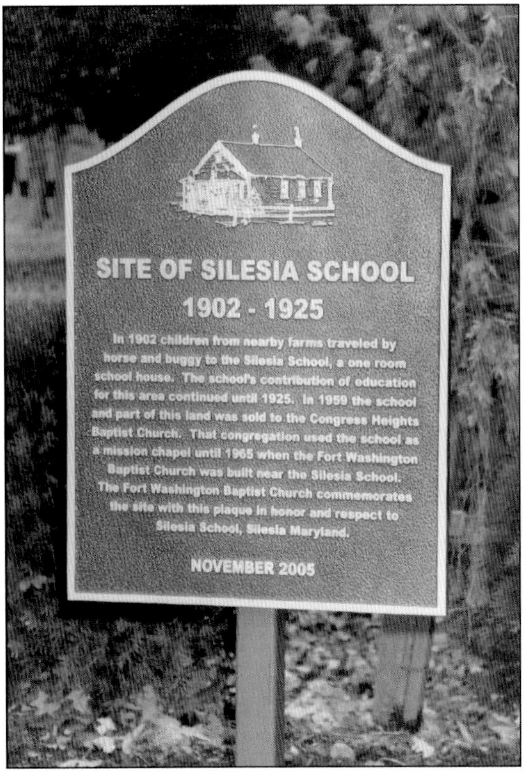

SILESIA SCHOOL. This school was constructed in 1902 on a one-acre lot purchased from James and Mary Edelen by the board of county commissioners. It was used for grades one through eight until 1925, when the Oxon Hill Consolidated School was built. In 1959, it was sold to Congress Heights Baptist Church, which used the building as its mission chapel until 1965, when Fort Washington Baptist Church was built. In 1981, Silesia School was designated as a historic site by the Prince George's County Council. Although area residents had proposed to restore the school, the church no longer wanted to be responsible for the building and wanted it removed from their property. All that remains is the marker commissioned by Fort Washington Baptist Church and Silesia Citizens Association. (Left, author's collection; below, courtesy of Fort Washington Baptist Church.)

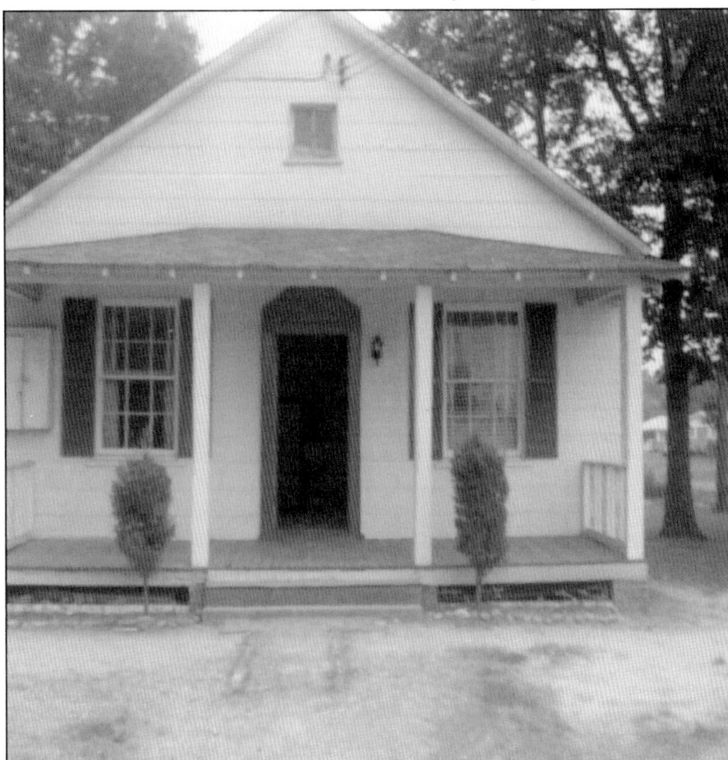

Seven

Where the Arts Come Out

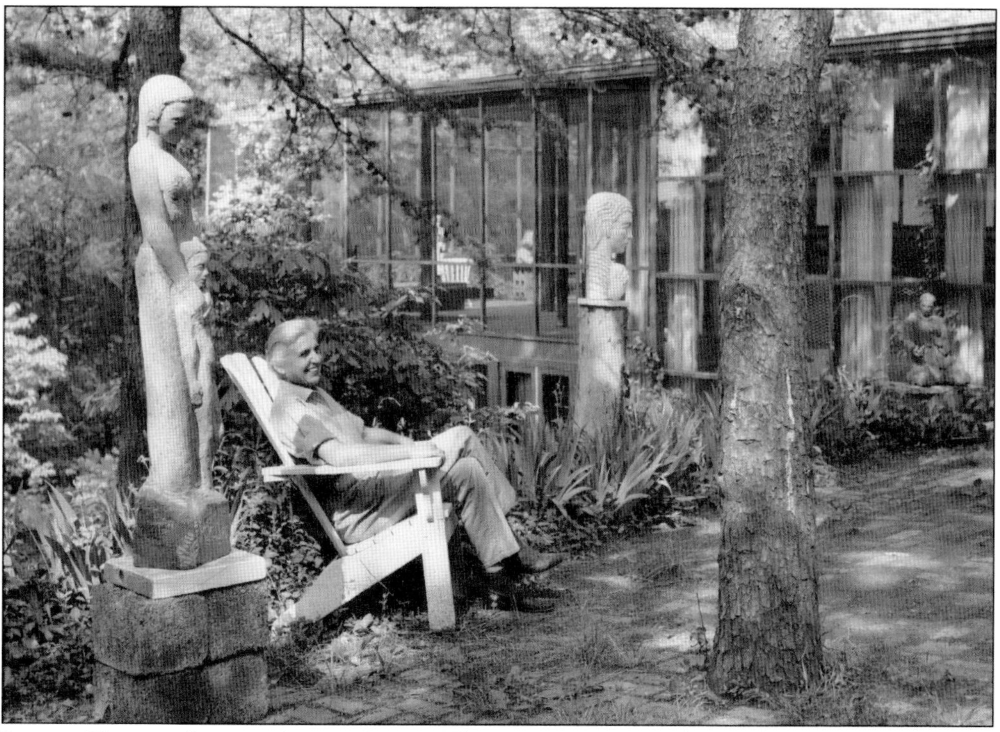

Lenore Thomas Straus, Artist. Lenore Thomas Straus is seen here at her home in Accokeek with two of her sculptures. In 1937, the Works Progress Administration commissioned Thomas to create sculptured art in Greenbelt. Part of her work consisted of bas-reliefs on the side of Center Elementary School. The school building now serves as the Greenbelt Community Center. (Courtesy of Nancy and Holly Wagner.)

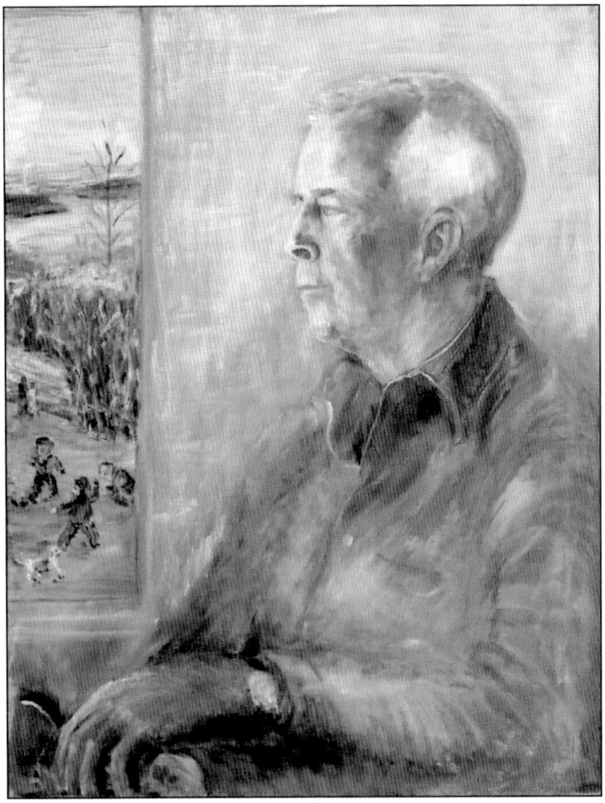

Ferguson Paintings. These two paintings of Henry "Fergie" Ferguson are in the main house at Hard Bargain Farm, now occupied by Alice Ferguson Foundation staff. The portrait at left was painted by Lenore Thomas Straus, and the one below was painted by Richard Kenah in 1958. Both artists had long-standing connections with the Fergusons. "Fergie" Ferguson recalled, "Dick Kenah was a member of the old volleyball gang before the Second World War. Lenore Thomas had been a resident at Longview. In 1941 she got married to Bobby Straus, who was living at Carver's Hill. In 1947 they moved to a house in Bond's Retreat, a large tract of land adjoining Hard Bargain Farm." (Both photographs by Alexandra Tice, courtesy of the Alice Ferguson Foundation.)

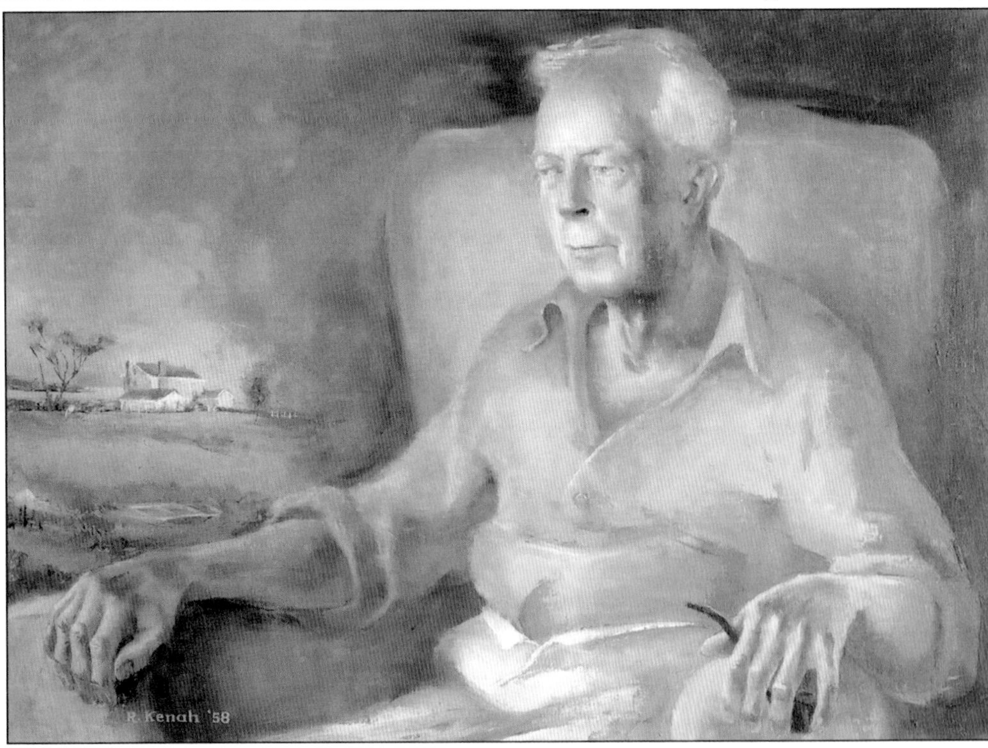

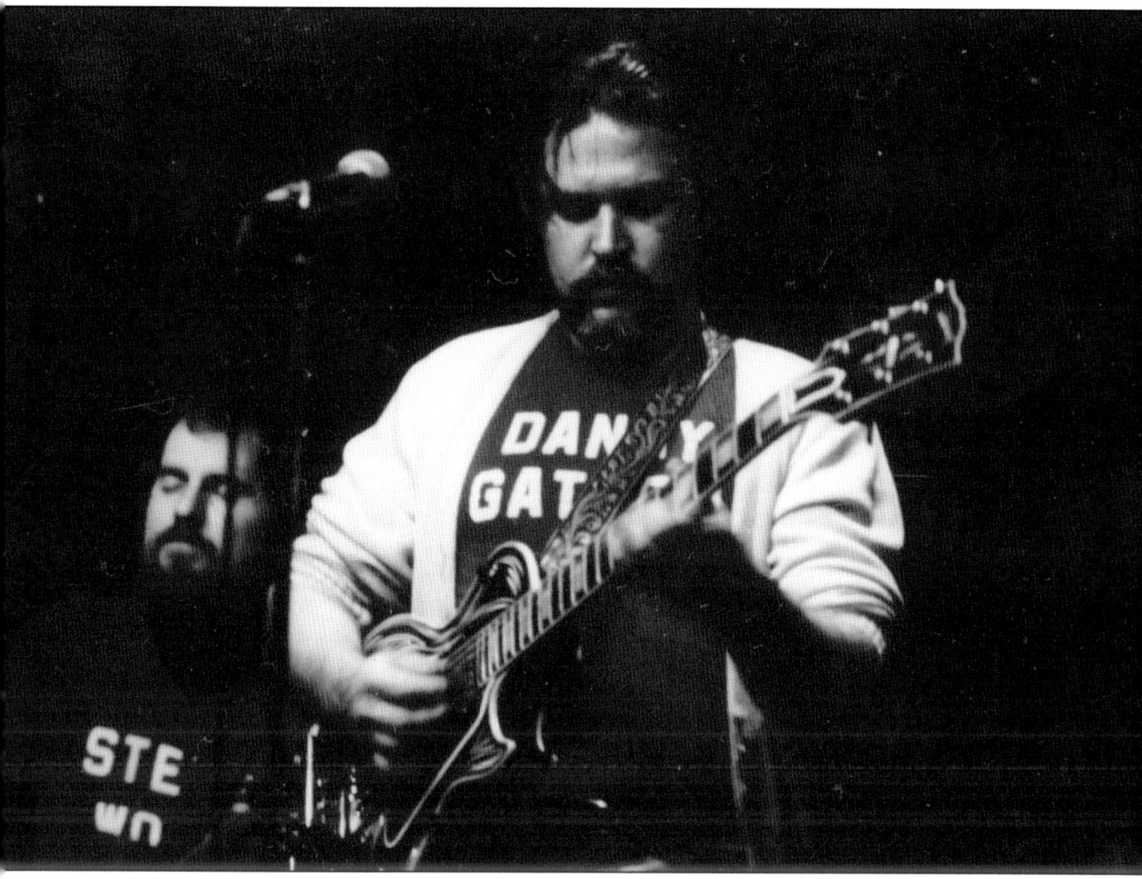

STEVE WOLF AND DANNY GATTON. Accokeek residents Steve Wolf (left) and Danny Gatton (right) are seen here in the late 1970s. A book by Ralph Heibutzki, *Unfinished Business: The Life and Times of Danny Gatton*, was published in 2003. In the introduction Heibutzki calls Gatton "The World's Greatest Unknown Guitar Player." The book provides detailed information about Gatton and the musicians he worked with in the 1970s, 1980s, and 1990s. One of these was Steve Wolf, who came down from Boston in early 1978 to work with Gatton on a project called The Redneck Jazz Explosion. The Rockabilly Hall of Fame website has a Danny Gatton page with links to his music and information about his life. (Courtesy of Steve Wolf.)

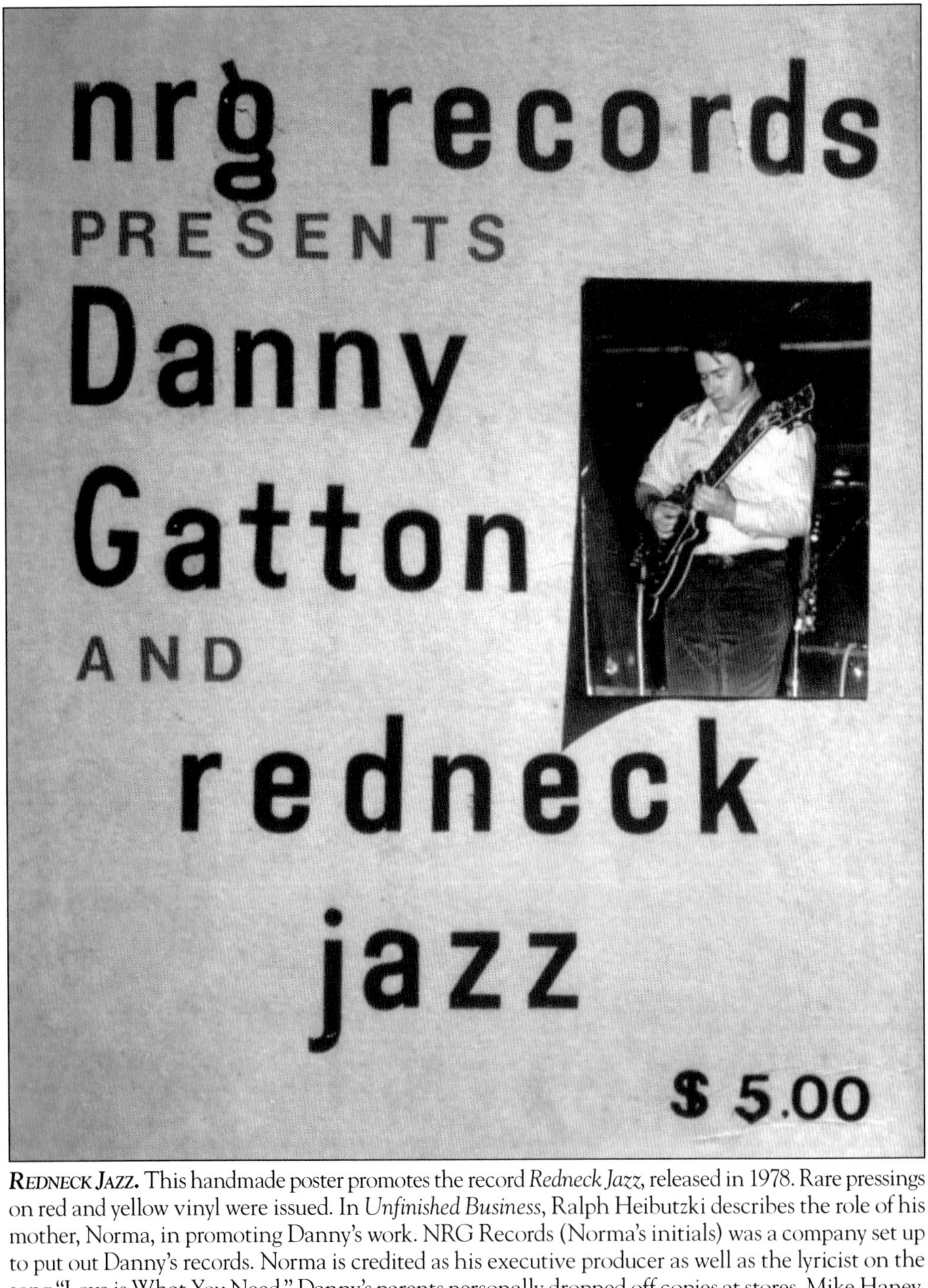

Redneck Jazz. This handmade poster promotes the record *Redneck Jazz,* released in 1978. Rare pressings on red and yellow vinyl were issued. In *Unfinished Business*, Ralph Heibutzki describes the role of his mother, Norma, in promoting Danny's work. NRG Records (Norma's initials) was a company set up to put out Danny's records. Norma is credited as his executive producer as well as the lyricist on the song "Love is What You Need." Danny's parents personally dropped off copies at stores. Mike Haney, assistant warehouse manager of the Penguin Feather chain, reported that *Redneck Jazz* outsold the Rolling Stone's *Some Girls* within two weeks after its release. It continued to be a top-five seller at the chain's four Washington stores. The term "redneck jazz" is used to describe Gatton's style, which combined jazz, blues, and rockabilly in an innovative fashion. The photograph of Danny Gatton on the poster is an iconic original that has been reproduced widely. (Author's collection.)

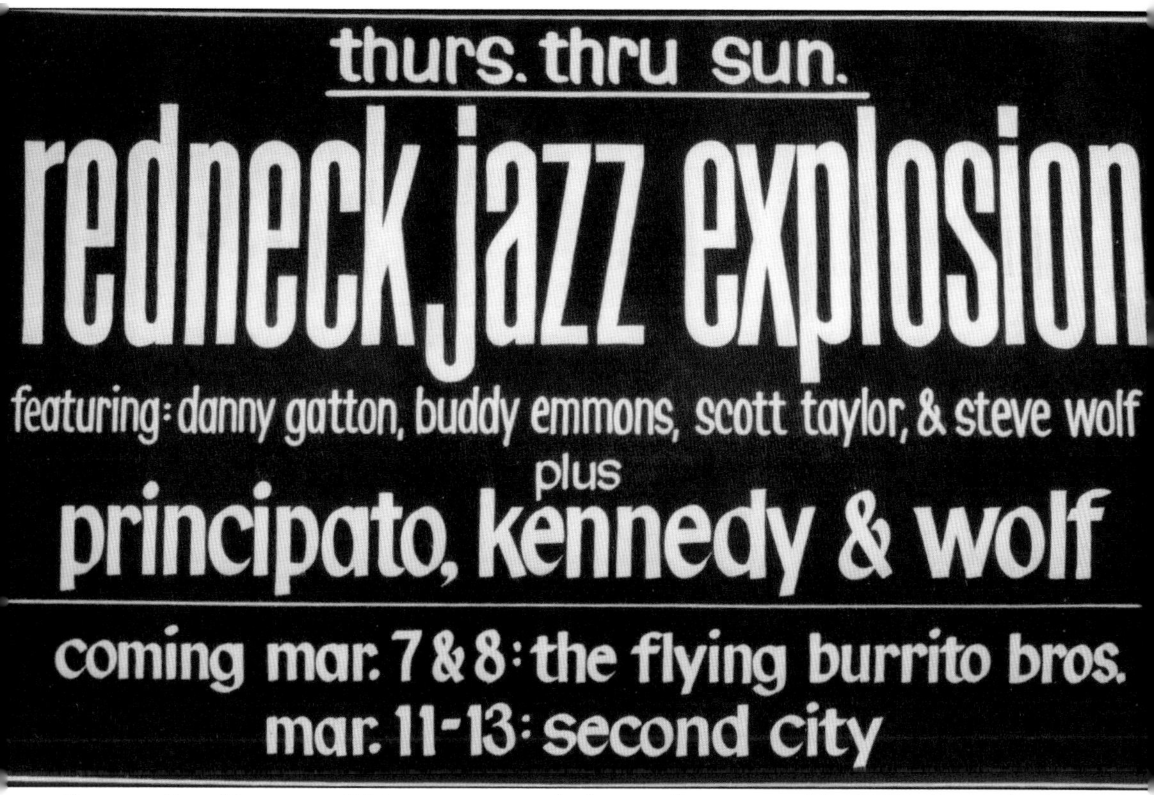

Redneck Jazz Explosion. This poster was made for a performance at The Cellar Door, which was at Thirty-fourth and M Streets in Washington from 1965 through 1981. According to Steve Wolf, one of the Redneck Jazz Explosion's first gigs was in Nashville at the now-defunct Randy's Pickin' Parlor. Guest performers with Gatton that evening were three top Nashville session players: guitarist Buddy Barrett, fiddle player Buddy Spiker, and pedal steel guitarist Buddy Emmons. Steve Wolf recalled: "The results were so much fun that Danny soon booked four nights in a row at the legendary Cellar Door in Washington, DC." Members of Danny's band for that gig included Steve Wolf, Buddy Emmons, and drummer Scott Taylor. The December 31, 1978, Cellar Door performance is preserved on the album *Danny Gatton's Redneck Jazz Explosion*, released in 1995. (Author's collection.)

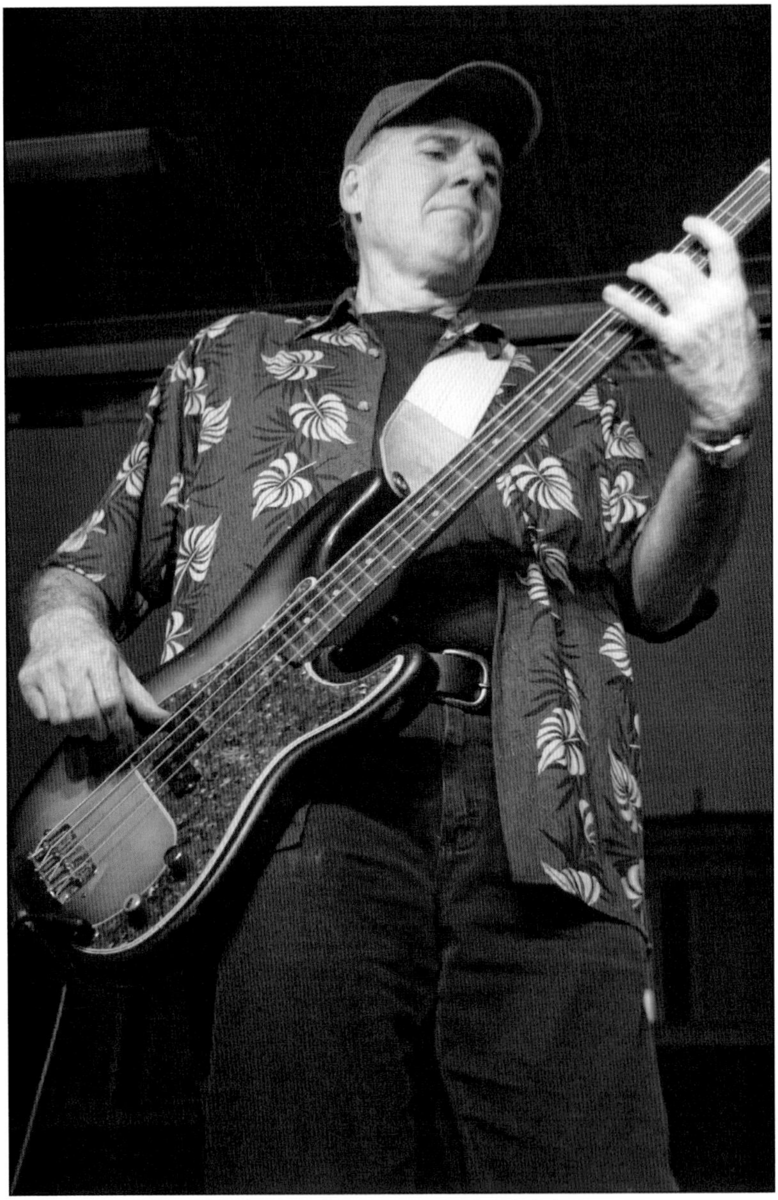

STEVE WOLF. A bassist, Wolf has been a fixture on the Mid-Atlantic music scene since the late 1960s. During that time, he has performed at major festivals and venues throughout the United States and Europe with such DC-area notables as Danny Gatton, Tom Principato, the Nighthawks, Catfish Hodge, Big Joe Maher, Deanna Bogart, Linwood Taylor, Ron Holloway, Cathy Ponton-King, Jesse Yawn, and a diverse group of national artists ranging from Chuck Berry, The Coasters, and Bo Diddley to Doctor John, Danny Gatton, Brian Auger, The Marvellettes, and Clarence Clemons, Bruce Springsteen's saxophonist. His well-respected work in the blues arena has led him to back Chicago blues legends Sunnyland Slim, Pine Top Perkins, Bob Margolin, Charlie Musselwhite, Luther "Guitar Junior" Johnson, Jimmy Thackery, and many others. For the past 20 years, Wolf has been leading the award-winning jazz and swing group Swing Speak. Their first album, *Well Spoken*, won the Washington Area Music Association Award for Best Traditional Jazz Recording. Wolf is a longtime Accokeek resident. (Courtesy of Alan Grossman.)

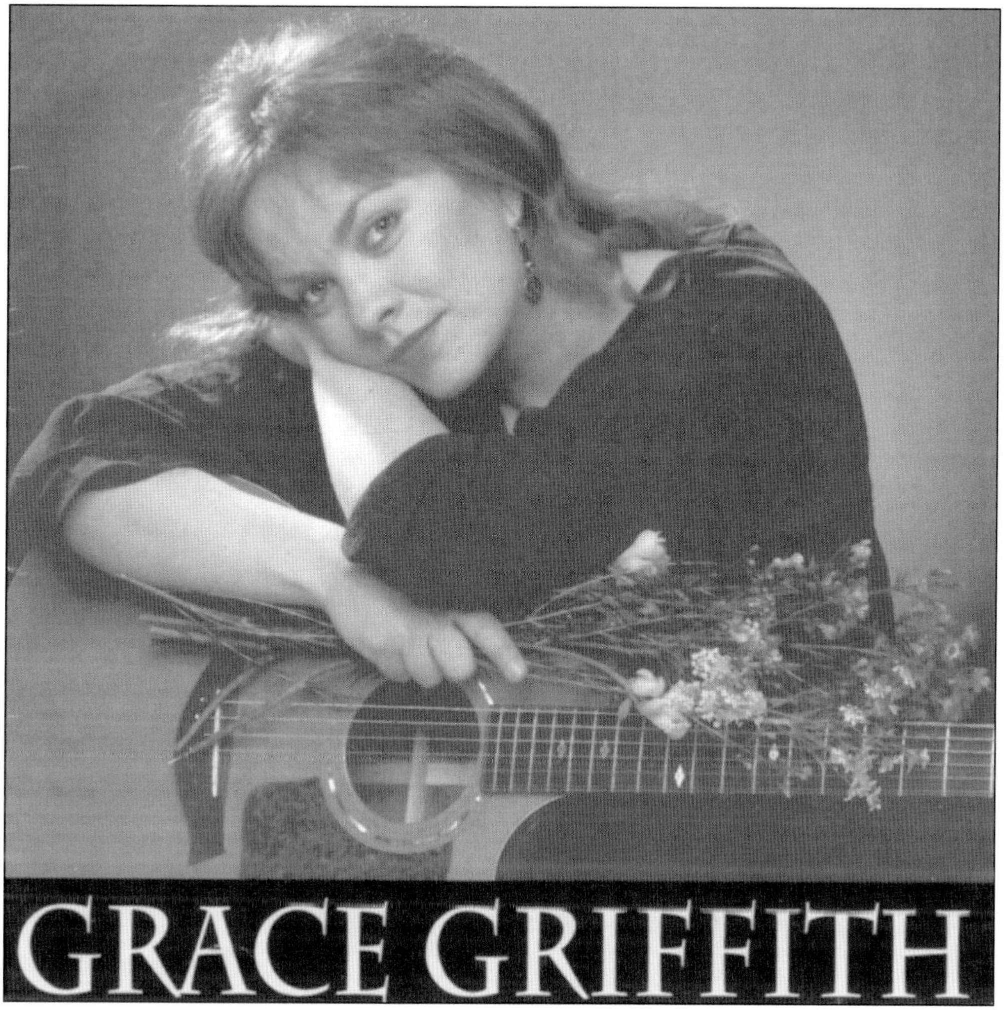

GRACE GRIFFITH. Grace Griffith was born in Washington, DC, and raised in a "handmade" country house, one of 10 children. Her father wished to establish a self-sufficient family farm. They were not rich, but they ate their own vegetables and the children had lots of time to play in the woods. "Town" meant Indian Head, but they got their mail at Bryans Road, the closest thing to town they knew. During college, one of Griffith's main musical inspirations was the Café Florian, which she ran for five years at the Unitarian Universalist church in Camp Springs. Her career in music has been a source of great personal and spiritual sustenance. She has been fortunate to receive the praise of her peers and much recognition from the Washington Area Music Association, which has awarded her about 25 awards over the course of her career. Griffith currently records for the West Coast record label Blix Street and enjoys mentoring younger musicians and aspiring performers. (Photograph by Christopher Moscatiello, courtesy of Grace Griffith.)

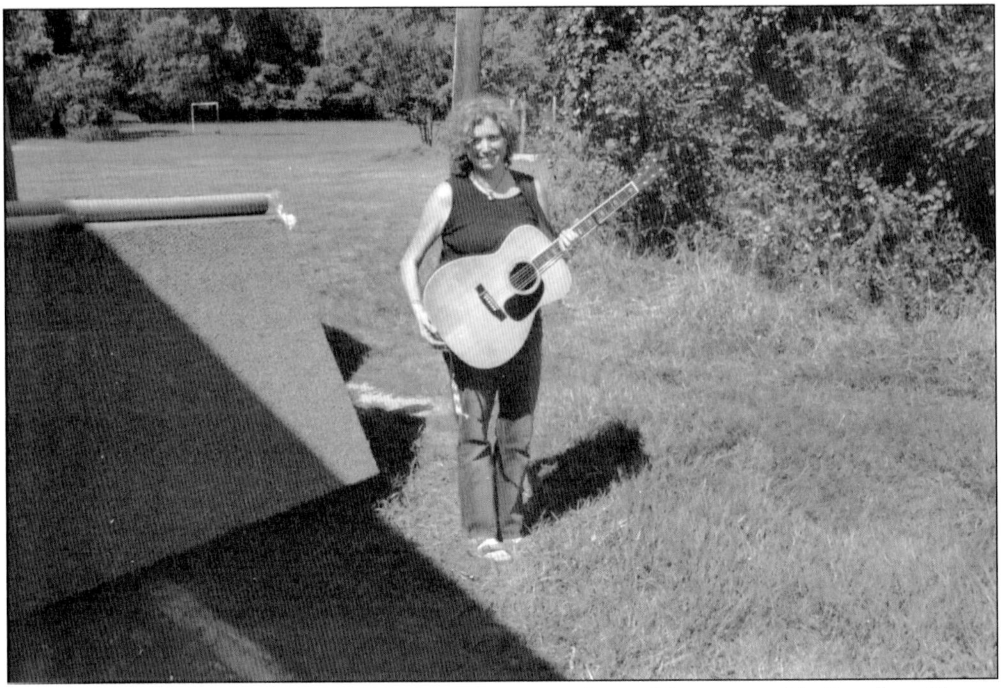

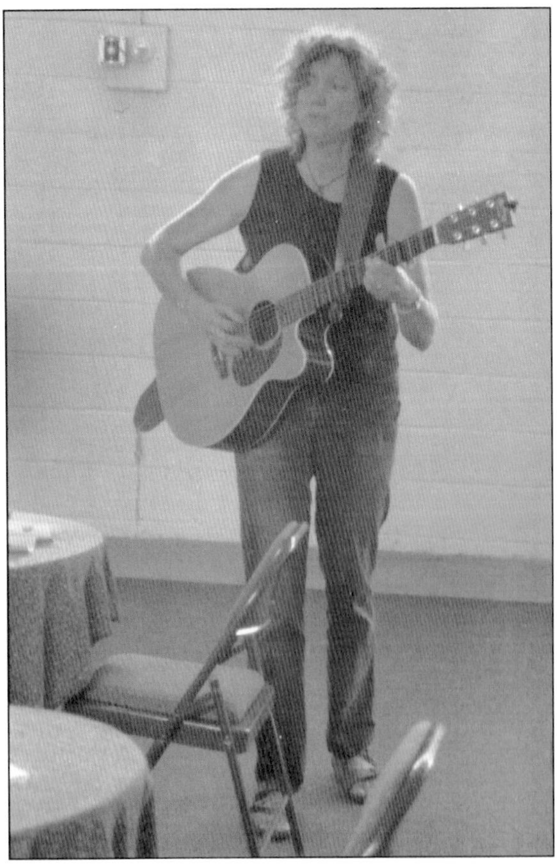

Lynn Hollyfield. Hailing from Staten Island, New York, Lynn Hollyfield picked up the guitar at age 10 and ran, with musical influences from great jazz artists like Ella Fitzgerald and Billie Holiday to the Beatles, Cream, and Crosby, Stills, Nash & Young. She launched into her own songwriting, infusing these influences to create a diverse repertoire of contemporary folk, pop, blues, and jazz. Her 2010 solo recording, a collection of 10 original songs, earned her three Washington Area Music Award nominations, for Best Contemporary Folk Recording, Best Debut Album, and Songwriter of the Year. Her songwriting received recent Honorable Mentions in the Mid-Atlantic Songwriting Contest and the Indie International Songwriting Contest's Folk category. Hollyfield lives in Accokeek, where she combines music with a professional practice. (Both, author's collection.)

Eight

OLD FAMILY PHOTOGRAPHS

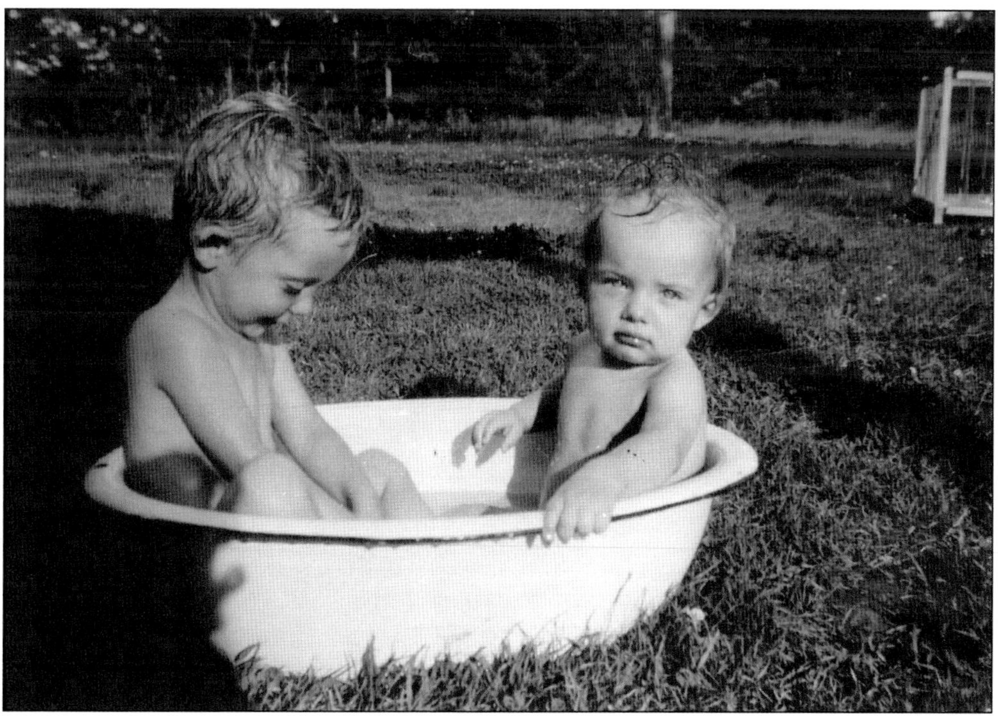

GORDON AND JON POWELL. The Powell brothers, Gordon and Jon, are seen here in a washtub in Accokeek around 1949. On hot July days, this was a good way for children to stay cool. Other residents could take advantage of being close to the Potomac River, where it was relatively cooler. (Courtesy of Gordon and Jon Powell.)

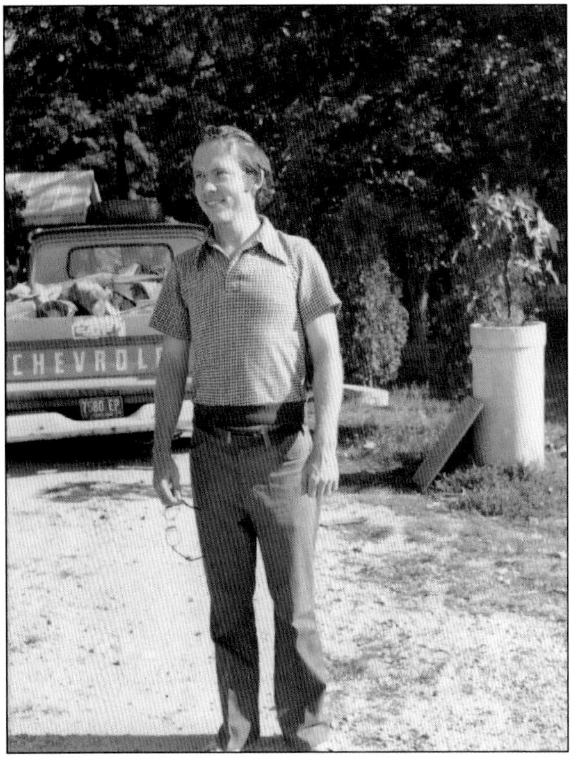

The Powell Brothers. Years later, Gordon (left) and Jon Powell (below), who both still live in Accokeek, are seen here as dignified adults, especially Jon, who is dressed up for a wedding. Remembering the photograph on the previous page, Jon Powell wrote, "64 years later brother Gordon and I are still in the same boat, the current boat being a project of cold fusion experimentation. E. Gordon Powell is a physicist and I tag along as machinist—each does a part. Gordon's side of the bath may have been deuterium bearing water with a touch of humor. My side was more infused with wine, women, song, and gears. As the twigs are bent so grew the trees." (Both courtesy of Gordon and Jon Powell.)

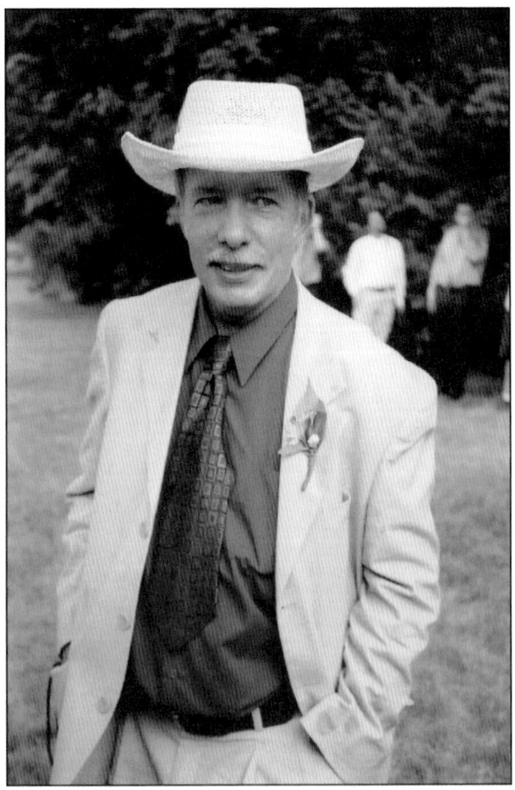

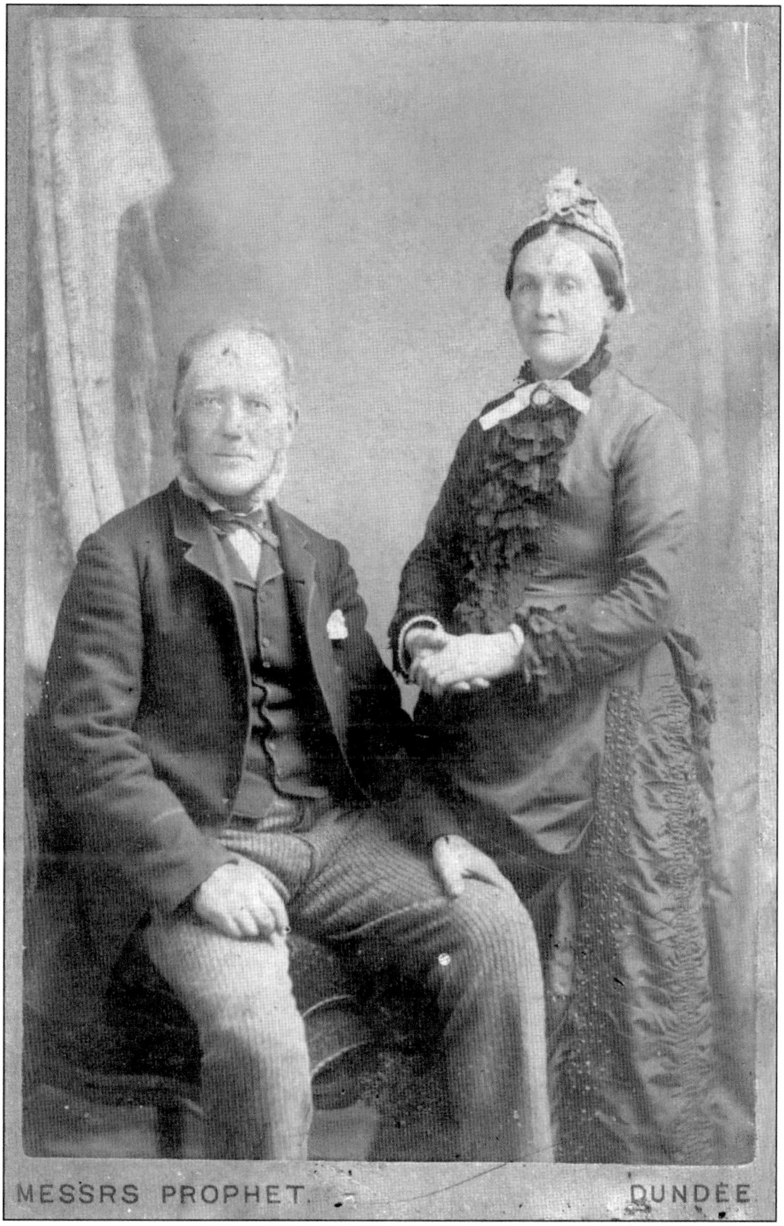

POWELL ANCESTORS IN SCOTLAND. According to Jon Powell, "Hilda Blanchard Powell gained a much beloved stepfather in the person of Bruce David Silve Gordon. Shown in [this] photograph are his parents photographed in Dundee, Scotland, before coming to North America. He was a lifelong farmer and well thought of in Manitoba, Canada. At last check the photographic enterprise, Messrs. Prophet and son, was still in business. Grandfather Bruce spoke of begging on the streets of Dundee for milk at the age of 7, and asking for the 'cap' [end] of a boiled egg where a bit of egg may be found. People came from all around to hear his stories." In his book *The Moyaone Reserve*, George Hanssen writes, "The majority of settlers were yeomen of meager means who could barely afford the cost of the voyage, persons under bond to pay transportation and service costs, and those who were sent under contracts that would be sold to bidders, for a specified term of years, upon arrival." (Courtesy of Gordon and Jon Powell.)

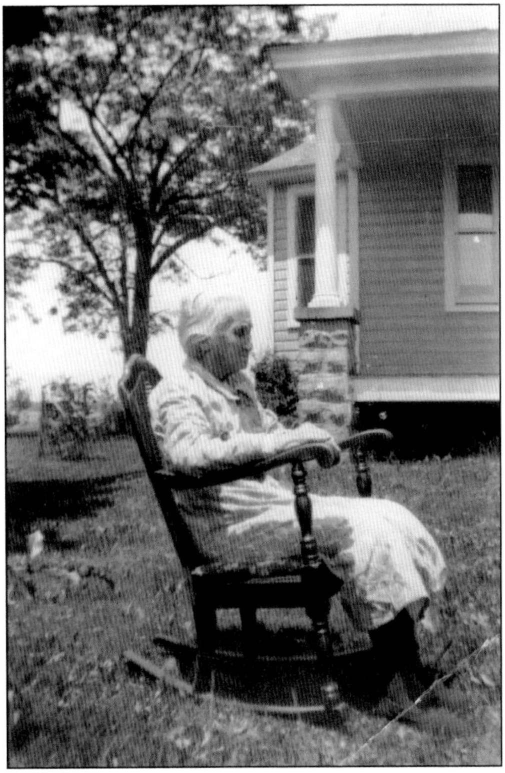

Berry Ancestors. Frances LaPoint Berry (left) was born in Malone, New York, on March 1, 1852. She married George Waters Berry (below), who was born on February 8, 1845. The Berrys are the grandparents of Hilda Blanchard Powell, Jon and Gordon Powell's mother. Berry Road is named in memory of these ancestors. Nowadays, except for a short section in Accokeek, Berry Road is a divided highway, Route 228, connecting Accokeek with Waldorf. (Both courtesy of Gordon and Jon Powell.)

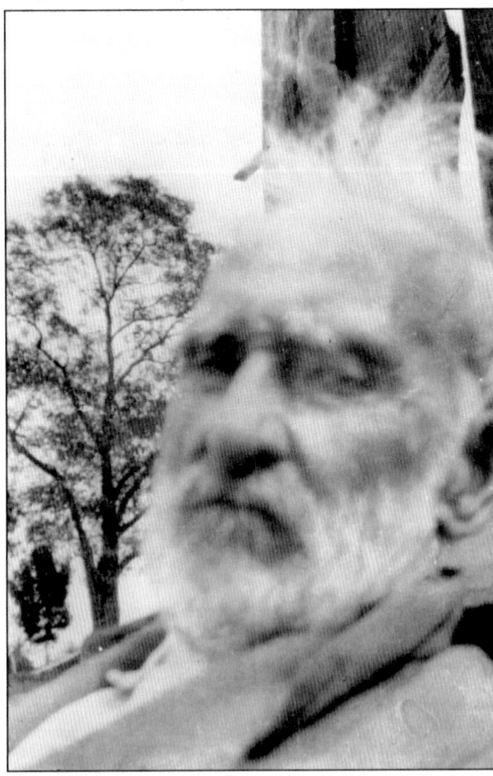

MATTIE VAN DORN JENKINS POWELL. Born Mattie Van Dorn Jenkins around 1882, Powell was the mother of Edward Carter Powell and the grandmother of the Powell brothers, Gordon and Jon. This elegant lady was a schoolteacher who passed on her love of reading to her grandchildren. (Courtesy of Gordon and Jon Powell.)

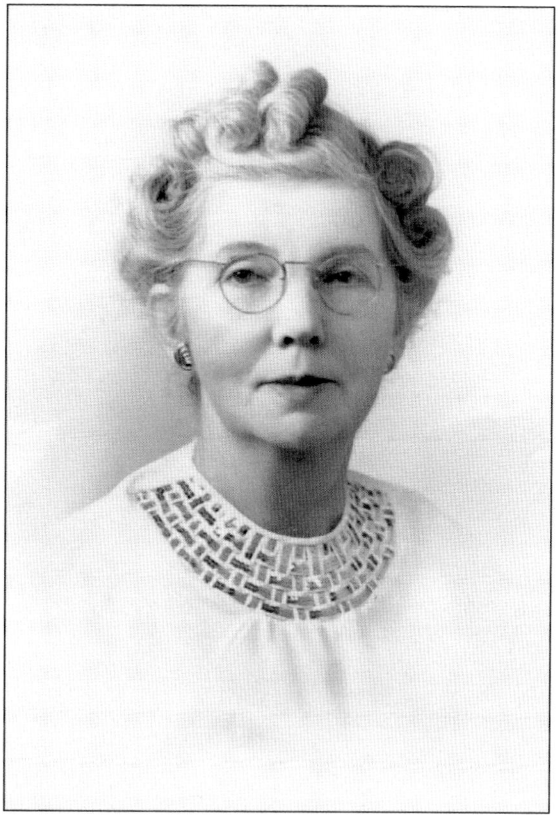

WILLIAM BLANCHARD AND THE *ARK*. The crew of the *Ark* (below) needed no charts to navigate Piscataway Creek. Crabs, fish, muskrats, waterfowl, and oysters could be caught in those days of cleaner water. This photograph from around 1911 shows the *Ark* at low tide with eight men, one dog, and a chef. Nothing was needed from a store to prepare a delicious meal except salt and pepper. The man at the far right is William Blanchard, the father of Hilda Blanchard Powell. (Courtesy of Gordon and Jon Powell.)

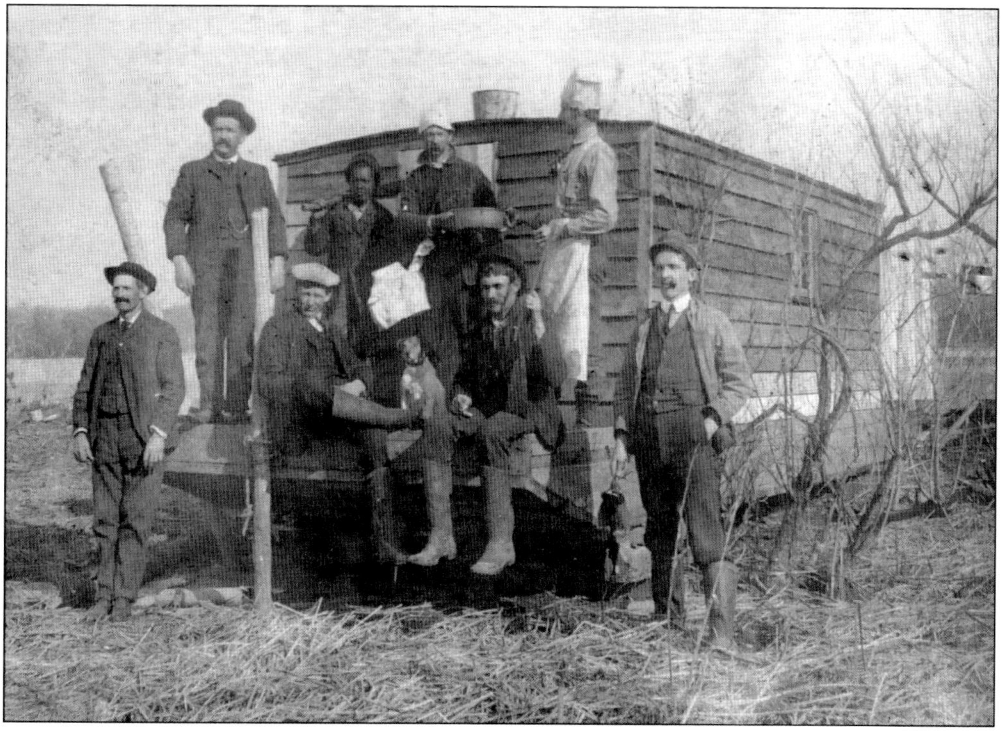

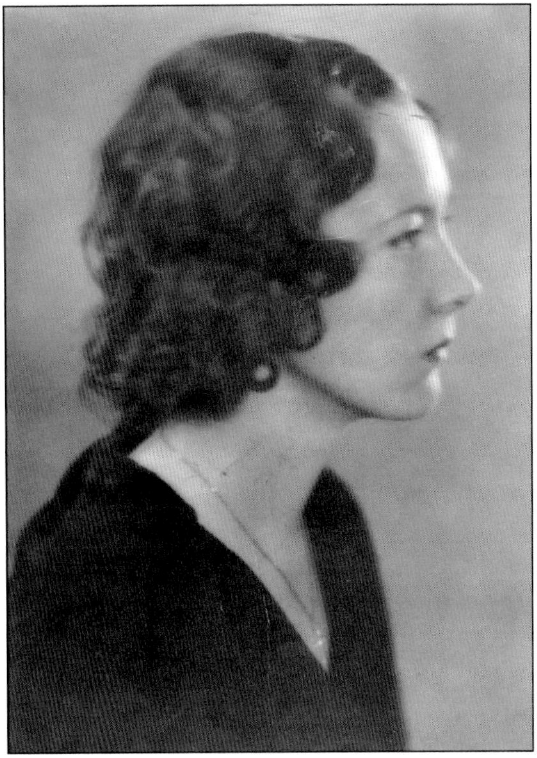

Hilda Blanchard Powell (1911–1996). The mother of the Powell brothers, Gordon and Jon, Hilda Blanchard Powell was born in Accokeek. Gordon recalls that, as a child, she caught a turkey vulture, painted it green, and released it. The released vulture then ascended to heaven, to the great wonderment of all observers. (Courtesy of Gordon and Jon Powell.)

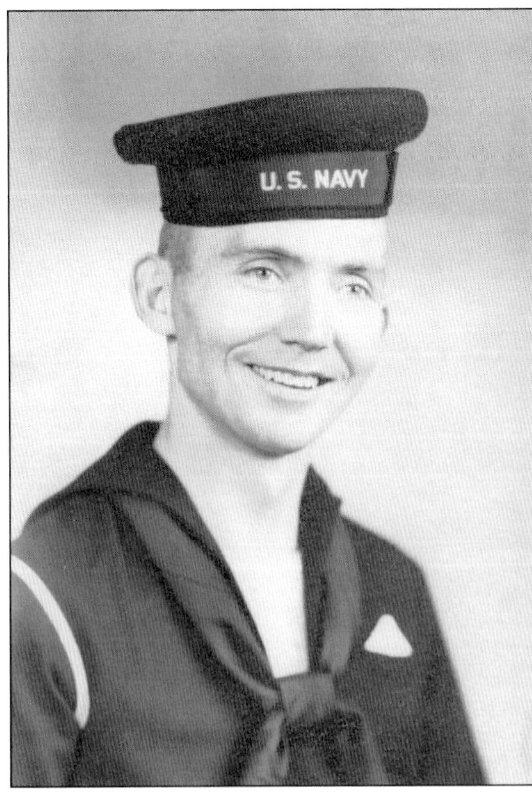

Edward Carter Powell (1906–1996). Ed Powell spent his early life in Wilson, North Carolina. After moving to Washington, DC, he worked at the State Department. When he was drafted, he was sent to Bainbridge Island, in Washington state. A "Q" specialist, he intercepted Japanese code groups and then transmitted them to Washington, DC, by teletype in Morse code. Ed died in 1996, one month after his wife, Hilda. He was the father of the Powell brothers, Gordon and Jon. (Courtesy of Gordon and Jon Powell.)

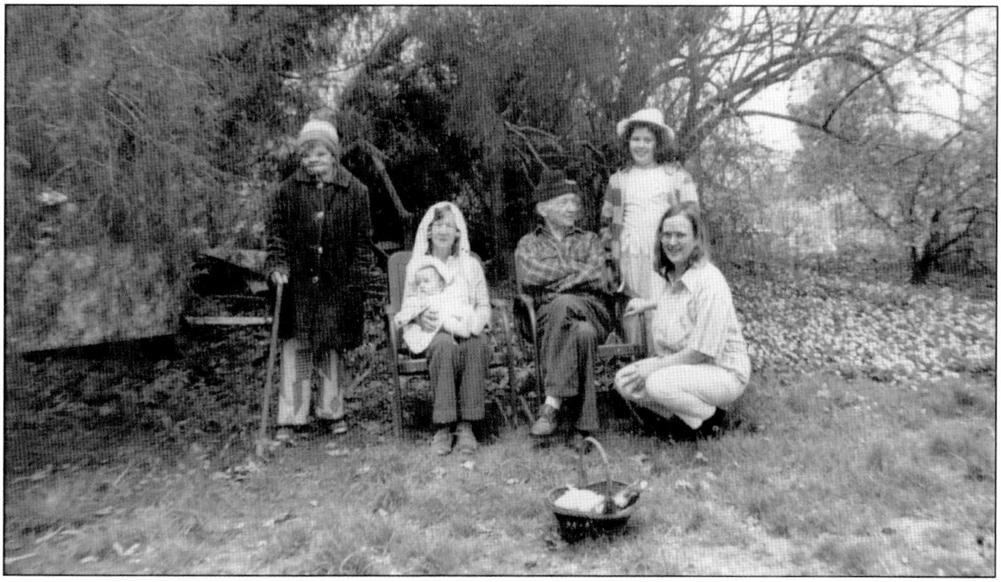

Powell Family Group. This photograph from around 1977 shows, from left to right, Amelia Fletcher, Leanna Celeste Powell, Hilda Rae Powell, Edward Powell, Emily Evenstar Powell, and Erin Jean Gatewood. Erin is the mother of Emily and Leanna, and Edward and Hilda are their grandparents. Fletcher, who was disfigured from birth, came from Indian Head, where she cared for Hilda's mother for 60 years. She was more of a family member than a domestic servant. (Courtesy of Gordon and Jon Powell.)

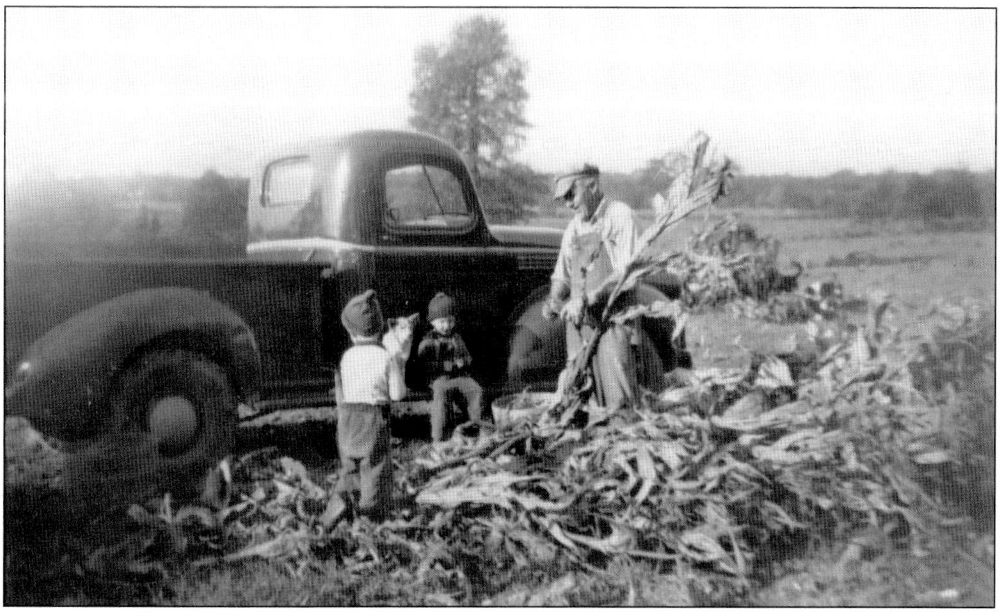

Bruce Gordon's Farm. This photograph from around 1951 shows, from left to right, Gordon Powell, Jon Powell, and Bruce Gordon, whose dog Trailer is playing with the boys. Bruce Gordon was the much-beloved stepfather of Hilda Blanchard Powell. This farm was bisected when Indian Head Highway was built. Beretta USA's gun factory now occupies the western portion, and Jon Powell lives on the eastern portion. To the left, outside the photograph, is the cowshed where Jon once surprised a prowling bobcat. (Courtesy of Gordon and Jon Powell.)

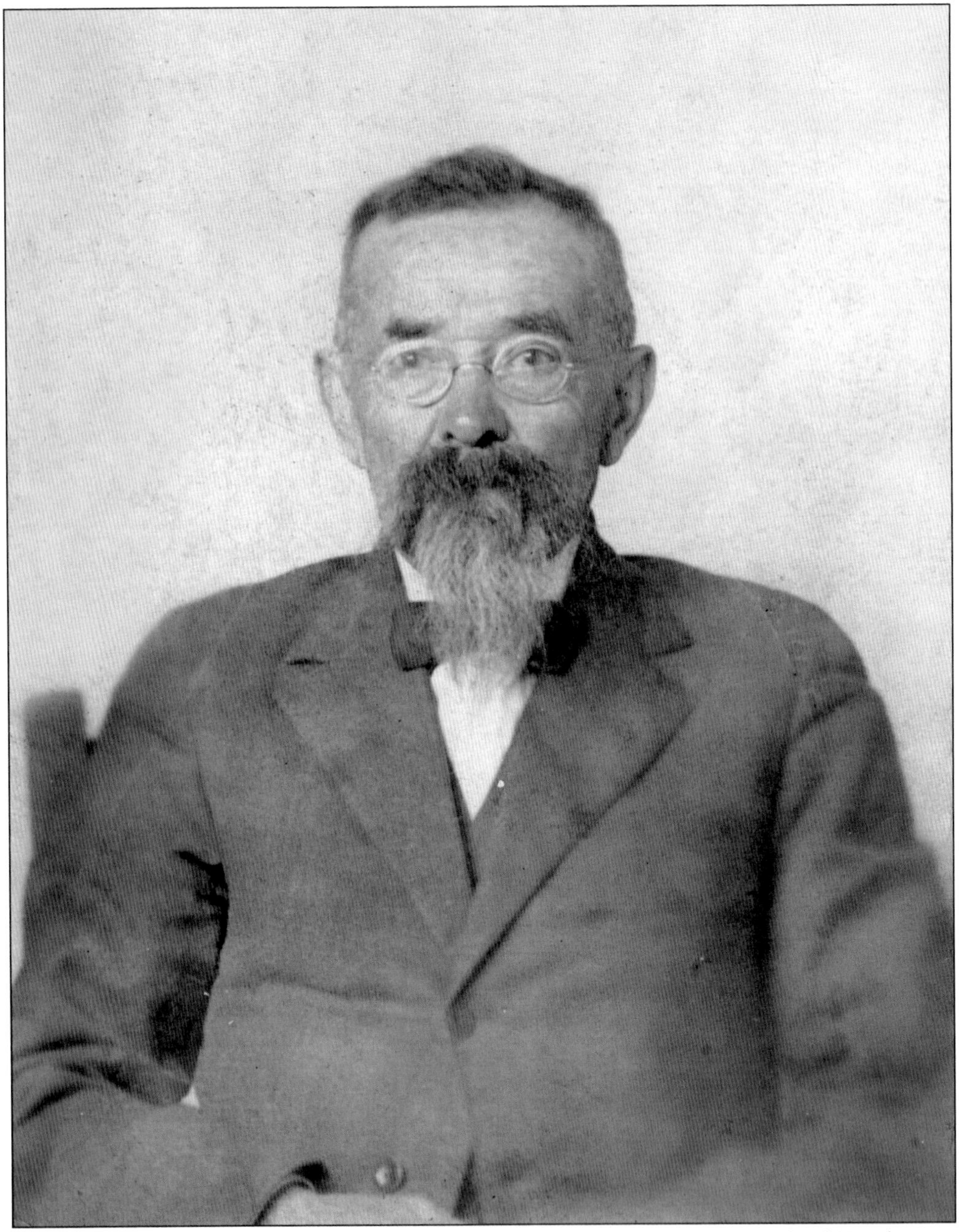

Gottfried Xander. When this photograph was taken, around 1920, Gottfried Xander was about 70 years old. A 1920 passport application on file at the National Archives and Records Administration includes a photograph of him when he was 27 years old, before he emigrated from Württemberg to the United States. This document includes a description of the young man as five-feet-four-inches tall with blue eyes and light brown hair. The name, year, and place of birth of his father are given as George Xander, born in Württemberg in 1810. On the application, Gottfried Xander declared that he became a naturalized citizen of the United States in 1894 and resided in Accokeek, Prince George's County, Maryland, where he had the occupation of farmer for 40 years. (Courtesy of Betty Dillon and Dorothy Showalter.)

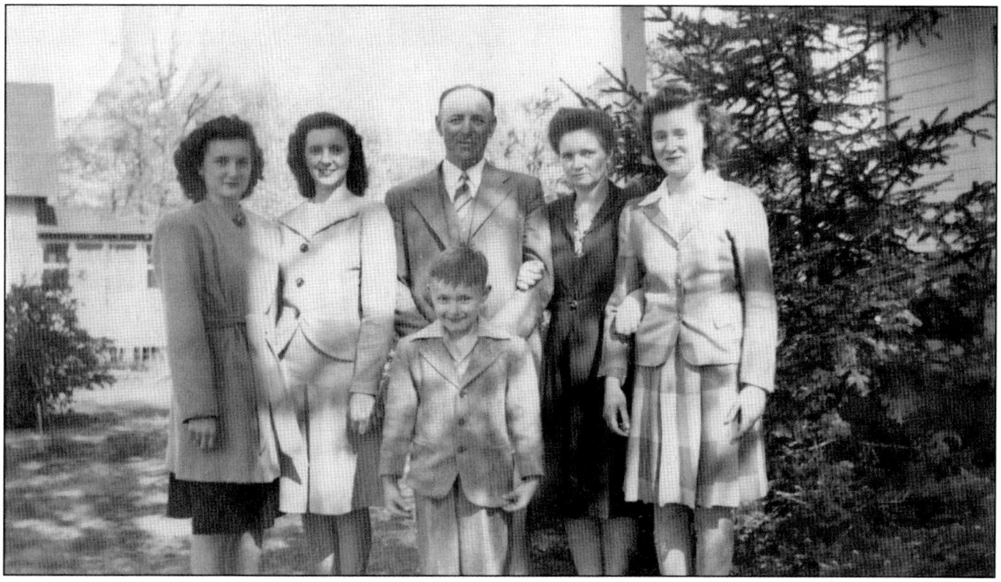

XANDER FAMILY. These two photographs show the descendants of Gottfried Xander, who came from Germany to Accokeek in 1880, when he was 30 years old. He was born in Württemberg on April 16, 1849, and sailed from Hamburg to New York on the German ship *Herder* on April 7, 1880. The photograph above, from around 1947, shows, from left to right, Elizabeth "Betty" Xander Dillon, Dorothy E. Xander Showalter, Henry A. Xander Sr., Henry A. Xander Jr. (in front), Wilhelmine (Thee) Xander, and Wilhelmine H. Xander Naive. The photograph below shows, from left to right, George Xander, Henry A. Xander Sr., Sophie Xander, Emma Xander Gallahan, Lottie Xander Wilson, and Fred Wilson. Gottfried Xander and his wife, Amelia, are buried at Christ Church in Accokeek, along with several other Xander descendants. (Both courtesy of Betty Dillon and Dorothy Showalter.)

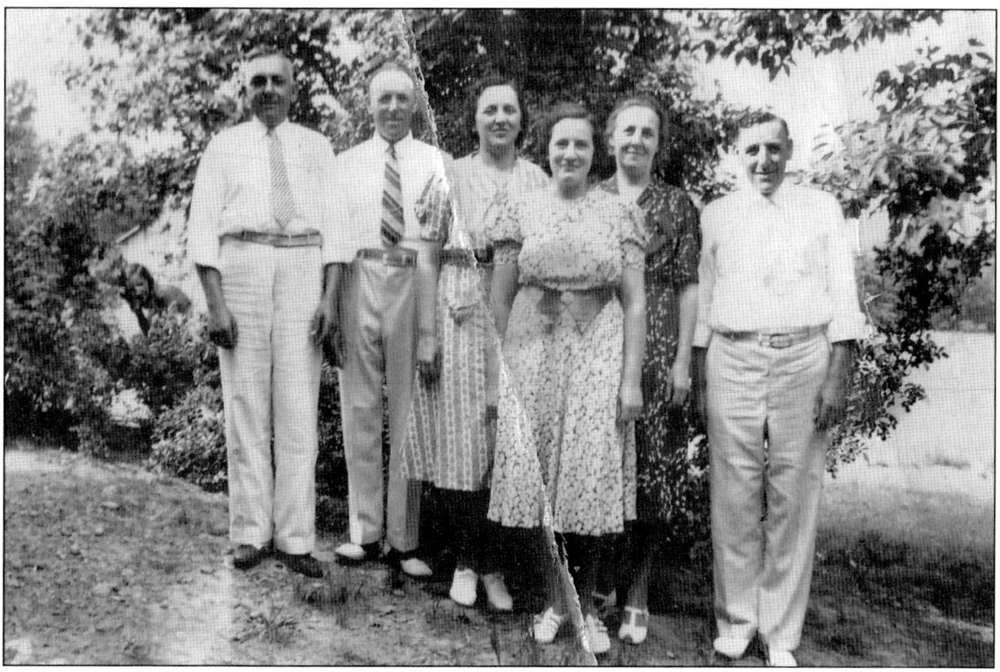

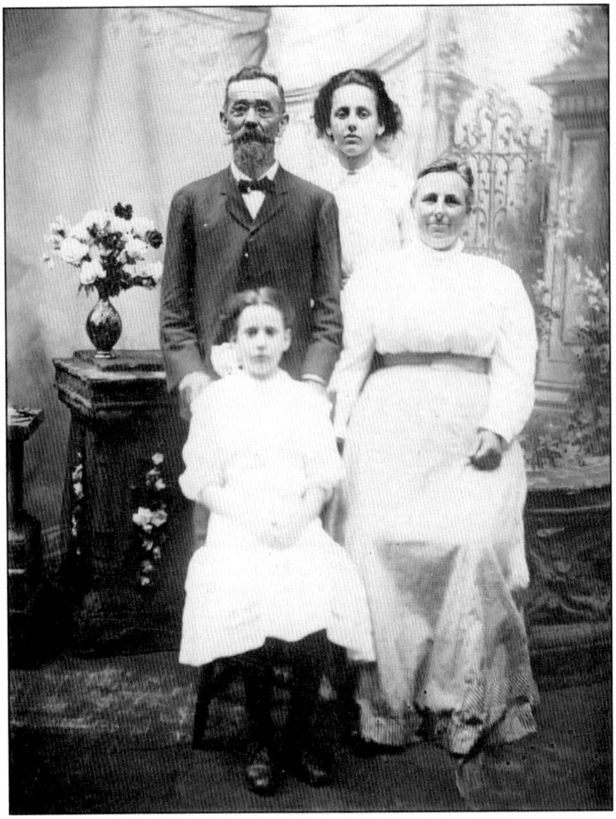

Gottfried and Amelia Xander and Children. These photographs show Gottfried Xander and his wife, Amelia M. Schmidt, who was born in Washington, DC, in 1863. By the time of the 1880 census, she had come to live in Piscataway. She and Gottfried were married at Concordia German Evangelical Church in Washington in 1884. They are seen at left with their daughters Sophia (1895–1978, standing) and Emma Theresa (1899–2000, seated). They are seen below with their daughters Sophia and Lottie (born 1887) and their son Henry Andrew (1893–1963). Their other children, not pictured here, were sons George William (born 1885) and Frederick Herman (born 1889). (Both courtesy of Betty Dillon and Dorothy Showalter.)

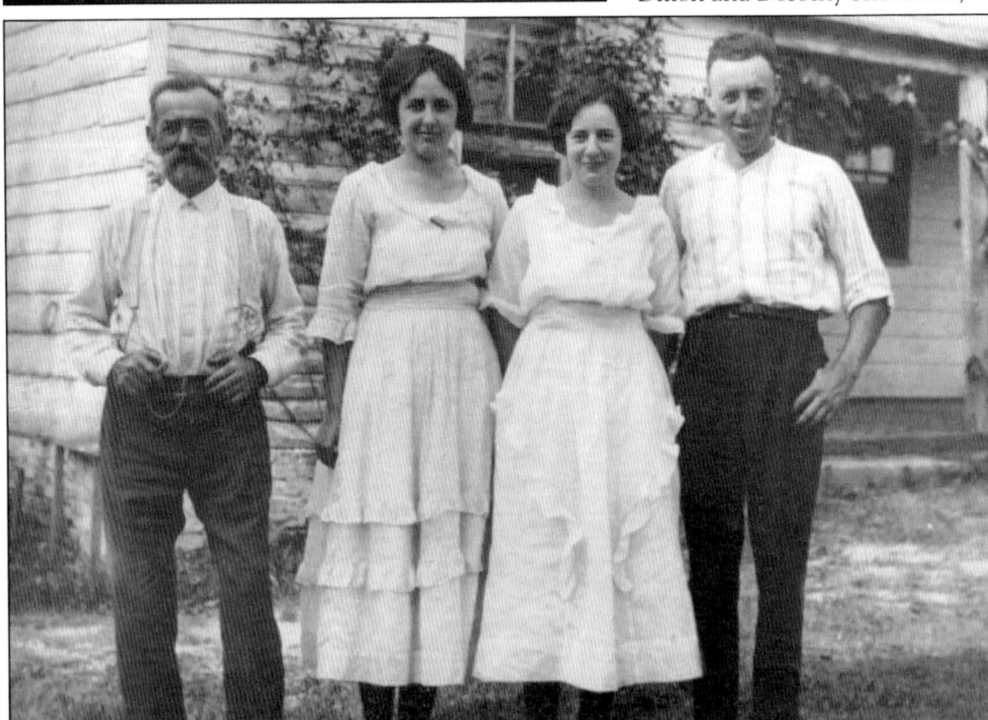

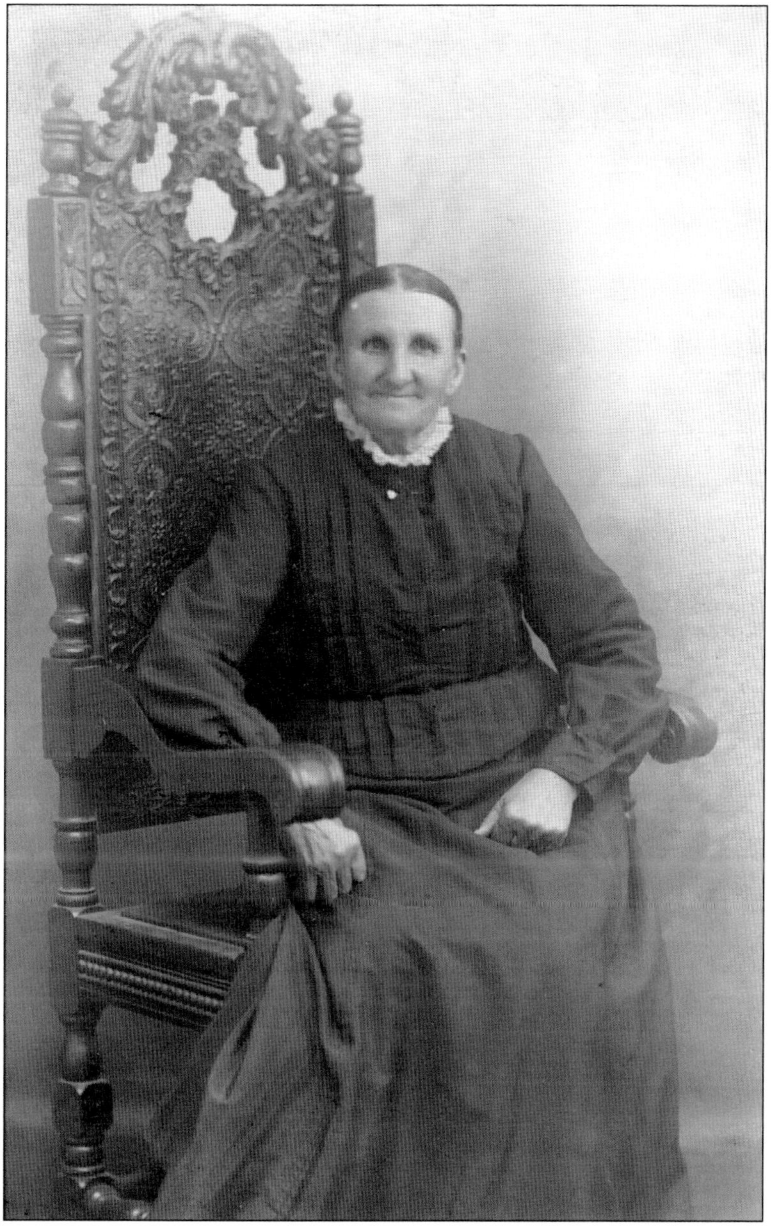

SOPHIA SCHMIDT. Johanna Maria Sophia Englert immigrated to North America in August 1860 from Schrozberg, Württemberg, Germany. She married Frank August Schmidt on March 8, 1863, at the Concordia German Evangelical Church in Washington, DC, which is located in Foggy Bottom on the corner of G and Twentieth Streets. It has been located there since 1833 and was rebuilt in 1932. It is a German-based church that has united the religions of the United Church of Christ and the United Methodist Church. It is also still a German language–based church, giving the majority of its services in German. Sophia died on March 11, 1911. She and her husband, Frank, who died on September 19, 1913, are buried at Christ Episcopal Church in Accokeek. The ornate chair on which she is sitting is similar to one in the church's storeroom. The family name, Schmidt, was later changed to Smith. (Photograph courtesy of Betty Dillon and Dorothy Showalter; caption courtesy of Rosalie Smith Puterbaugh.)

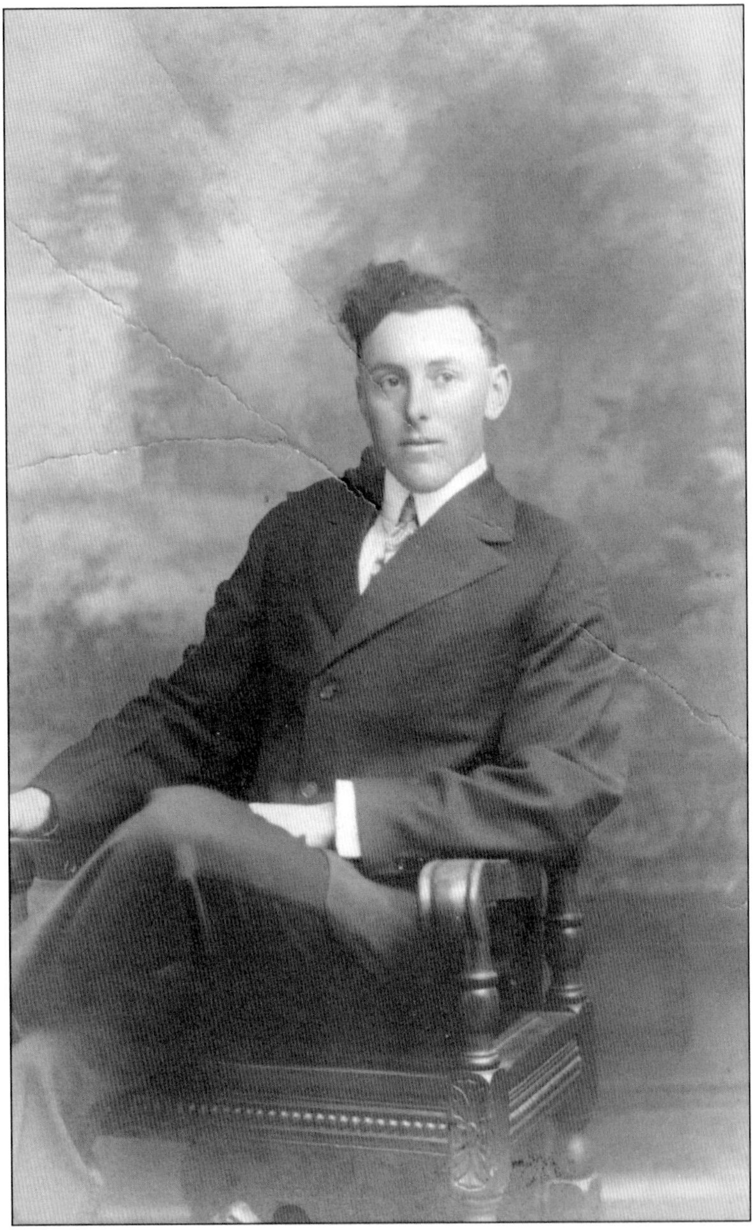

HENRY A. XANDER. Born in Washington, Henry Xander moved to Accokeek when he was two years old. For 41 years, he was the manager of Hard Bargain Farm for Henry and Alice Ferguson. He was a member of the board of directors of the Rural Electric Administration (REA), which was created by Pres. Franklin Roosevelt's administration in 1935 to bring electricity to rural areas. He served for 20 years. As a member of Christ Episcopal Church, he served for many years as a senior warden and a vestryman. Xander married Wilhelmina Thee on June 2, 1928. She was born in New York and raised on a farm in Fenwick, Maryland, before graduating from Steward College of Business. They had four children. When the children were older, she worked for the powder factory in Indian Head, from which she retired in 1970. She then worked as the manager and secretary of Hard Bargain Farm until 1985. She died in 1989. (Courtesy of Betty Dillon and Dorothy Showalter.)

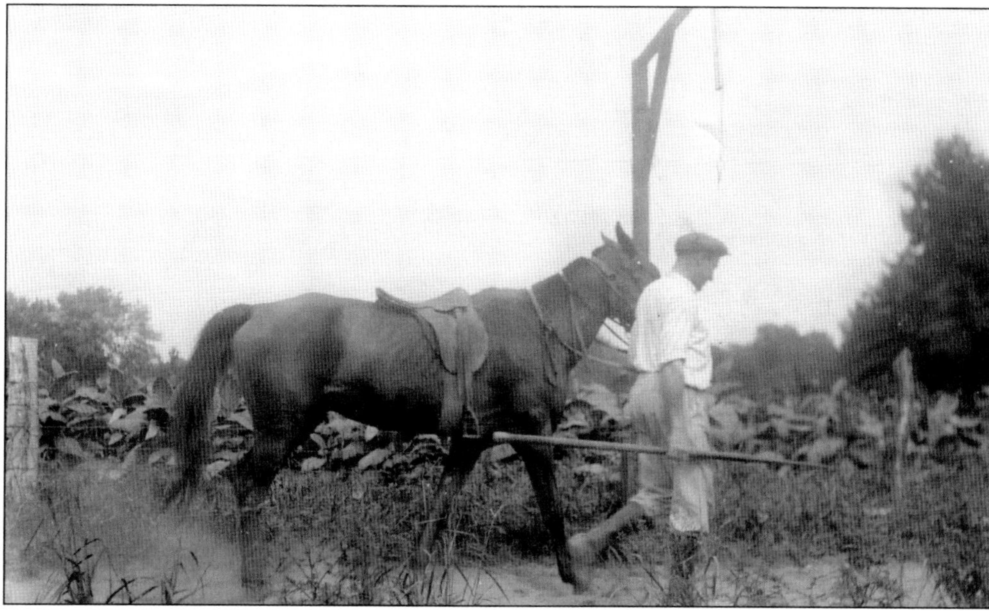

Practicing Jousting. Henry Xander is seen here practicing for a jousting tournament in the lower fields of Hard Bargain Farm, where tobacco was grown. In jousting, each knight gallops his horse down a dirt track beneath three arches. Suspended from each arch is a metal harness ring wrapped with white cord. As the knight charges through the arches in a time limit of nine seconds, he attempts to spear the metal rings on his long, steel-tipped lance. Rings vary in size from 1.75 inches in diameter to 0.25 of an inch in diameter. After each contestant has received three rides at the larger rings, those with tie scores are given one charge at rings of a smaller size. If there are still ties, a smaller-sized ring is used until only the victorious knight remains in the contest. (Both courtesy of Betty Dillon and Dorothy Showalter.)

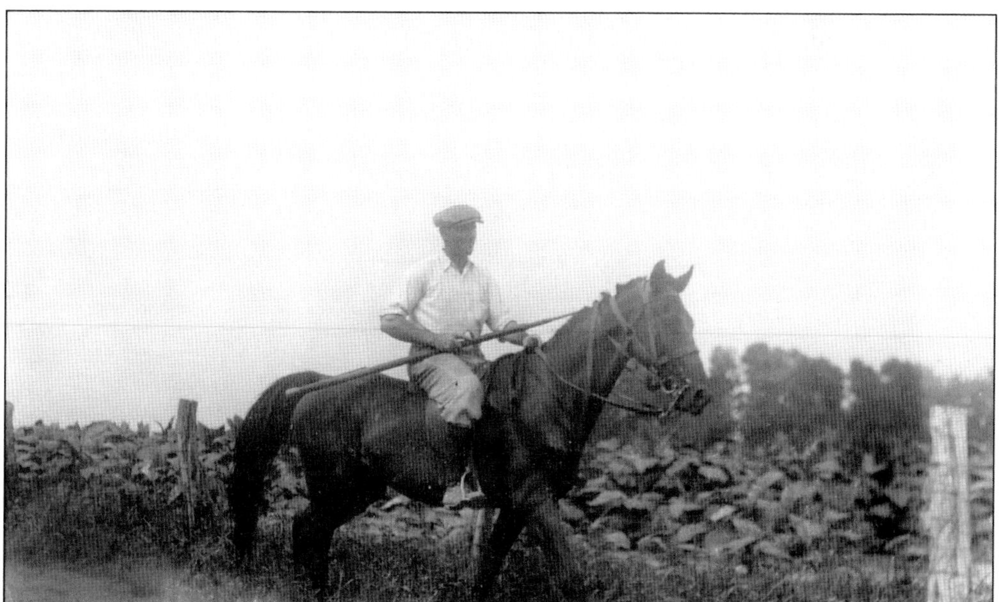

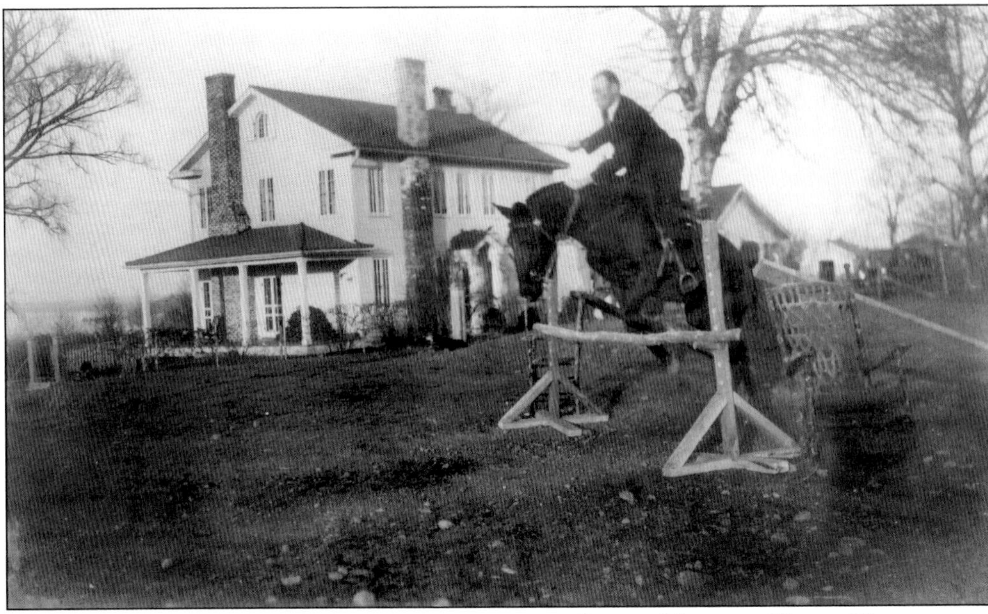

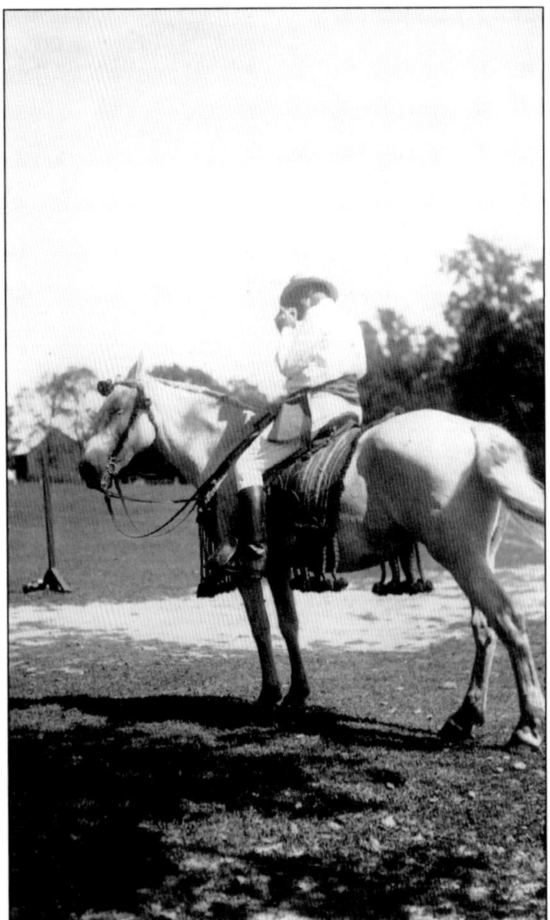

Grand Marshal Henry Xander. Henry Xander was fond of equestrian sports. He is seen above practicing jumping. At left, he is astride his horse Bonus and dressed in finery for the jousting tournament held at Christ Episcopal Church. He had the important role of grand marshal of this tournament for several years before World War II. This annual event was a fundraiser for the church, but also an opportunity for community members to get together, join in the fun as spectators, and enjoy traditional food and dancing in the parish hall. (Both courtesy of Betty Dillon and Dorothy Showalter.)

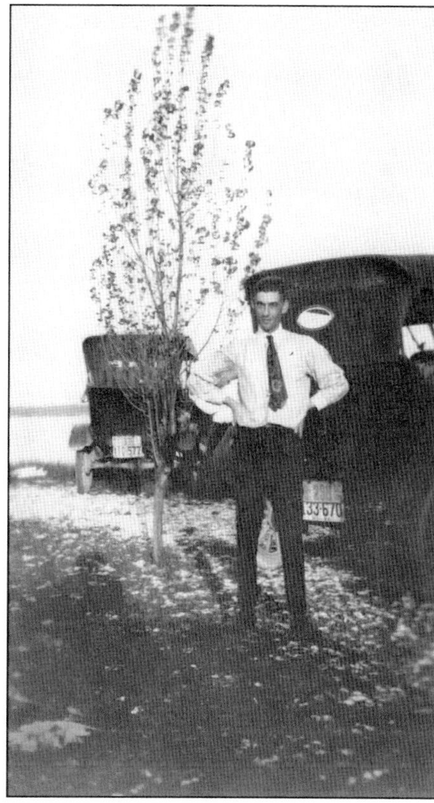

Henry Xander and Family. Henry Xander is seen at right as a young man. The Ford Model T in the background, according to Manning Clagett, an automobile expert, indicates the year as being between 1922 and 1925. Xander is seen below with family members. In addition to his children, he was also close to other family members. The Accokeek community was small, and the families living there were close. Some, like the Clagetts, were neighbors. Others, like the Smiths, were cousins. Christ Episcopal Church was a community center for worship and entertainment, the annual jousting tournament, and other events throughout the year. (Both courtesy of Betty Dillon and Dorothy Showalter.)

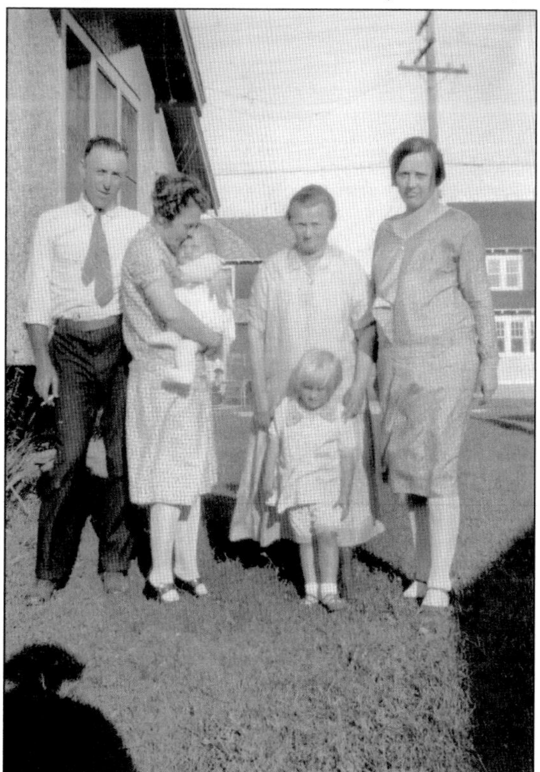

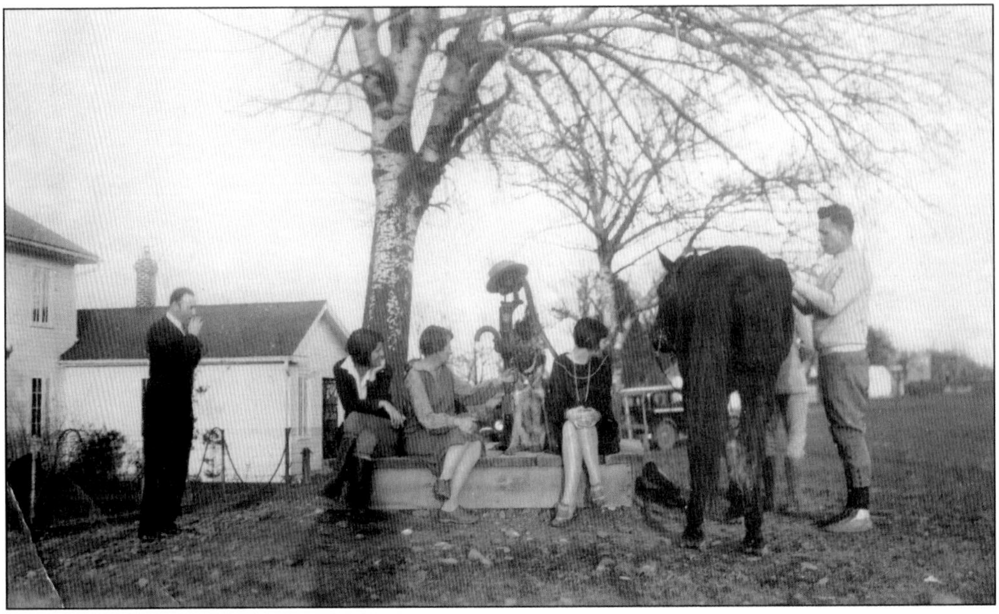

Hard Bargain Farm. Photographs of the Xanders were often taken at the farm of Henry and Alice Ferguson, where Henry Xander was the manager for many years. The photograph above shows Henry Xander standing on the far left at the farm. Alice Ferguson is the second woman from the left. Horses were an important part of life on Hard Bargain Farm. Henry Ferguson loved weekend polo games with "Fergie's gang." The automobile below, a 1925 Cadillac, according to Manning Clagett, was renovated into Accokeek's first fire truck. (Both courtesy of Betty Dillon and Dorothy Showalter.)

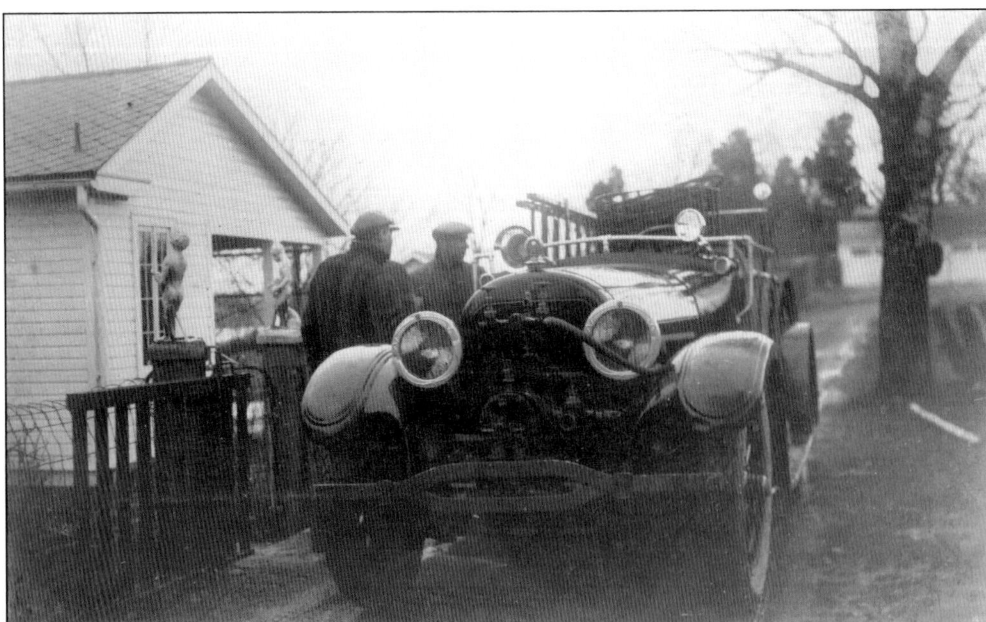

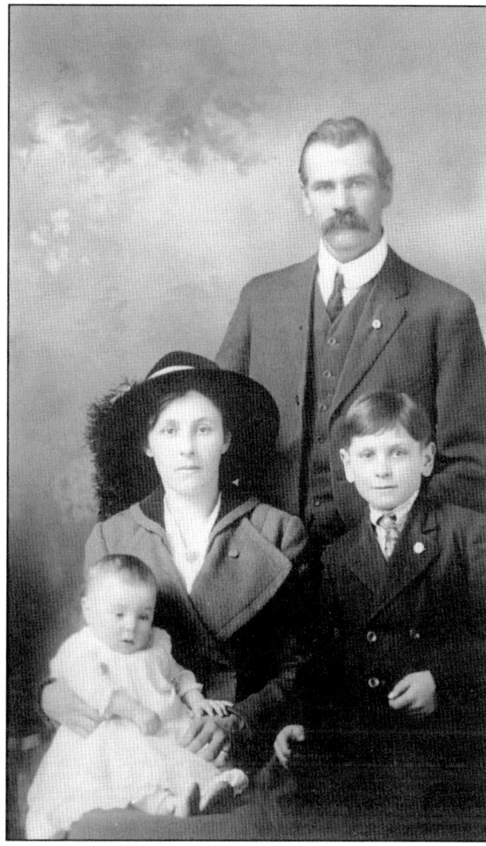

Gilbert and Lottie Xander Wilson and Their Children. Gilbert Wilson (1878–1955) operated a very successful sawmill and a gristmill behind his home in Accokeek. He was also the justice of the peace for the surrounding area and a volunteer fireman. When there was a fire, his wife, Lottie, would ring a large bell and men from the community would respond. These two photographs show the Wilsons and their children. Lottie (1887–1969) was a daughter of Gottfried and Amelia Xander. Gilbert and Lottie's four children were Lucille Wilson Hennings (1920–1995), Wakefield Wilson (1906–1995), Mildred Wilson Dent (1915–1988), and David Wilson (1918–2003). (Both courtesy of Betty Dillon and Dorothy Showalter.)

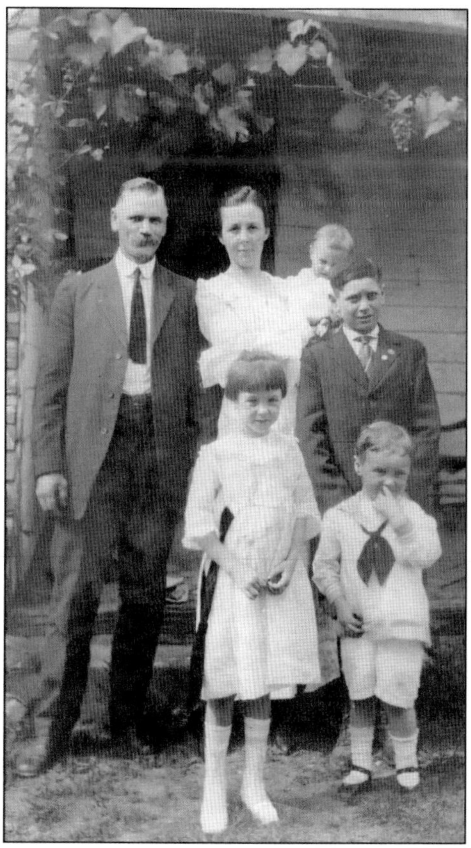

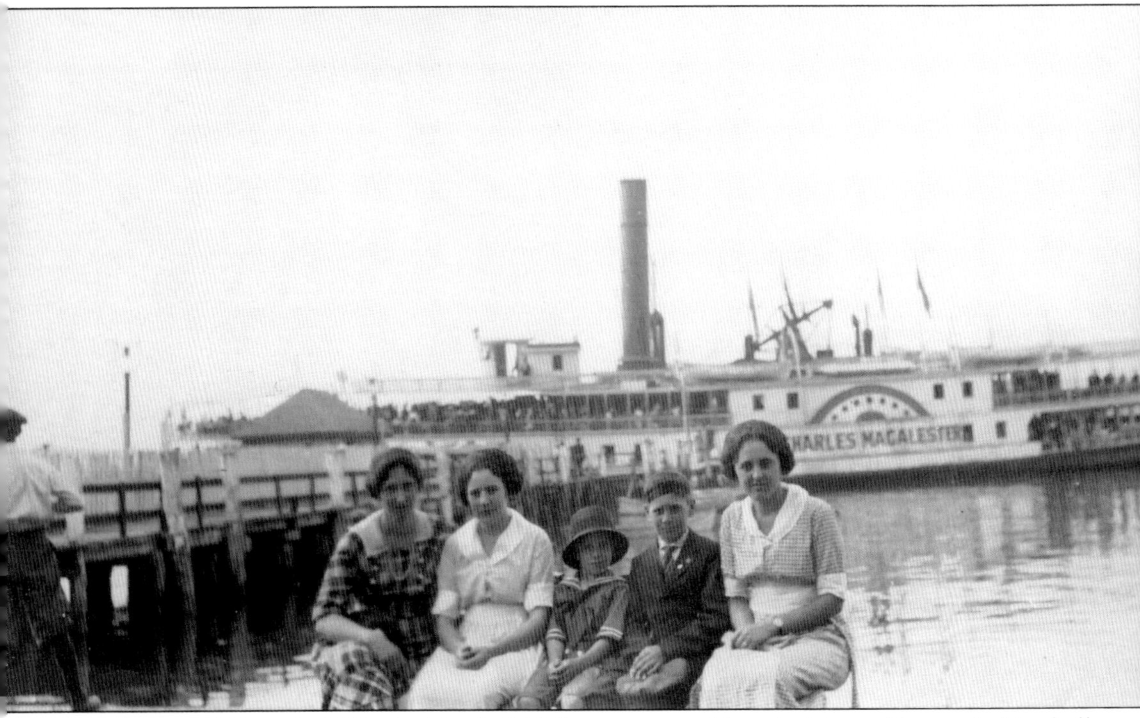

MARSHALL HALL. In 1889, the Marshall Hall estate was sold to the Mount Vernon & Marshall Hall Steamboat Company. The steamboat *Charles Macalester* was also built in 1889. It left twice a day and on midsummer evenings from Washington to Mount Vernon and Marshall Hall, a small Victorian amusement park. From the beginning of the park's history, jousting tournaments took place there each year. In 1966, the property was sold to the Marshall Hall Development Corporation. Many of the late-19th-century park structures stood until the mid-20th century, when, along with most of the 18th-century farm buildings, they were demolished to make way for a modern amusement park. In October 1974, the US government authorized the National Park Service to purchase 446 acres at Marshall Hall. A 1976 bill, Public Law 93-444, set January 1, 1980, as the phase-out date for Marshal Hall Amusement Park. This photograph shows the pier at Marshall Hall, along with Emma Xander (far left), Sophia Xander (far right), and other family members. (Courtesy of Betty Dillon and Dorothy Showalter.)

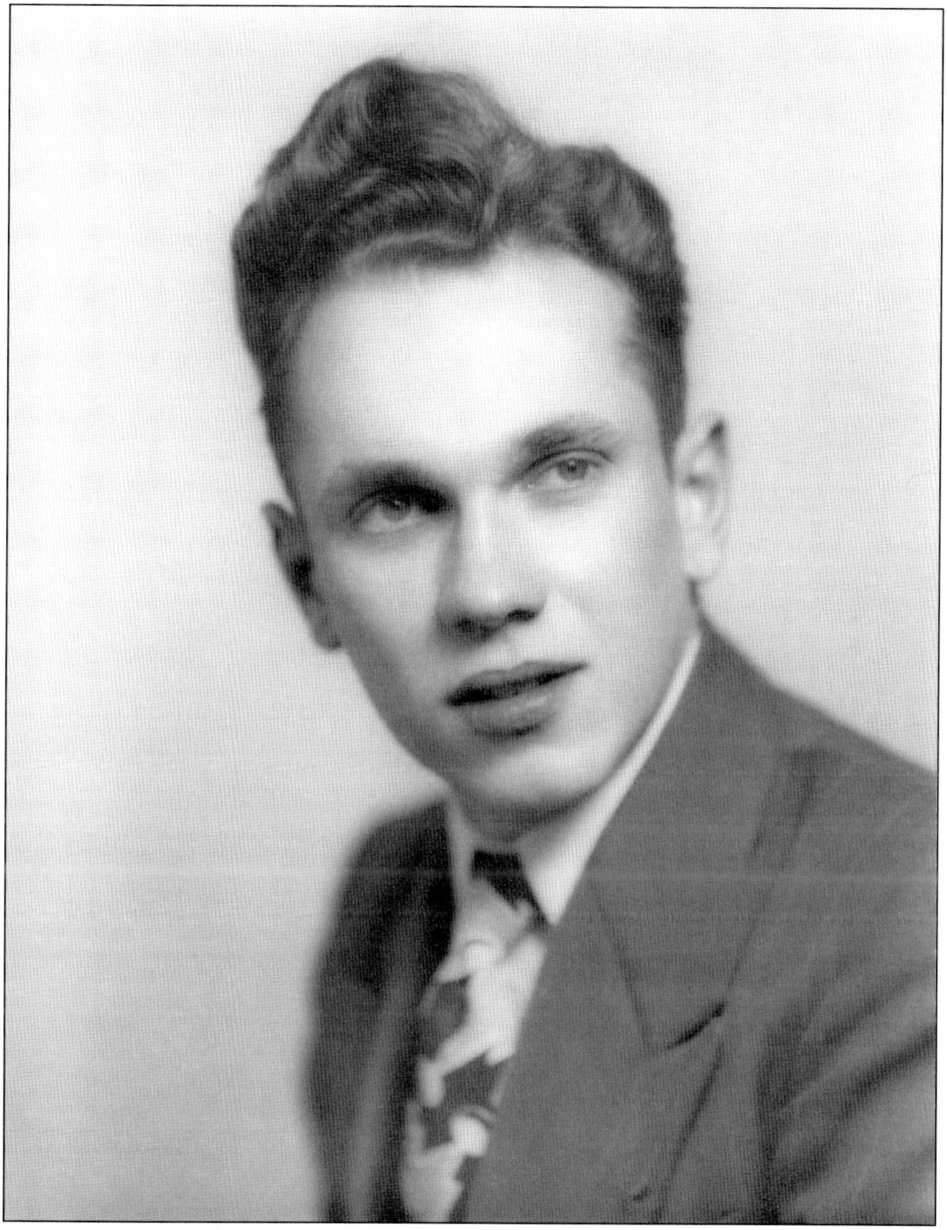

Manning Clagett. This photograph from around 1948 shows a young Manning Clagett. He was born on May 2, 1925, to Henry and Lizzie Manning Clagett. The Clagetts were living in Accokeek, where Henry was a farmer. Clagetts had originally emigrated from England to the United States. Originally, in the 1400s, the family name was Claygate, according to one family tree. Maryland branches of the family adopted two different spellings of the family name. Thomas John Claggett, who was born in Prince George's County in October 1743, was the first to use the double "g." This spelling is said to indicate loyalty to the English crown. Thomas John Claggett became the first Episcopal bishop of Maryland and the first Episcopalian bishop consecrated in America. The Accokeek Clagetts spelled the family name with a single "g" to indicate their opposition to English oppression at the time of the American Revolution. (Courtesy of Chuck and Manning Clagett.)

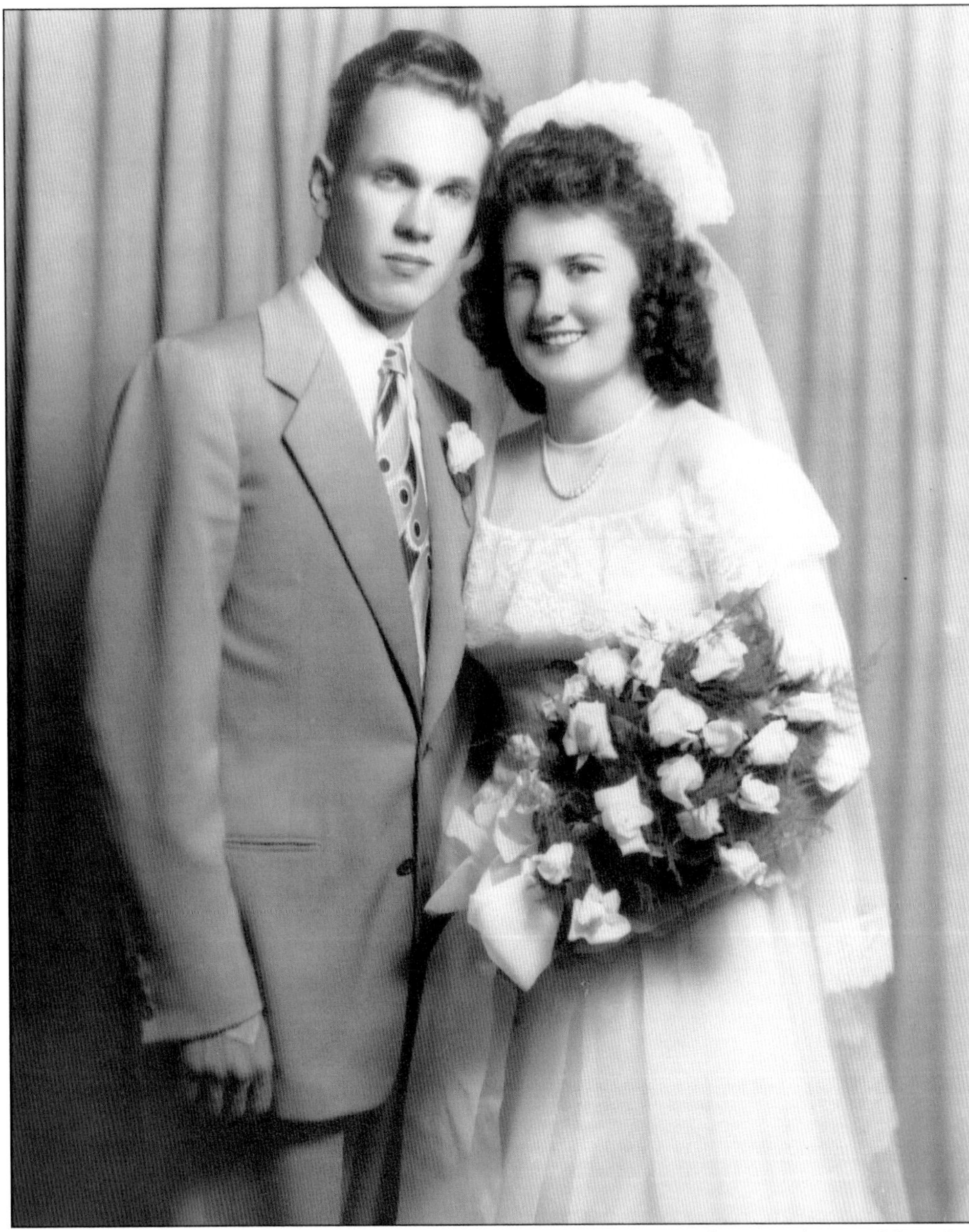

Manning and Christine O'Brien Clagett. The Clagetts are seen here on their wedding day, May 28, 1948. The O'Briens are a Kansas family, and Christine had come to Washington for a federal government job. She lived with an unmarried O'Brien sister who worked at Sholl's Colonial Cafeteria, which was famous for its popularity among tourists and government workers. Scholl's closed in 2001. When World War II was over and the troops came home, men took over many of the jobs that women had been doing. Soon, Christine O'Brien was without a government job. Manning Clagett worked for a Buick dealership in Washington at that time, and Christine came to work in the office of that firm. They met and were married soon thereafter. After the wedding, they moved to a home in Accokeek, where they still live today. (Courtesy of Chuck and Manning Clagett.)

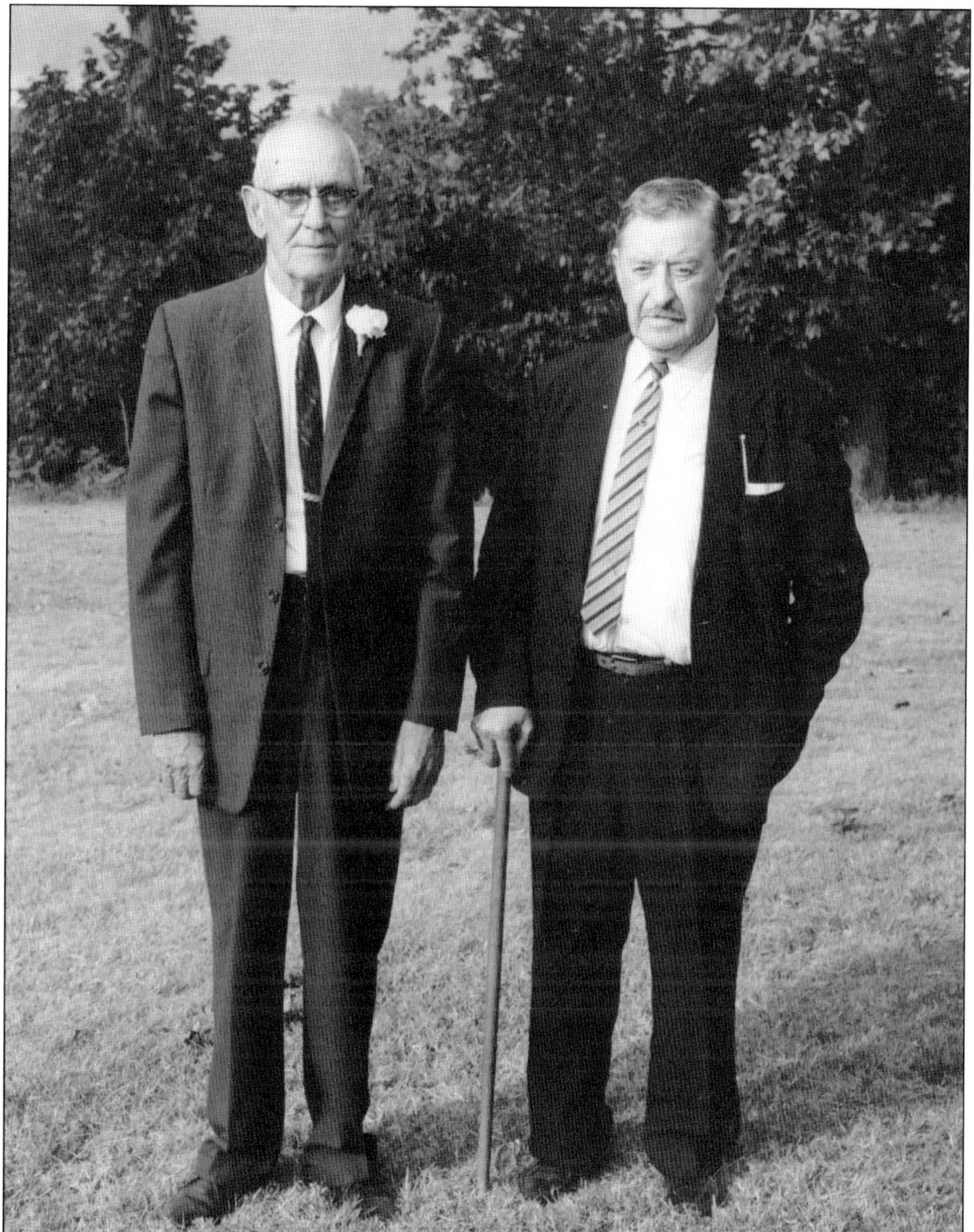

HENRY AND JOHN H. CLAGETT. This 1963 photograph shows Henry Hawkins Clagett and his brother John H. Clagett, who died in 1970 at the age of 100. In 1899, John H. Clagett married Carolyn (Caroline) Bryan. Bryan Point Road in Accokeek is named for the Bryan family. The 1920 census lists five children of John and Carolyn: Ella H. (age 14), Catherine B. (12), John H. Jr. (7), Bryan A. (5), and Catherine H. (under 1). Subsequent generations of the family include John H. Clagett III and John H. Clagett IV. All four John H. Clagett men have been important to Christ Episcopal Church. In 1908–1909, John H. Clagett I was listed as a vestryman. The official history of the church was written by John H. Clagett IV. (Courtesy of Chuck and Manning Clagett.)

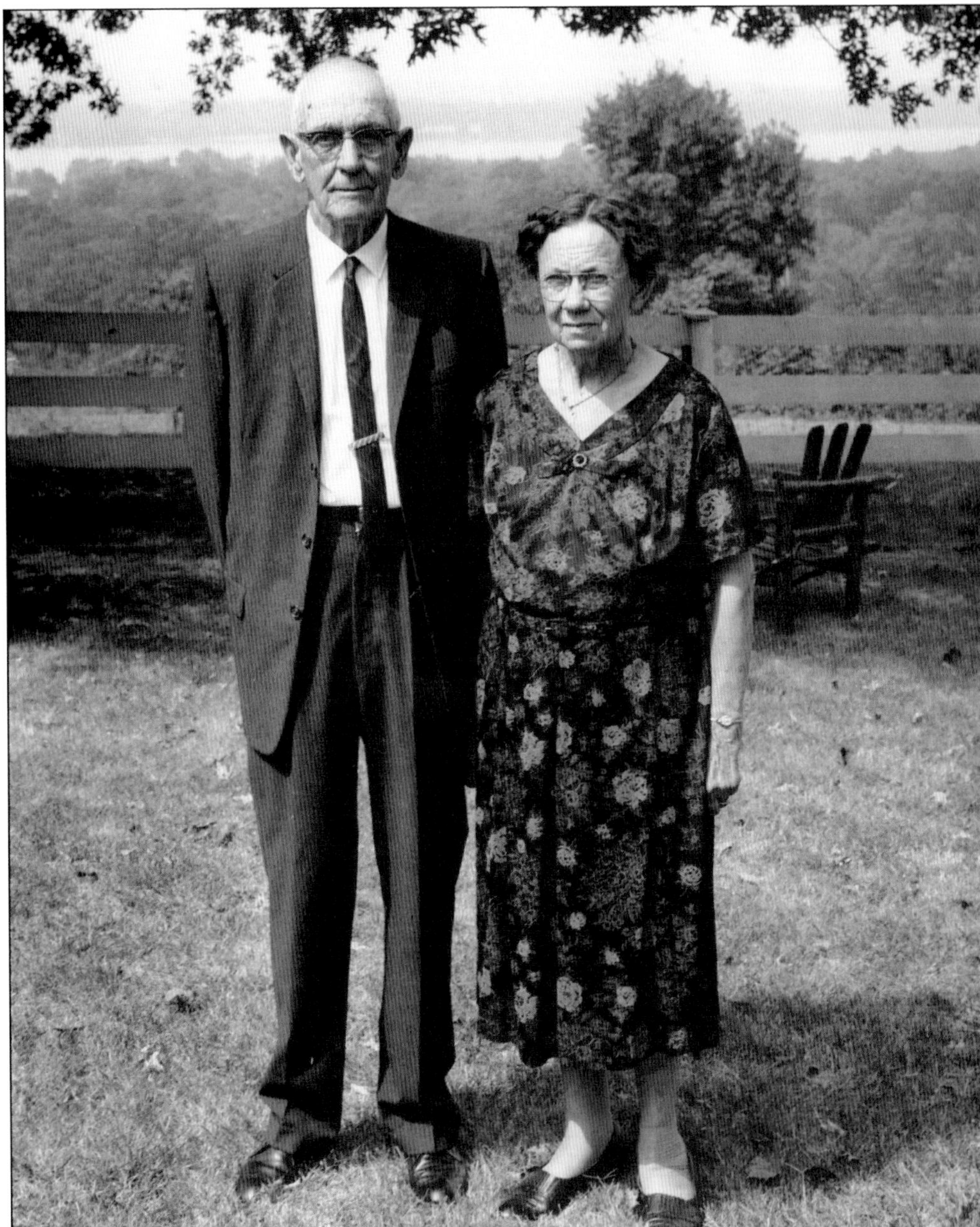

Henry and Lizzie Clagett. This 1963 photograph shows Henry Hawkins Clagett and Elizabeth "Lizzie" Manning Clagett, the parents of Manning and Oswald Clagett. Manning Clagett's full name, Henry Manning Clagett, incorporates the names of both of his parents. Henry Hawkins was born on September 20, 1883, and Lizzie was born in 1891 or 1892. Lizzie's parents were Robert Lee Manning and Juliana Steed Hatton Manning. Robert Lee Manning was born on February 4, 1865, and died on July 17, 1926. His parents were John Manning and Mary Elizabeth Ditty Manning. According to the 1900 census, Lizzie Manning's brothers and sisters were Addie (age 7), Ellenor (5), John R.L. (2), and Francis R. (under 1). Henry and Lizzie were married in 1913. This and following pictures show the happy couple, with children and grandchildren, on the occasions of their 50th and 60th wedding anniversaries. (Courtesy of Chuck and Manning Clagett.)

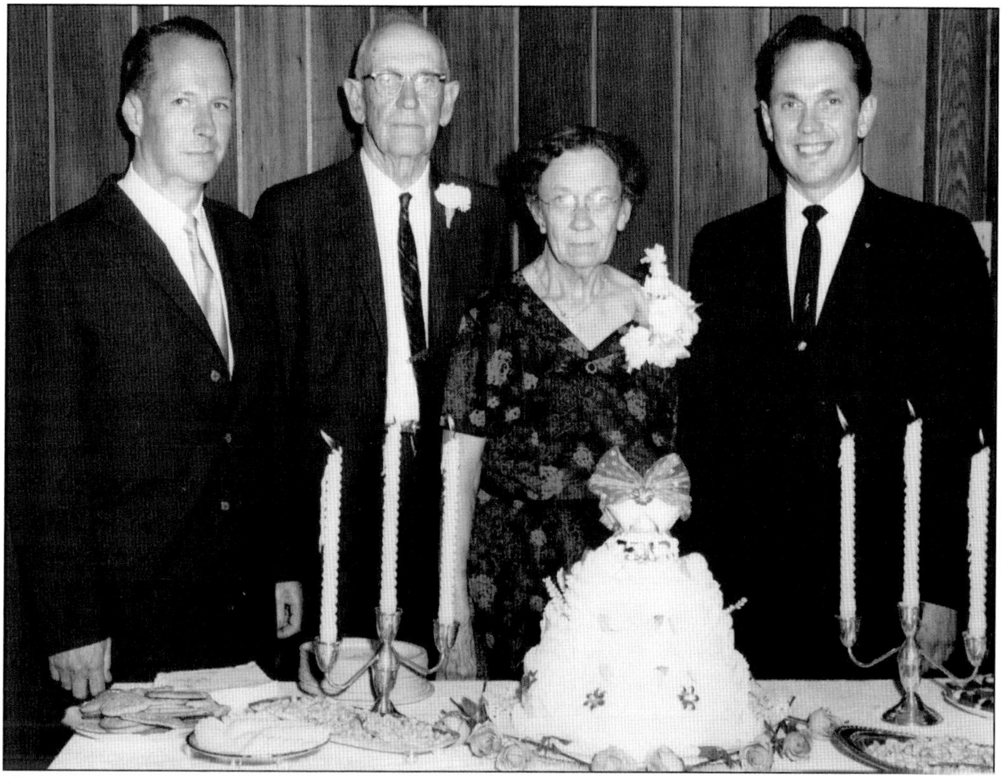

Henry and Lizzie Clagett 50th Anniversary Dinner. In 1963, Henry Hawkins Clagett and Lizzie Manning Clagett celebrated 50 years of happy marriage. Seen above, from left to right, are Oswald Clagett, Henry Clagett, Lizzie Clagett, and Manning Clagett. It is appropriate that the dessert on this occasion was a large wedding cake. Many members of the Accokeek community expressed their congratulations and best wishes to Henry and Lizzie Clagett. The photograph at right shows Oswald Clagett in his World War II Navy uniform about 1945. (Both courtesy of Chuck and Manning Clagett.)

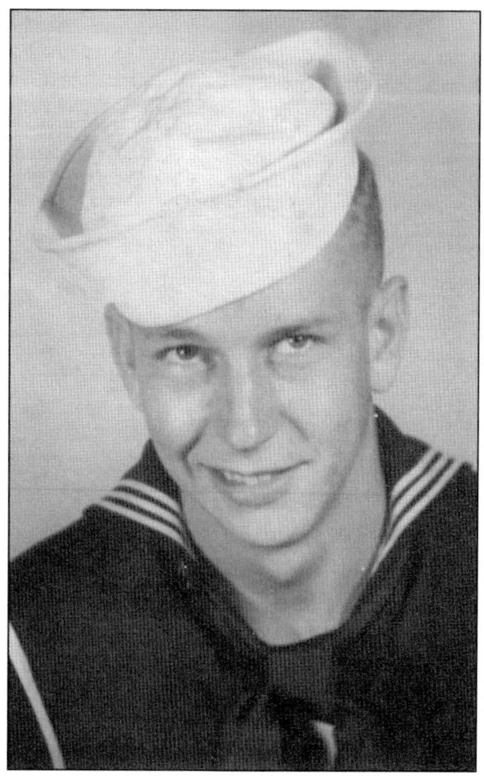

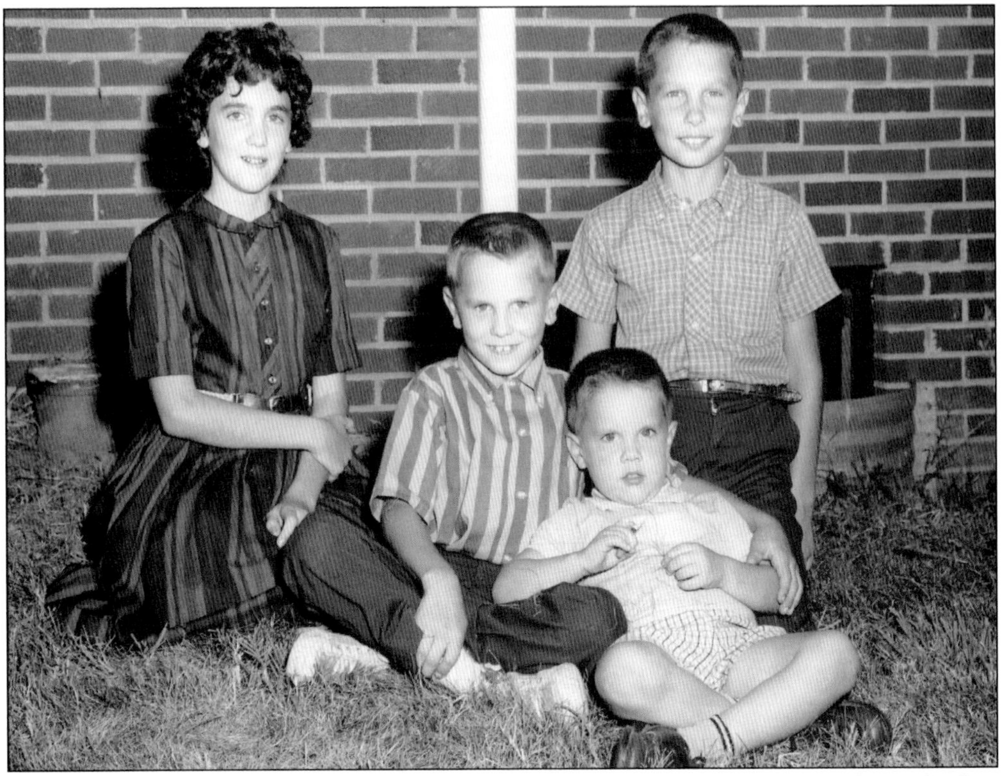

GRANDCHILDREN OF HENRY AND LIZZIE CLAGETT, 1963. The photograph above shows the four children of Manning and Christine Clagett, the grandchildren of Henry and Lizzie Clagett. They are, from left to right, Diane, Lee, Chuck, and Jim. The group picture below shows, from left to right, (first row) Jim, Diane, and Lee; (second row) Christine, Chuck, Manning, Henry, Lizzie, and Oswald. (Both courtesy of Chuck and Manning Clagett.)

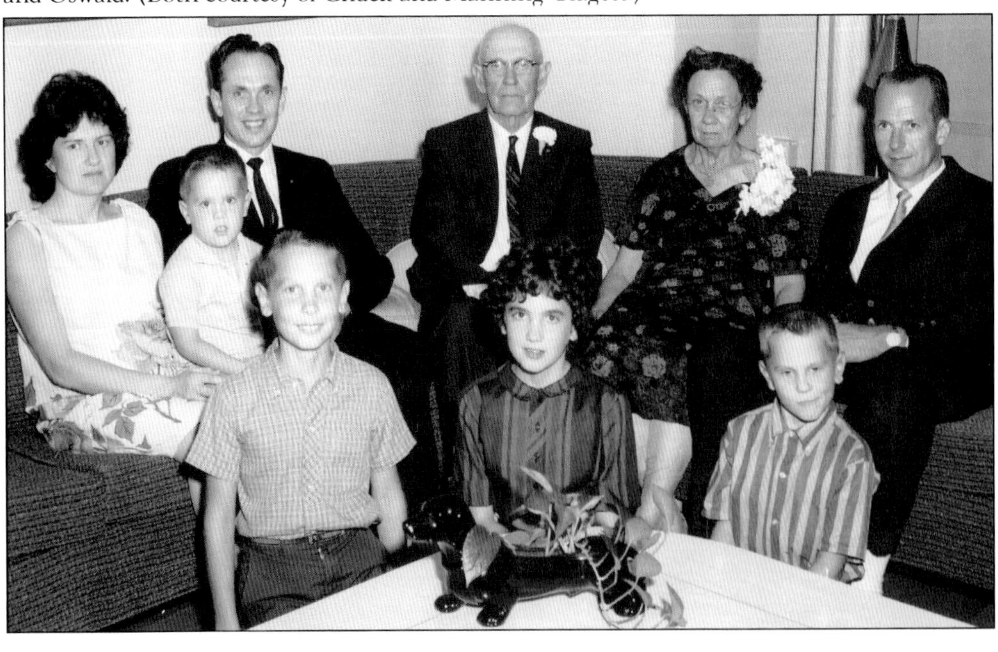

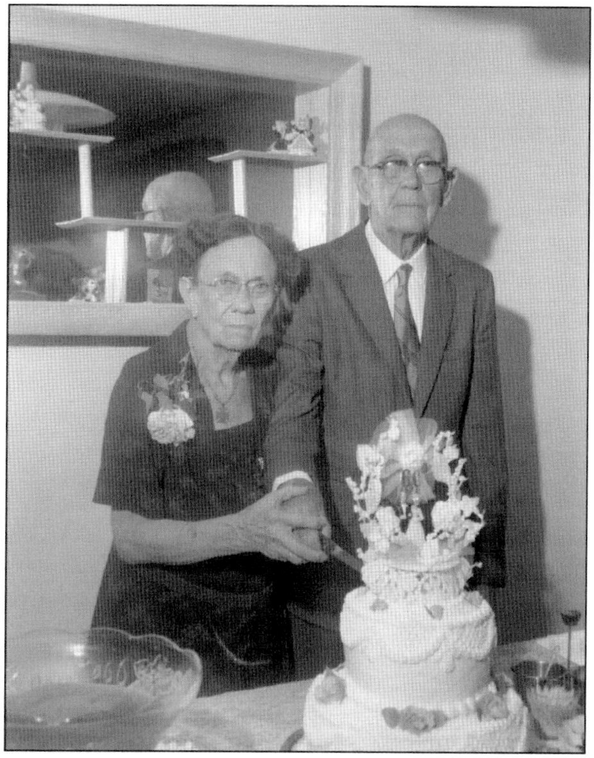

The Clagetts' 60th Wedding Anniversary. These 1973 photographs show Lizzie and Henry Clagett celebrating their 60th wedding anniversary. The photograph at right recalls a similar scene in 1913, when they were newly married. Pictured below, the Clagetts are about to enjoy some of the cake. Standing behind the couple are, from left to right, son Oswald, granddaughter Diane, and son Manning. This modest event at home fits the Clagett lifestyle. Over the years, other events in the parish hall of Christ Episcopal Church or a local restaurant have involved more people. (Both courtesy of Chuck and Manning Clagett.)

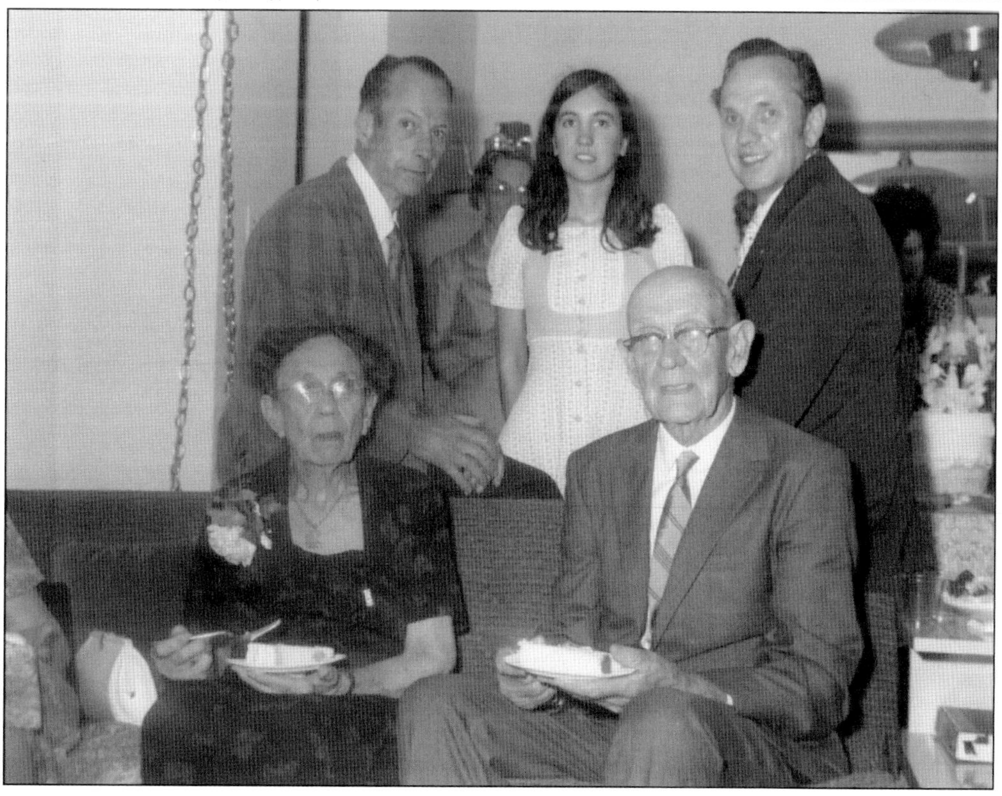

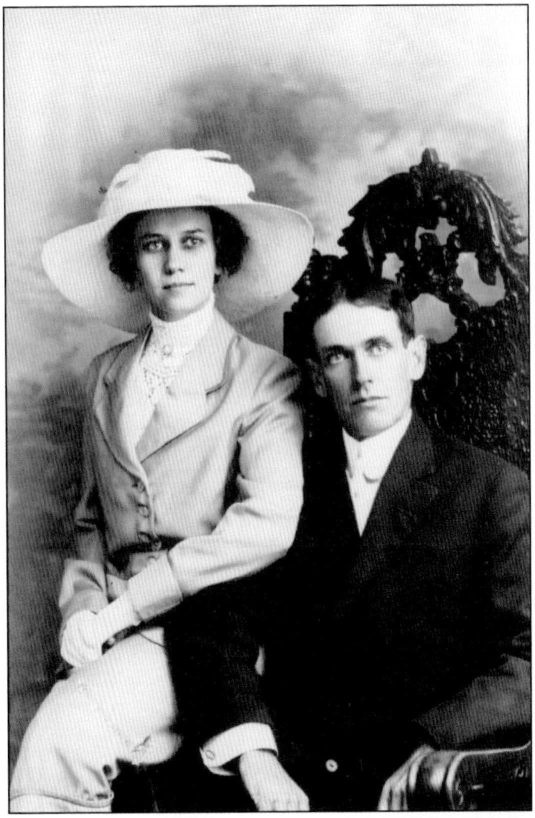

Henry and Lizzie Clagett, 1913. Pictured are Henry Hawkins Clagett and Lizzie Manning Clagett on their wedding day in 1913. Both members of this handsome couple were in their twenties at the time of their wedding at Christ Episcopal Church in Accokeek. On the preceding pages are photographs from their 50th and 60th wedding anniversaries. (Courtesy of Chuck and Manning Clagett.)

Philip and Bertha O'Brien. Pictured are Philip J. O'Brien and his wife, Bertha Scheidt O'Brien. They were Christine O'Brien Clagett's father and mother. The 1930 census includes Philip (age 52) and Bertha (46), as well as Christine (3) and her brothers and sisters. The O'Brien family lived in Kansas. (Courtesy of Chuck and Manning Clagett.)

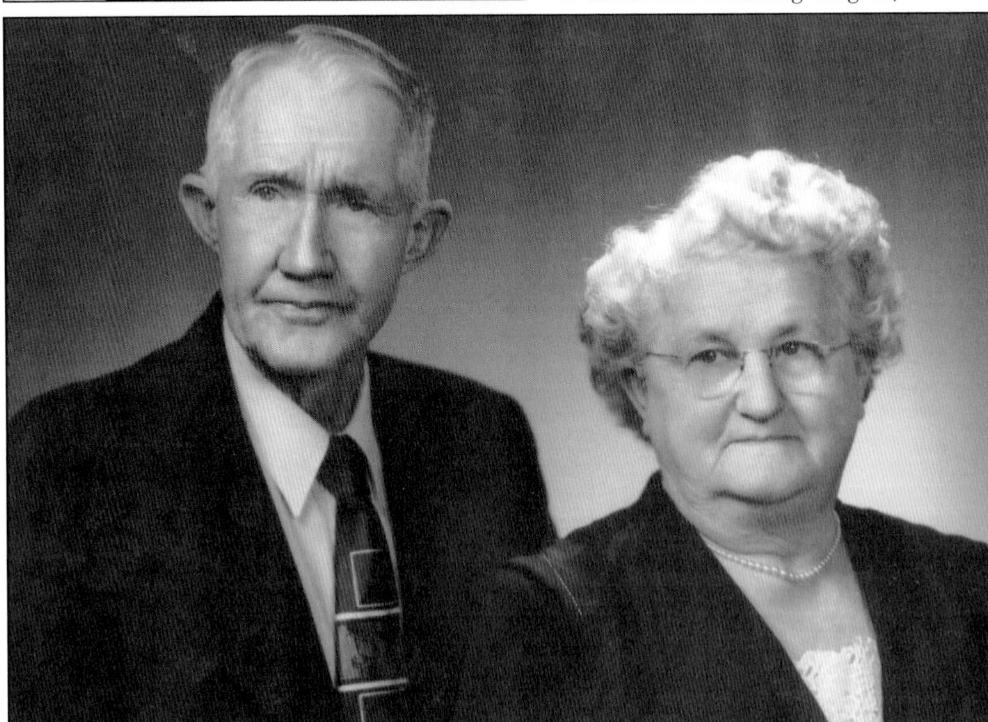

Parents and Grandparents of Christine O'Brien Clagett. At right is the wedding photograph of Philip J. and Bertha Scheidt O'Brien. They were married on June 9, 1903, in Labette County, Kansas. Philip's parents were William O'Brien (1831–1912) and Ellen Dunn (1838–1891), who were both born in Ireland and immigrated to Parsons, Labette County, Kansas. Below are Weimar Scheidt and Julia Kneipher Scheidt, the parents of Bertha Scheidt O'Brien. They are the maternal grandfather and grandmother of Christine O'Brien Clagett. Photographs on the next page, taken about 1950, show a large number of O'Brien relatives in Kansas. (Both courtesy of Chuck and Manning Clagett.)

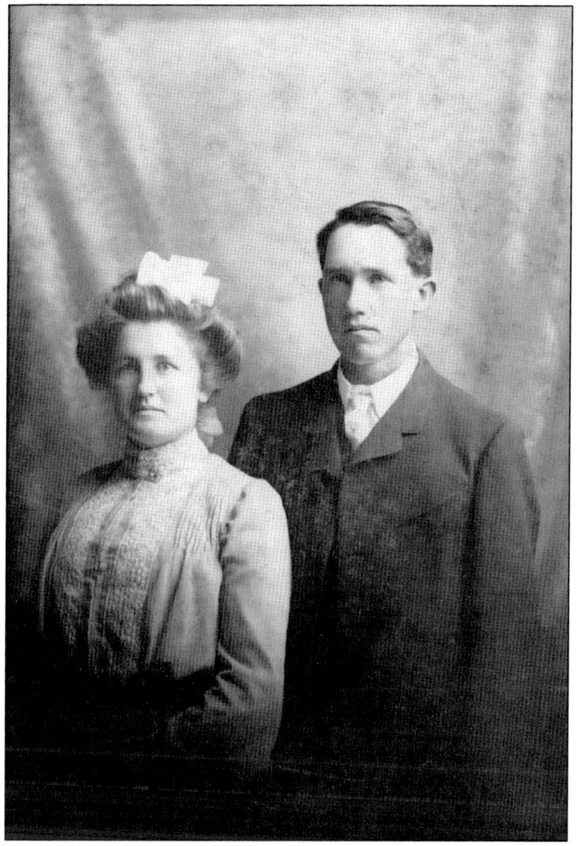

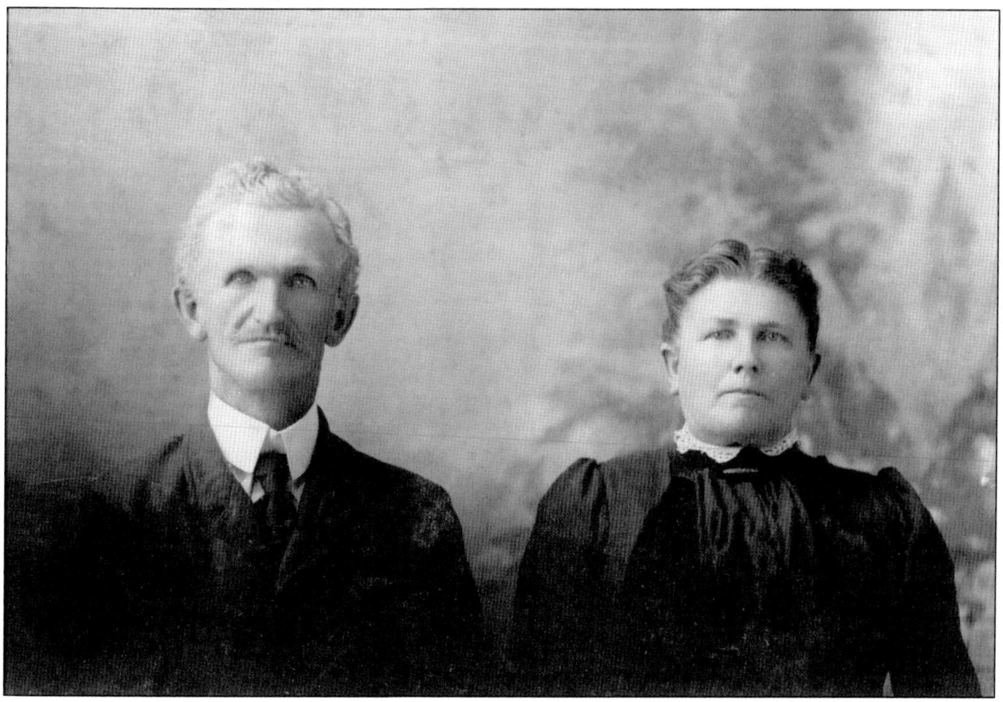

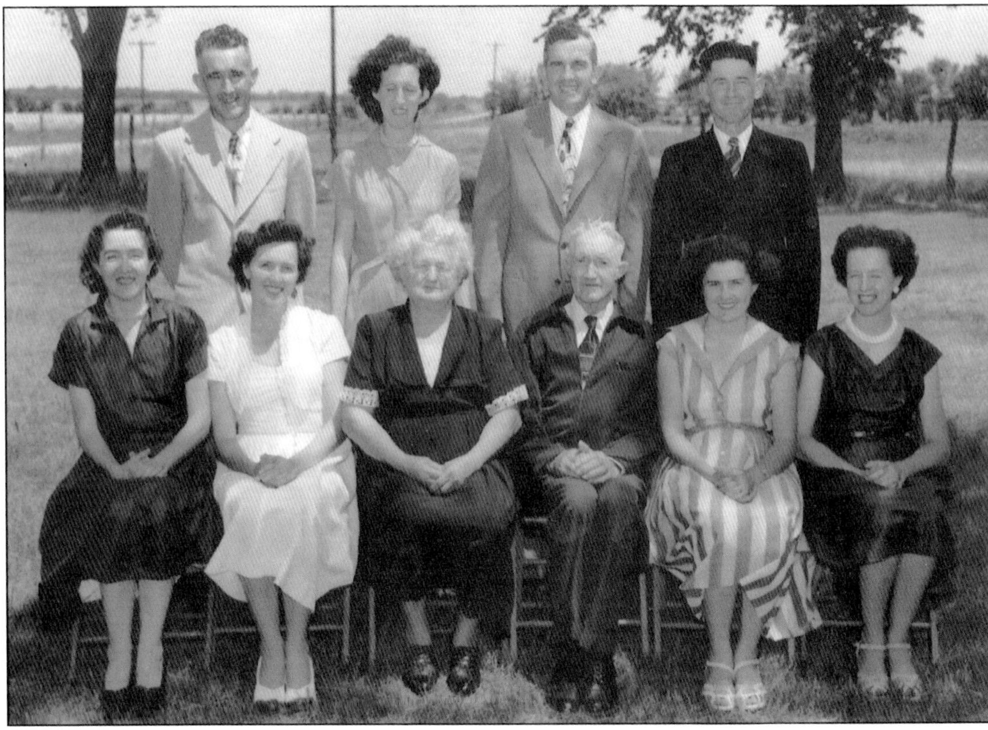

O'Brien Reunion in Kansas. These two photographs show a gathering of O'Briens in Labette County, Kansas. In both photographs, Christine O'Brien's parents, Philip and Bertha O'Brien, are in the center of the first row, seen with their children, grandchildren, and other close relatives. Philip O'Brien died on December 26, 1954, in Parsons, Kansas, at the age of 76. Bertha died in 1969. These photographs were probably taken around 1950. (Both courtesy of Chuck and Manning Clagett.)

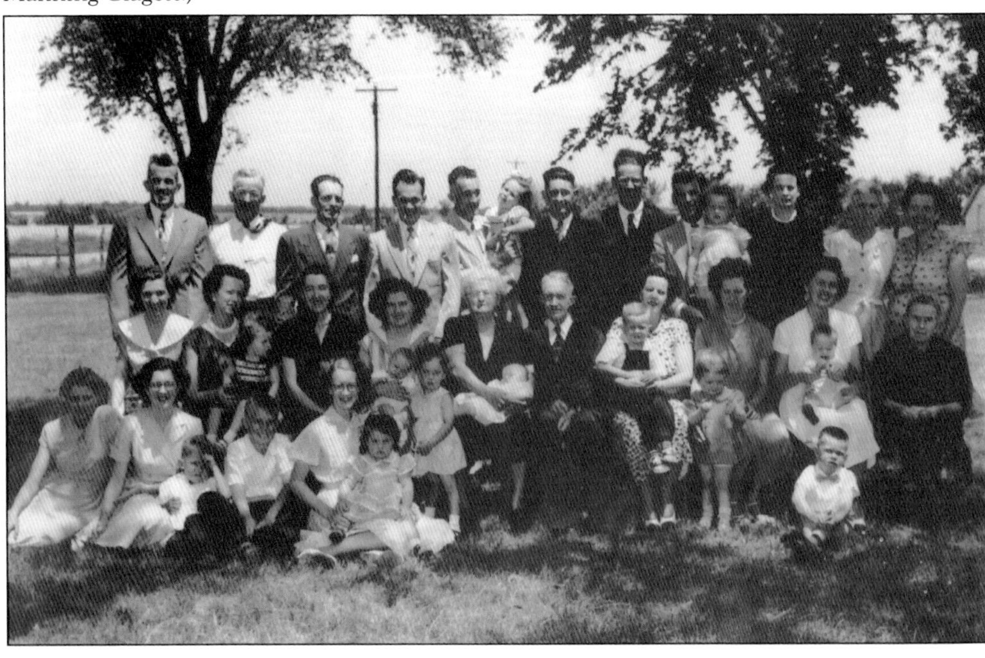

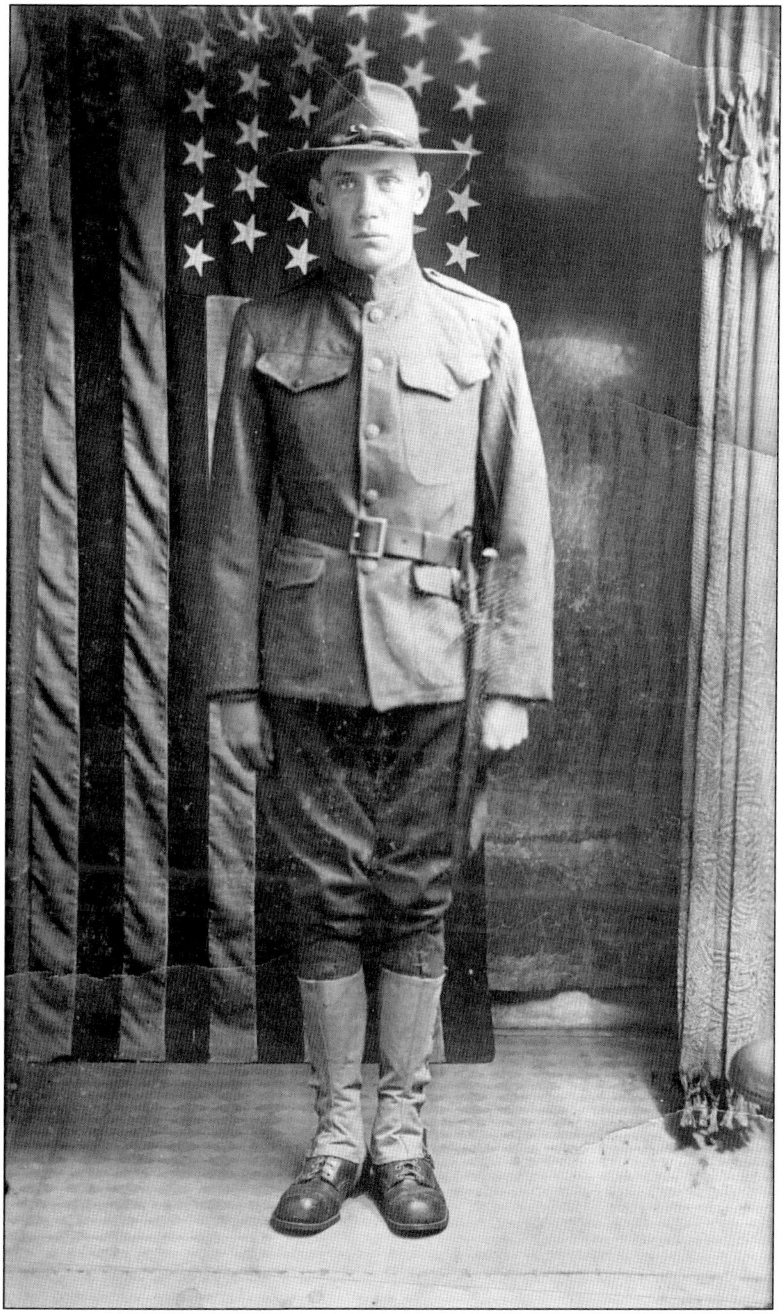

Robert Lee Manning Jr. Tall and sturdy in his Army uniform, Robert Lee Manning Jr. joined the Army on June 23, 1917, in Columbus, Ohio. He was about 19 years old at the time. Henry Hawkins Clagett also registered for the draft on September 12, 1918, in Upper Marlboro, Maryland. He was 34 years old, a government clerk for the US Engineering Department in Fort Washington, Maryland. Because of his age and employment status, it is very unlikely that he saw wartime service, but Manning did see active duty. The United States was a formal participant in World War I from April 6, 1917, until the war's end on November 11, 1918. (Courtesy of Betty Dillon and Dorothy Showalter.)

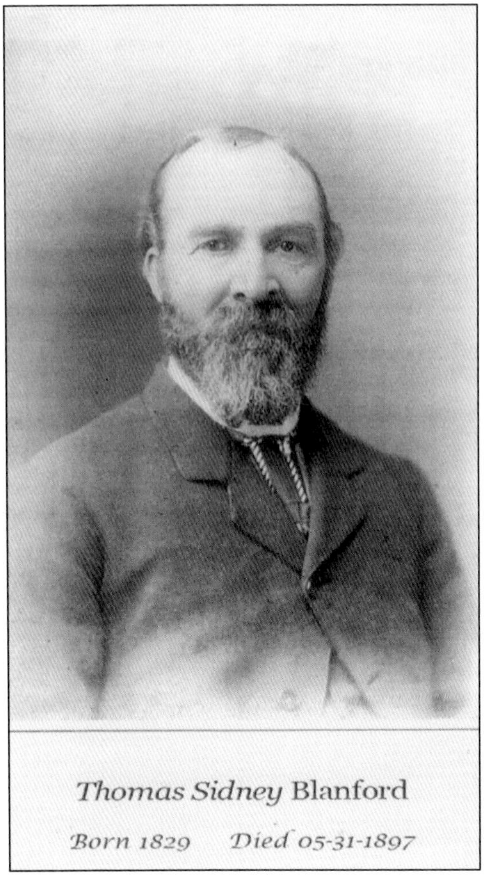

THOMAS SIDNEY AND CATHERINE SPAULDING BLANFORD. The Blandford name goes back quite a long time in Accokeek. On page 30, the name T.S. Blanford is listed in the middle of old Accokeek on the 1861 Martenet map. The spelling of the name changed from Blanford to Blandford at some point. These photographs show Thomas Sidney Blanford (1829–1897) and his wife, Catherine Spaulding Blandford (1837–1905). The Blandfords lived on Bryan Point Road in Accokeek. (Both courtesy of Virginia Robey.)

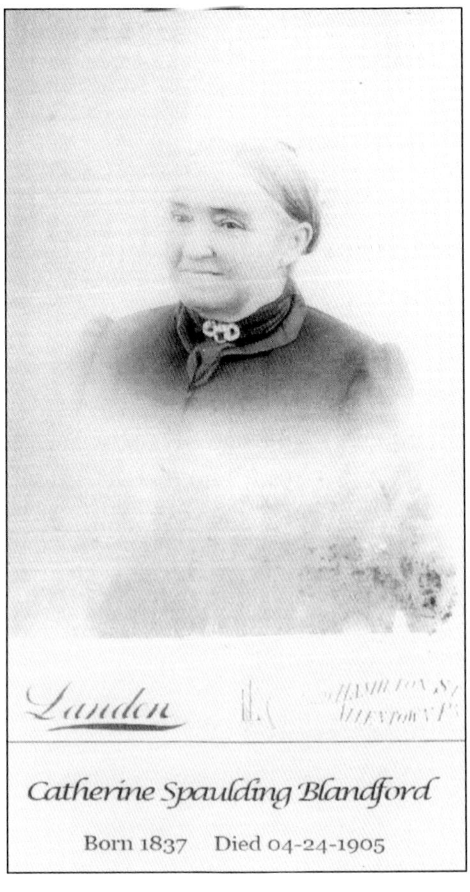

THOMAS SIDNEY AND EMMA CARROLL BLANDFORD. These Blandfords lived on Livingston Road in Accokeek. Their home was located directly behind the current location of the Accokeek Fire Department. Thomas Sidney Blandford was born on March 9, 1874, and died on February 17, 1933. He was the son of Thomas Sidney and Catherine Spaulding Blandford. His brothers and sisters included Catherine Sarah (born 1860), Charles T. (born 1862), Benjamin S. (born 1866), William Dominic (born 1869), Mary E. (born 1872), George Basil (born 1875), and John Eugene (born 1876). Thomas Sidney Blandford married Emma Theresa Carroll in 1895. On the 1880 census, Thomas Sidney Blandford's occupation was listed as farming. (Both courtesy of Virginia Robey.)

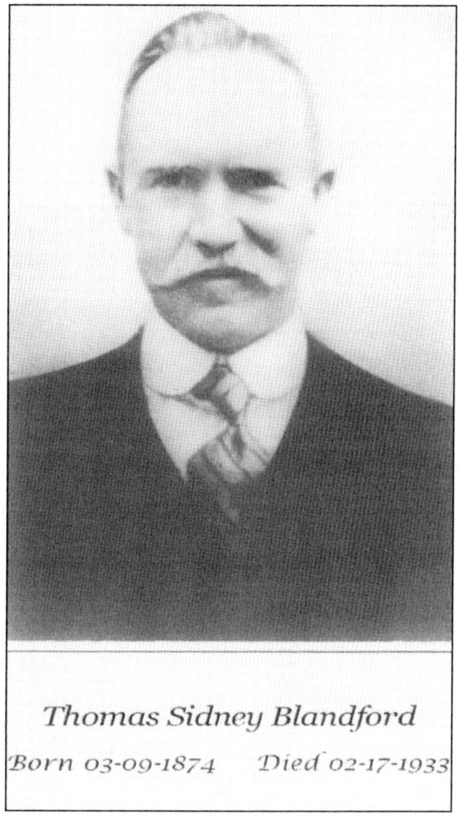

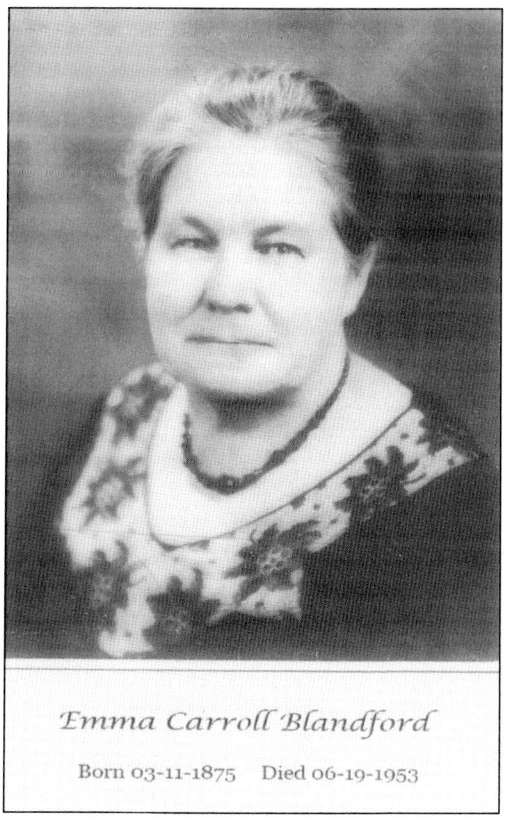

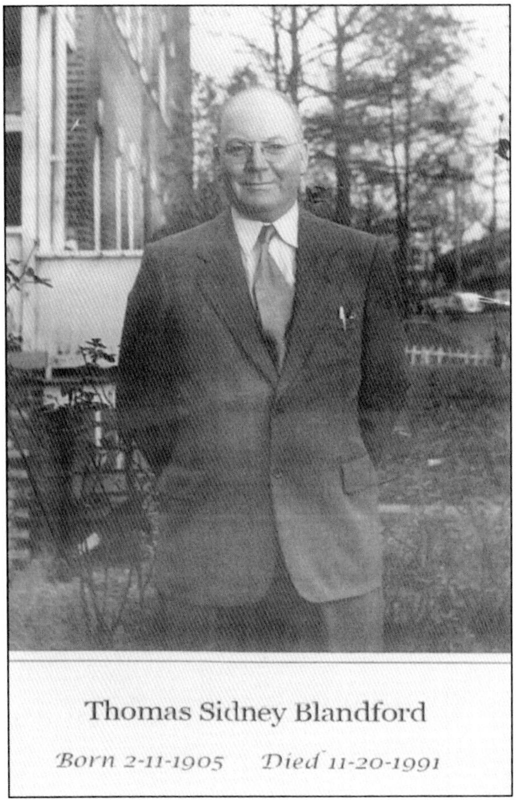

THOMAS SIDNEY BLANDFORD AND THOMAS SIDNEY BLANDFORD. Two other Thomas Sidney Blandfords are seen here. The first was born on February 11, 1905, and died on November 20, 1991. He married Elsie May Burgess on August 20, 1940, in Washington, DC. She died in 1996. His parents were Thomas Sidney Blandford and Emma Theresa Carroll Blandford, who are on the previous page. His brothers and sisters were Helen M. (1898–1979), Irving Paul (1900–1988), Walter F. (1901–1954), Blanche V. (1904–1990), Emma T. (1906–1980), Bernard Basil (1909–1966), Catherine Cecilia (1911–2001), and Claude Spaulding (1919–1986). The Thomas Sidney Blandford born August 19, 1934, was the son of Irving and Gladys Blandford. (Both courtesy of Virginia Robey.)

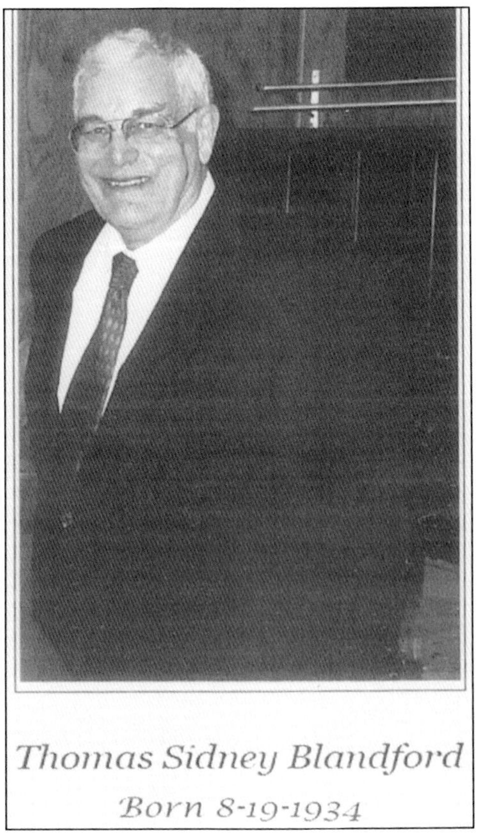

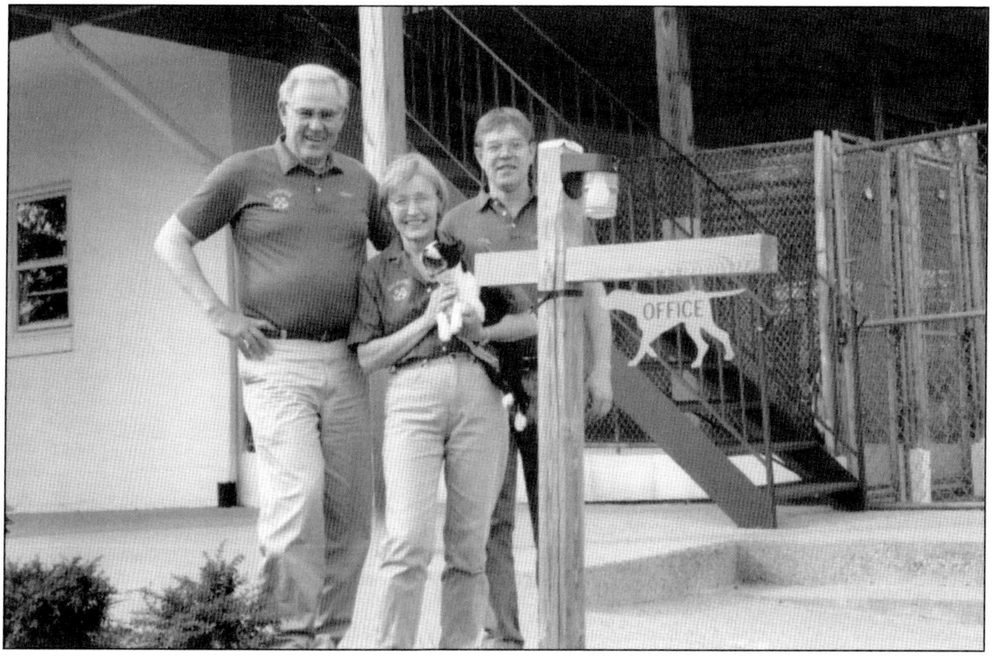

Marilyn Randall and Anchors Kennel. The Randalls are a relatively new "old family" in Accokeek. The Randall family has owned Anchors Kennel for over 25 years. The business is on Indian Head Highway on a former part of the Powell farm. Jon Powell is their next-door neighbor. Marilyn Randall retired from the federal government and has been involved with the kennel since the beginning. She has been breeding and showing American Kennel Club–registered Boston Terriers for 40 years. She is active in specialty dog clubs and Accokeek community activities. Marilyn's husband, Norman, and her son Scott, both of whom are seen above, are deceased. (Both courtesy of Marilyn Randall.)

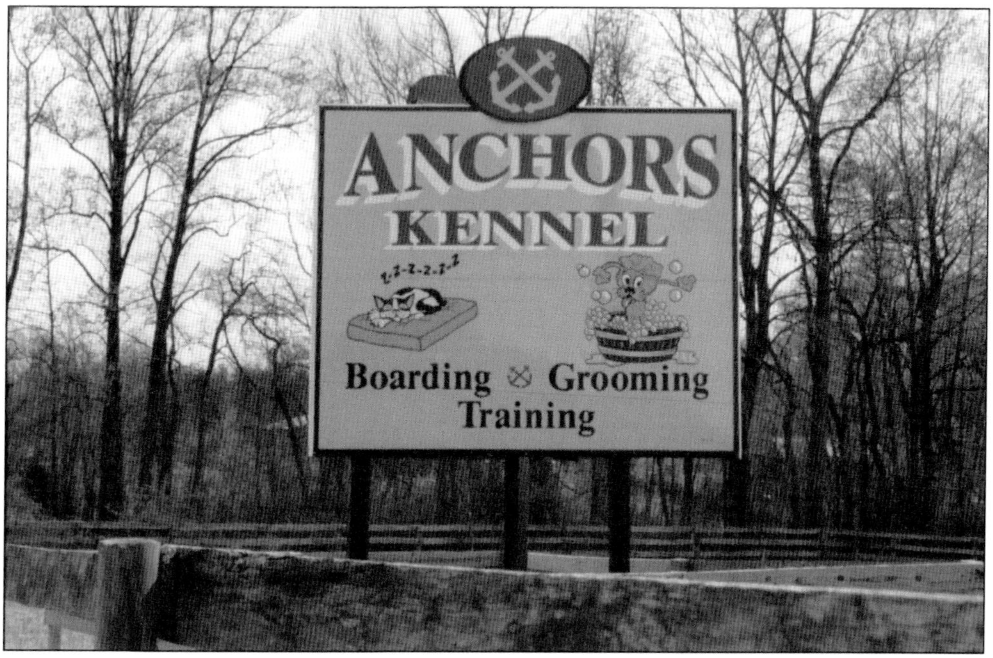

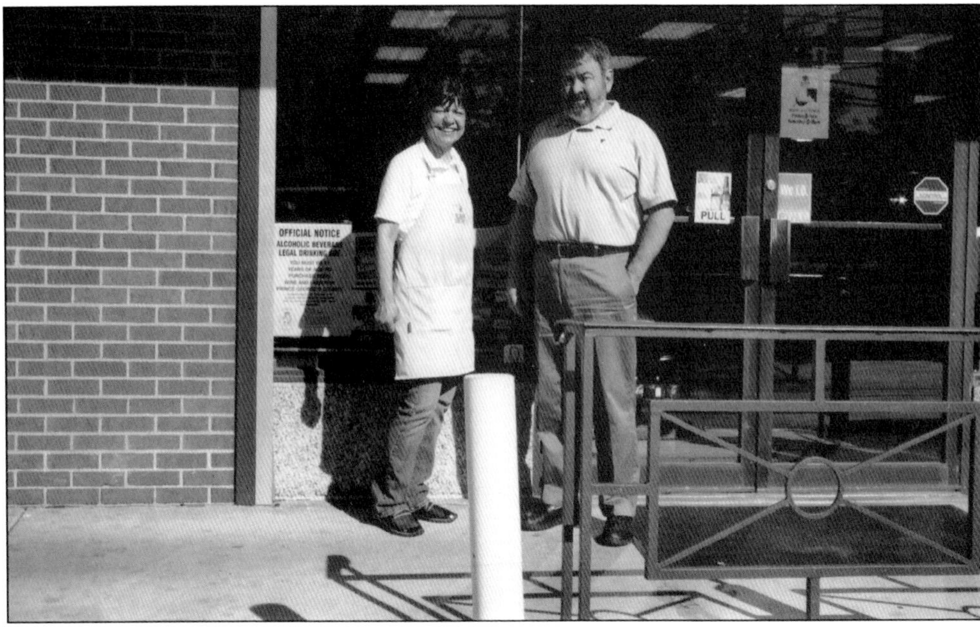

Ray and Karen Tilch. Ray Tilch and his wife, Karen, are young members of an old family. They and their ancestors have been living in Silesia, just north of Accokeek, for more than 100 years. The first Tilchs moved here from Silesia, then part of Prussia, at the end of the 1800s. Robert "Papa" Tilch arrived in 1895, when he was only one year old. When he was 15, he joined the family business and operated Tilch's General Store for 65 years. In 1935, he built a tavern adjacent to the store. On that site today, Ray Tilch owns and operates Silesia Fine Wines and Spirits, while Karen operates Silesia Carry-Out. These two businesses are the center of activity for Silesia and the surrounding communities of Fort Washington and Accokeek. (Both, author's collection.)

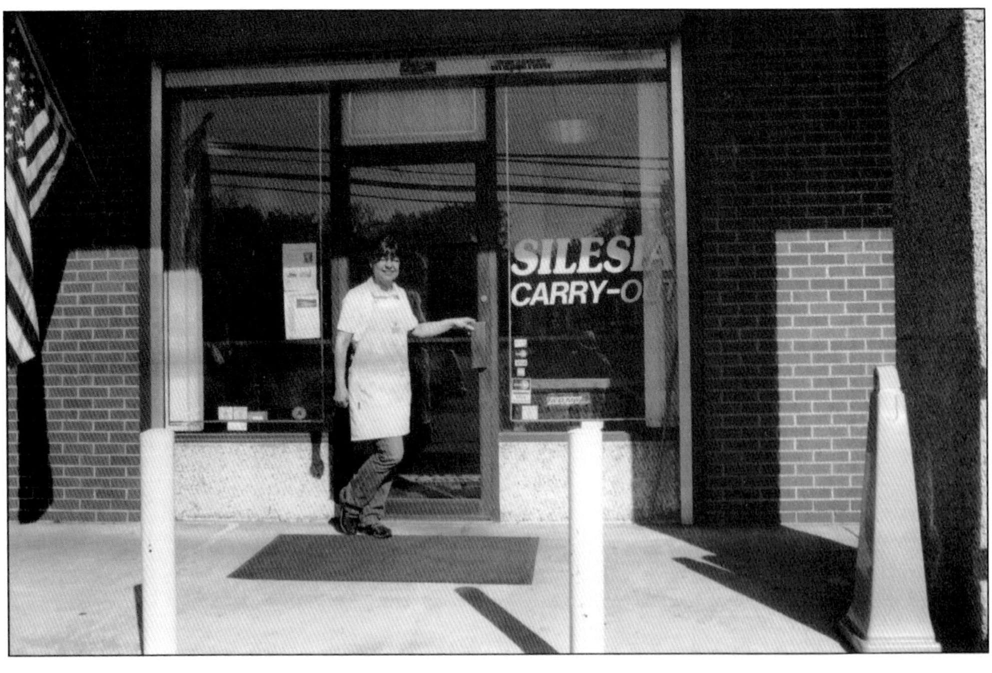

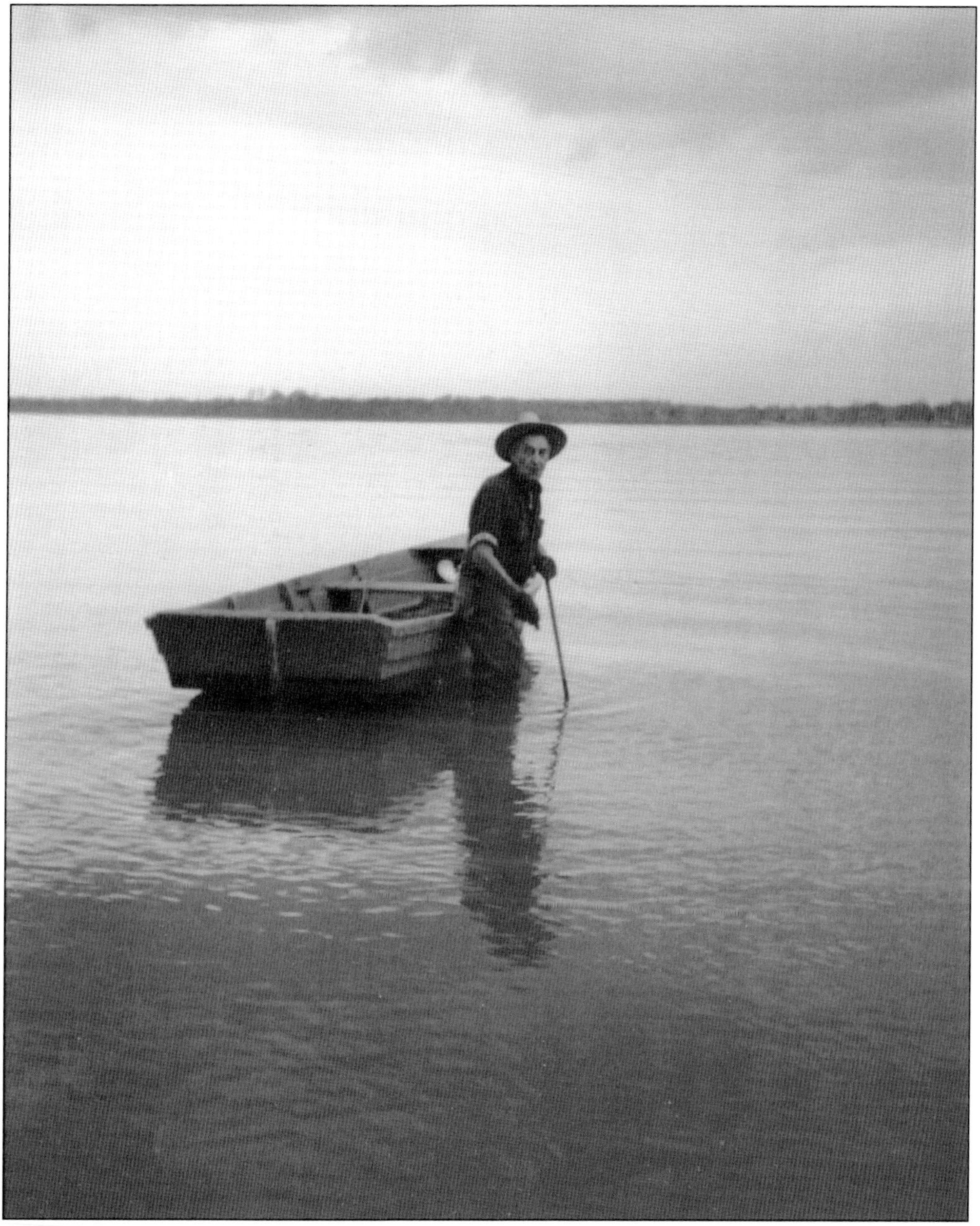

CLYDE ALLEN. Clyde Enoch Allen was born the day after World War I ended, November 11, 1918, which was designated as Armistice Day. He was just a boy when he began fishing on the Potomac River with his father and uncle. In 1925, he got a job at the fish hatchery on the cover of this book. Allen married in 1927 and moved with his bride into a one-room house, where four sons were born in rapid succession. All six Allens shared the one-room house for a number of years. Charles Dillon remembered Clyde Allen as a "substantial commercial fisherman" and recalled that he hauled carp to market in Philadelphia and New York. Although he had no formal training, he simply figured things out himself. Dillon was awed by Allen's mechanical genius and exceptional skill as a boat designer and builder. In 1954, he built a white oak shaped-plywood boat for Charles Dillon. (Courtesy of Nancy and Holly Wagner.)

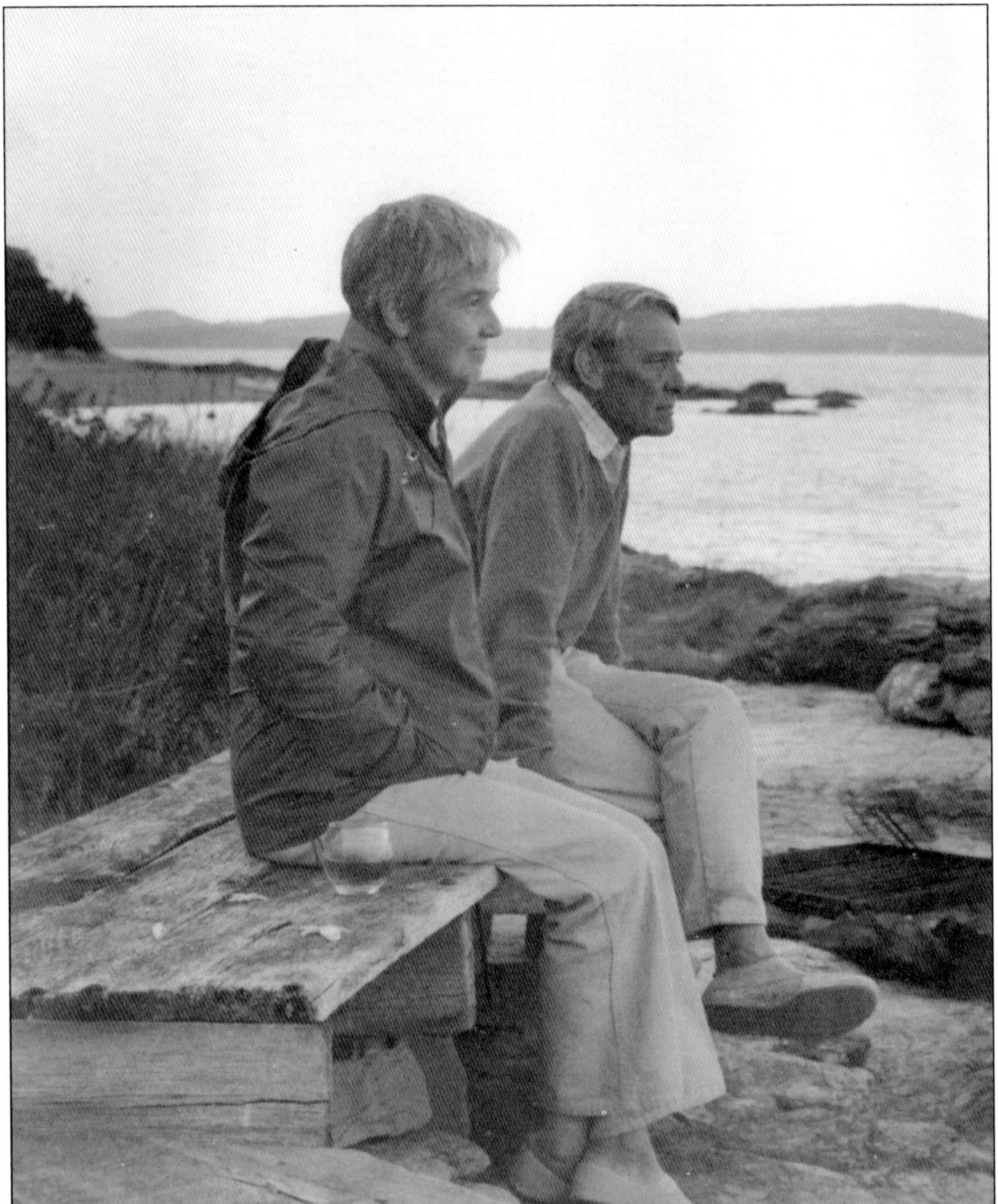

Charles and Nancy Wagner. Charles Wagner (1909–1998) moved to Accokeek in 1936. As an architect, he played an important role in the development of the Moyaone Reserve. After designing and constructing his own home in 1946, he designed and built 15 additional homes. He also designed the community center and the first swimming pool in Accokeek. Nancy, who was born in 1919, was instrumental in creating the Accokeek Cooperative Nursery. In 1953, at the behest of Henry Ferguson, Nancy, with Louise North and Mary Thornhill, organized the Alice Ferguson Foundation. In the mid-1950s, Nancy created *Smoke Signals*, a monthly newsletter for the Moyaone Reserve. With a family of four young children, a full-time job teaching nursery school, and a full social schedule, Nancy edited the newsletter, something she continued to do for more than 50 years. Recently, Nancy's many contributions were recognized when the board of the Alice Ferguson Foundation gave her the "Fergie" award. (Courtesy of Nancy and Holly Wagner.)

James and Polly Whyte. James Huntington Whyte (1909–1962, right) operated the James Whyte Book and Art Gallery on Connecticut Avenue and Dupont Circle in Washington. His friends in the art world included Franz Bader and James Leonard Mack. Bader and his first wife, Antonia, fled to the United States after the German annexation of Austria in March 1938. Upon arriving in Washington, Franz Bader worked in James Whyte's bookstore, selling foreign-language books and maps as well as modern art. James Leonard Mack recalls that Whyte would occasionally host receptions for artists he was exhibiting. The receptions usually included black, white, and Haitian artists and friends. James Whyte also wrote *The Uncivil War*, a complete history of the Reconstruction era in Washington. Whyte's wife, Polly (1919–1989, below), loved to host parties at their home in Accokeek. (Both courtesy of Juli Whyte.)

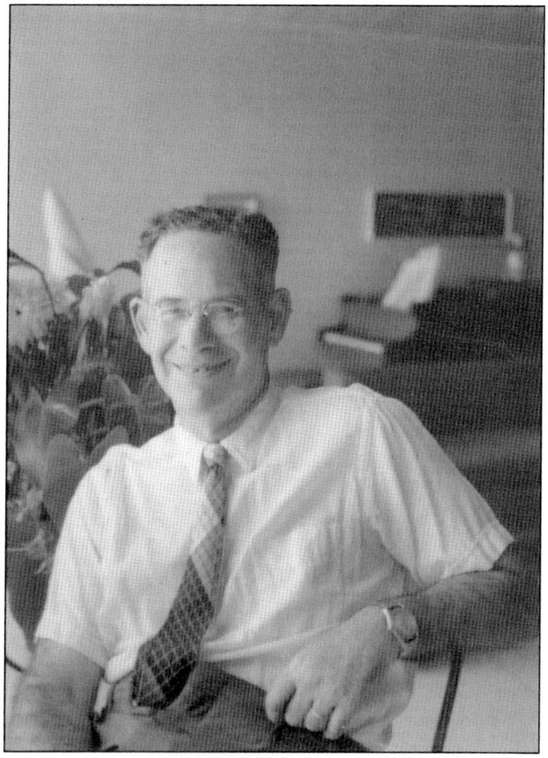

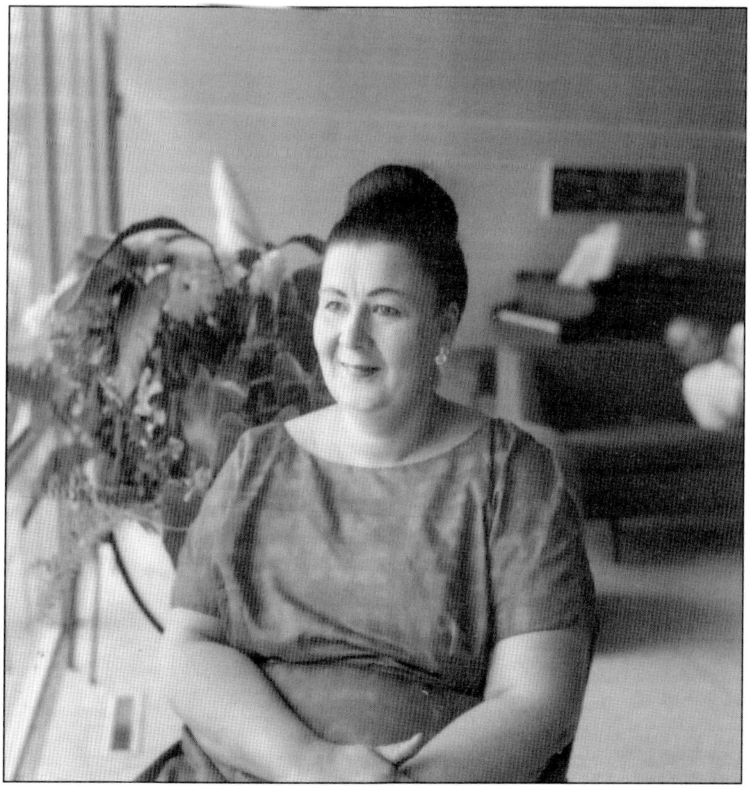

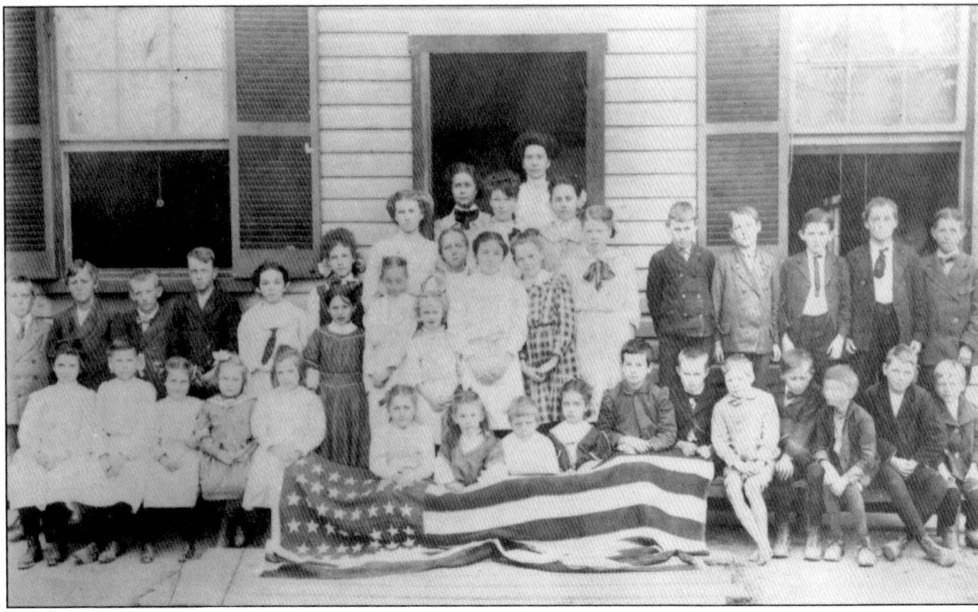

ACCOKEEK SCHOOL, 1910. Pictured are 38 students with their teacher, standing in back. The boys on the right end of the second row are, from left to right, Frank Smith, Malcolm Clagett, Stephen Davis, Ralph Clagett, and Al Wilson. Standing in the last row are, from left to right, Florence Wilson, Eleanor Manning, ? Coombs, Margaret Underwood, and Sophie Xander. (Courtesy of Betty Dillon, Dorothy Showalter, Virginia Robey, and Thomas Sidney Blandford.)

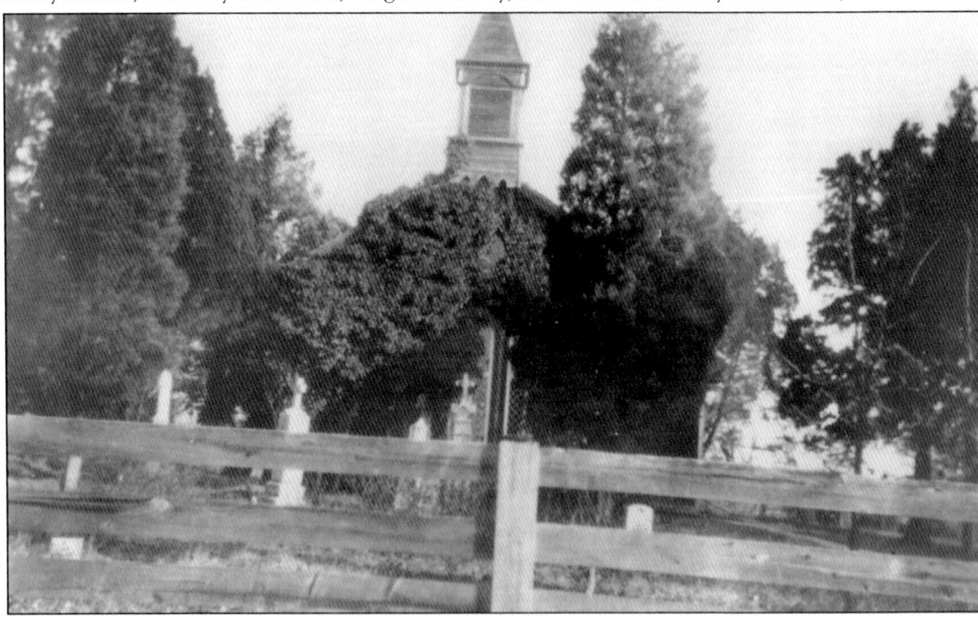

PRESERVATION OF CHRIST EPISCOPAL CHURCH. This photograph shows historic Christ Church overgrown with English ivy. In 1964, the vestry considered restoring the church to its 1740s appearance. Finding this impractical, however, they decided to renovate it instead. Some work needed to be done to the exterior, but significant interior renovation was required, including repairing the plaster, strengthening the balcony, and replacing the pews. (Courtesy of Betty Dillon and Dorothy Showalter.)

Nine

CHANGING TIMES

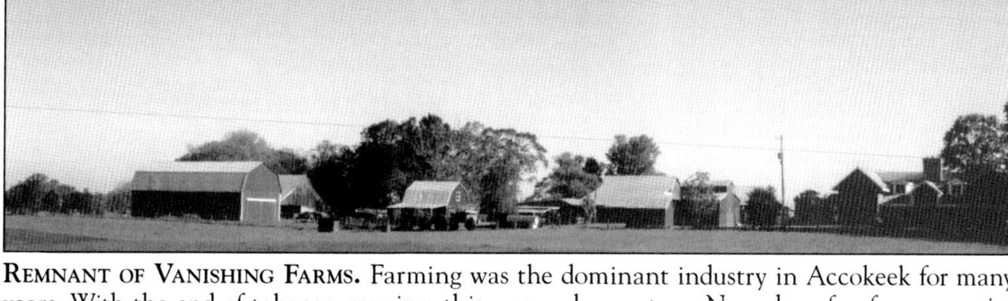

REMNANT OF VANISHING FARMS. Farming was the dominant industry in Accokeek for many years. With the end of tobacco growing, this was no longer true. Nowadays, few farms remain, but Rosalie Puterbaugh still operates this farm on the north side of Bryan Point Road. It is near the National Colonial Farm, a living history museum showing life on a small farm at the time of the American Revolution. (Author's collection.)

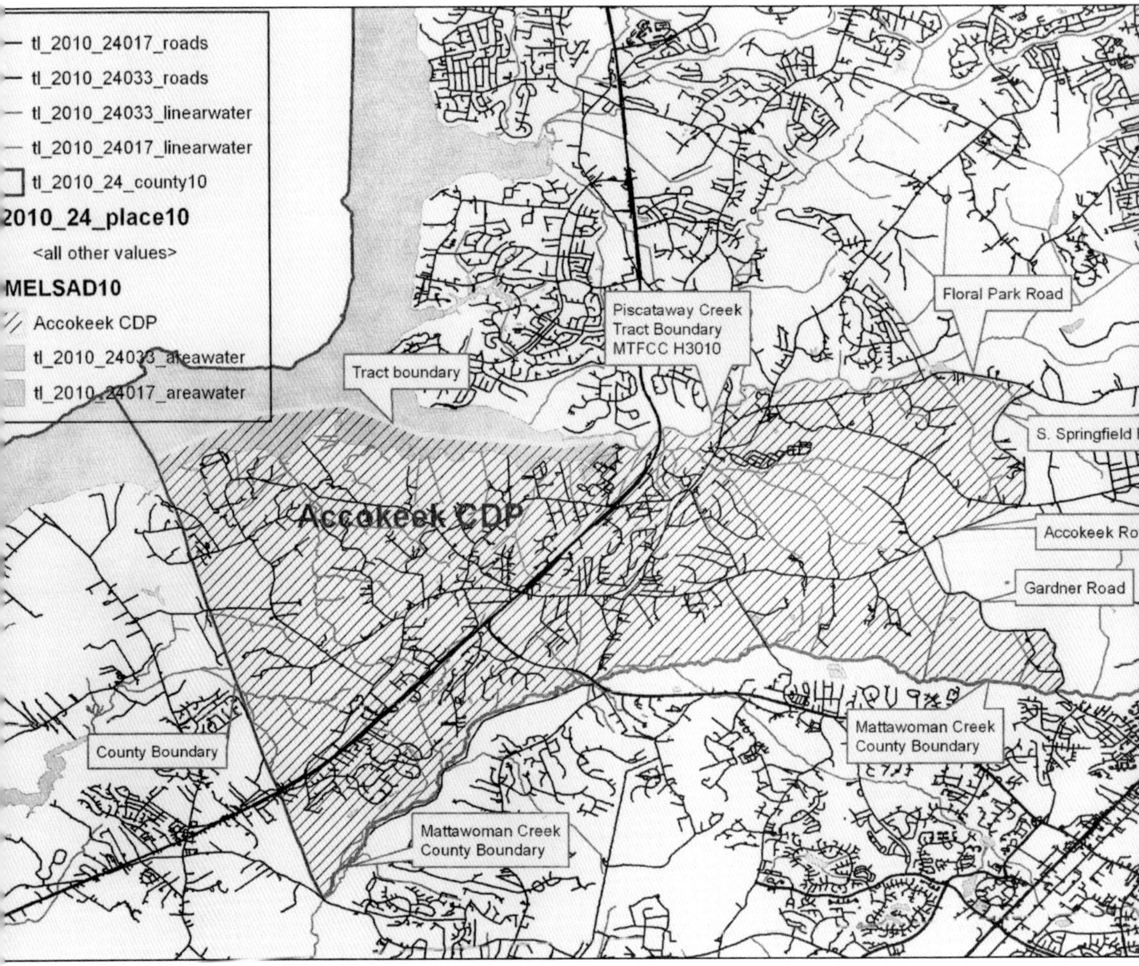

CENSUS BUREAU DELINEATES ACCOKEEK. For the 1990 census, the official boundaries of the Accokeek Census Designated Place (CDP) were established. That census recorded that Accokeek had a population of 4,477, with 84 percent white residents and 12 percent African American residents. By the 2010 census, the population of the Accokeek CDP had increased to 10,573, with two-thirds of the population listed as African American and 5.5 percent listed as Asian. Wat Tummaprateip Thai Buddhist Temple is now an Accokeek landmark. The median household income in the CDP is $112,780, and only 1.2 percent of people in Accokeek live in poverty, according to a 2007–2011 profile. More than 90 percent of people own their homes, and the median value of owner-occupied housing units is about $400,000. (Courtesy of the US Census Bureau.)

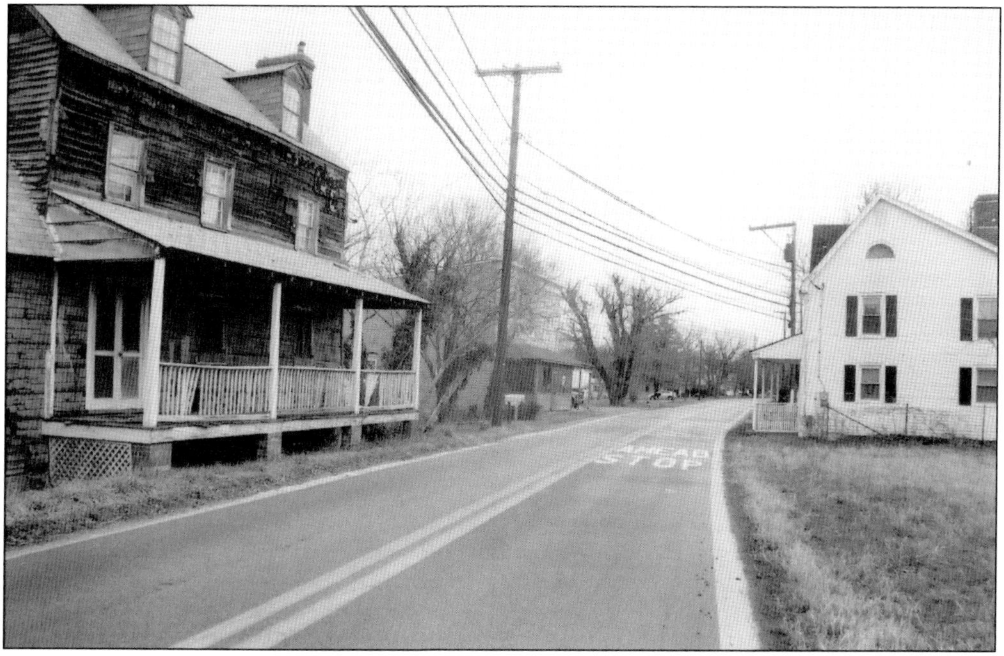

Piscataway Village Historic District. In December 2011, Piscataway Village Historic District was listed in the National Register of Historic Places. The period of the village's significance began with the establishment of a tobacco inspection warehouse in 1747 and ended in 1943 when the Piscataway post office closed. Historically, Piscataway Village provided goods and services to surrounding farms. Currently, three former stores, two former taverns, the former post office and doctor's office, and St. Mary's Roman Catholic Church remain. Some of the structures in the historic district are in poor repair. Being added to the National Register is a source of local pride, but it provides no resources for maintaining the heritage of the village. (Both, author's collection.)

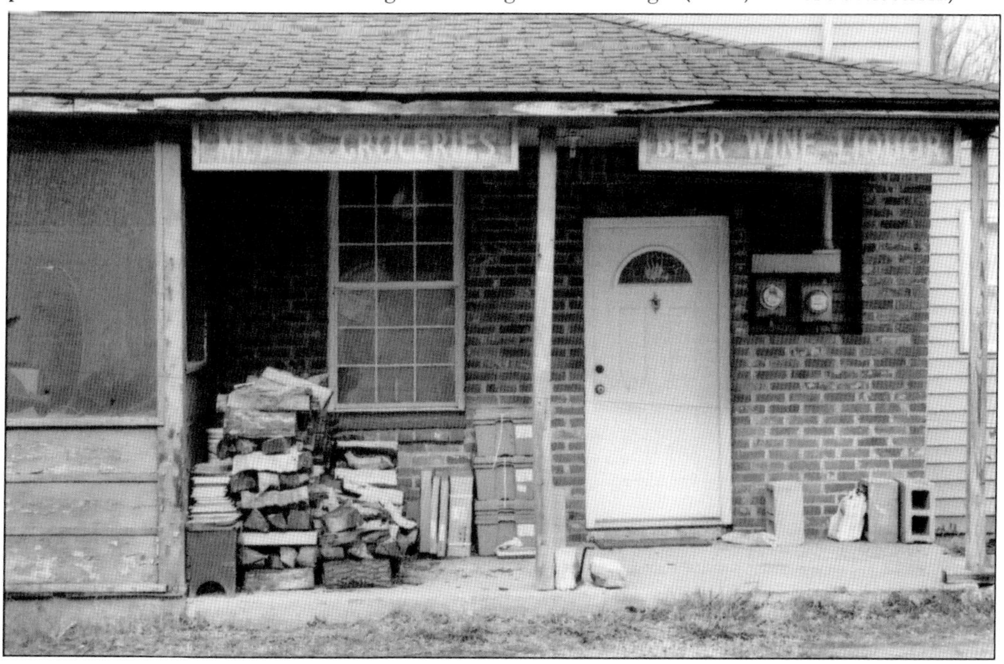

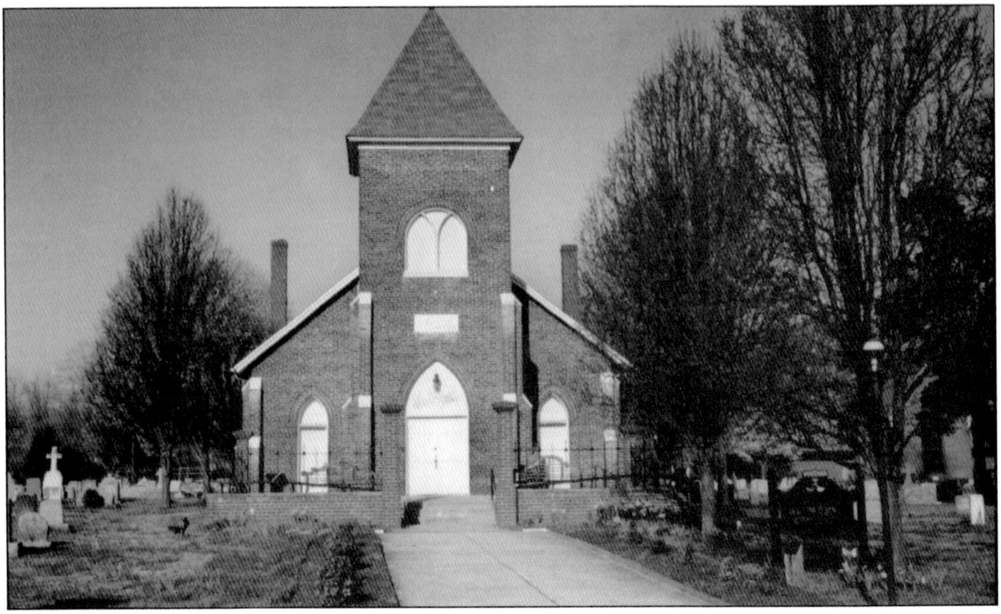

St. Mary's Catholic Church. The church seen here was constructed to replace an earlier church on this site. A foundation block located at the buttress of the bell tower reads, "St. Mary's A.D. 1906." A stone plaque above the entrance reads, "Come to me all who labour or are heavy laden and I will refresh you, 1838." This is one of several structures on the property, at 13401 Piscataway Road, including a large church built in 1988, a school, a rectory, and an office building. The old church is referred to as Our Lady's Chapel to distinguish it from the new church. St. Mary's Catholic Church of Piscataway marks its 375th anniversary in 2015. The church staff, under the leadership of Bill Kemig, is developing a publication on the history of the parish and the Catholic community in the region. (Author's collection.)

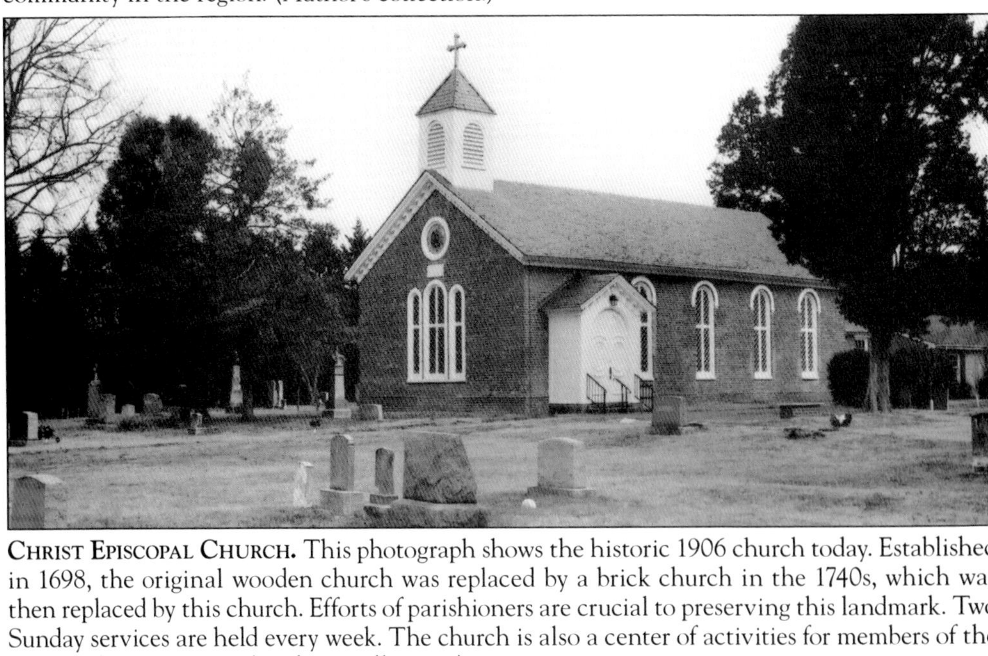

Christ Episcopal Church. This photograph shows the historic 1906 church today. Established in 1698, the original wooden church was replaced by a brick church in the 1740s, which was then replaced by this church. Efforts of parishioners are crucial to preserving this landmark. Two Sunday services are held every week. The church is also a center of activities for members of the Accokeek community. (Author's collection.)

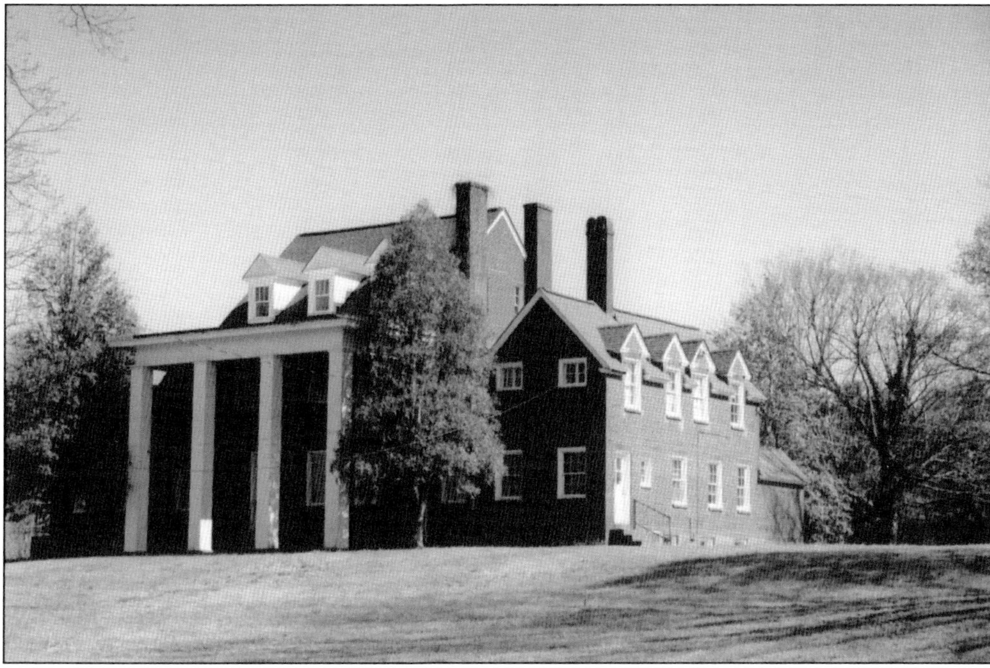

Edelen House. The Edelen House stands on a hillside overlooking Piscataway Village. The house and the surrounding 450 acres were owned by Horace Edelen until his death in 1882. Beginning in 1886, the property was sold out of the family and passed through a succession of owners. In 1926, the property was acquired by the Maryland Tobacco Planters Company. The company remodeled the Edelen House, covering the main block with brick veneer and adding a two-story portico with wooden pillars. In 1930, the company went into receivership, and David Bailey bought the property. It has been known since then as Bailey Tobacco Plantation, and two generations of Baileys have resided in the remodeled Edelen House. In 1989, the large acreage was sold again to a real estate development company. (Both, author's collection.)

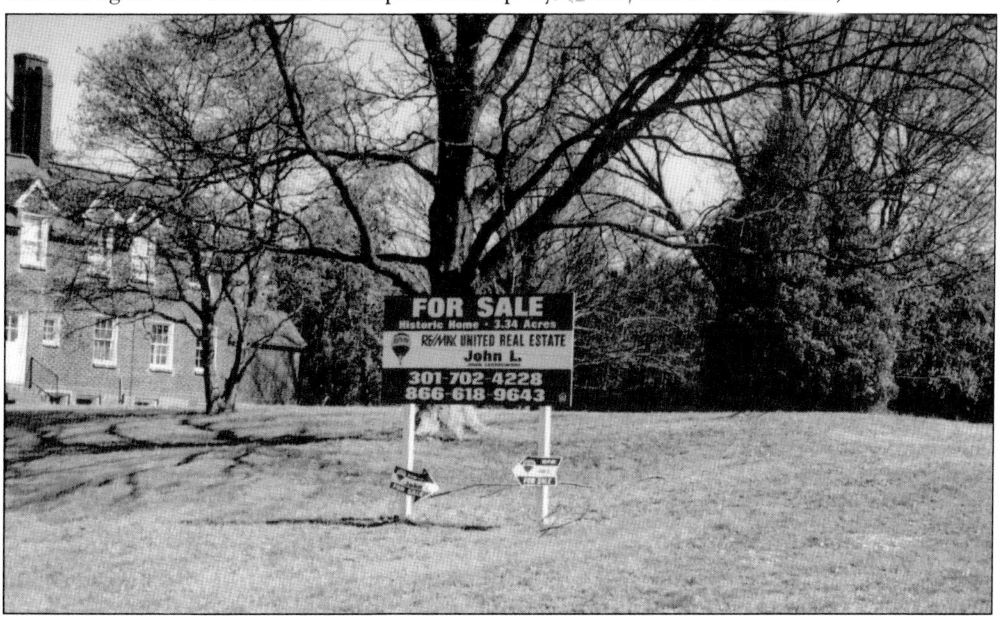

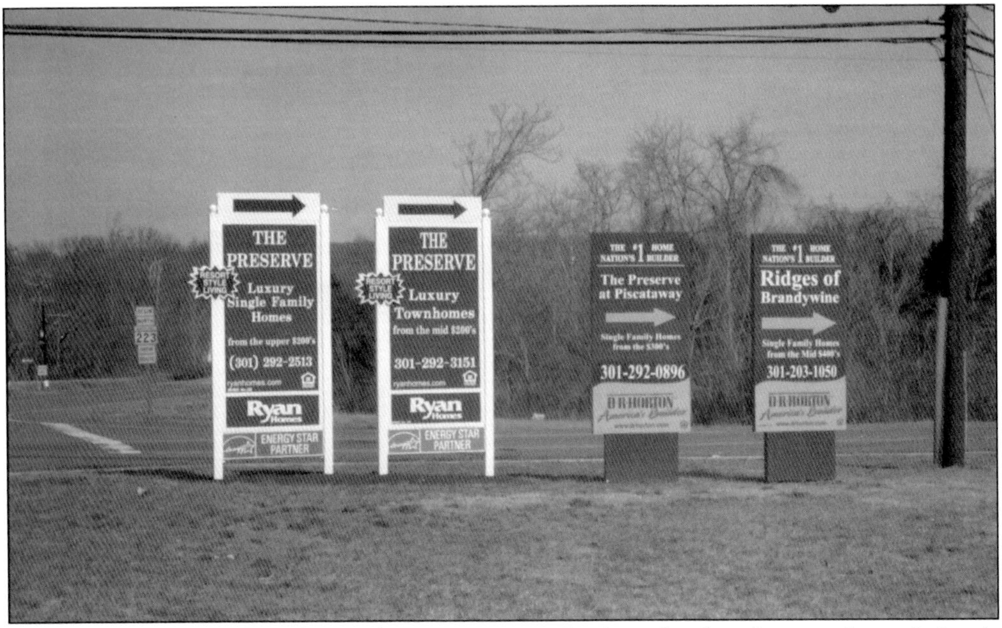

The Preserve. The Bailey Tobacco Plantation property has been developed as a site for single-family homes and townhouses. The property is now known as The Preserve. Construction of residences is continuing, and, eventually, it will consist of 1,100 dwellings. Townhouses are immediately adjacent to Edelen House, which has been for sale for several years. Ryan Homes's promotional materials advertise that The Preserve is rich with amenities, featuring a 25-meter swimming pool and a community center (currently under construction). Plans for a golf course, however, were abandoned. The Preserve consists of several villages, each with picnic tables, benches, and tennis courts. Two different townhouse floor plans and several different single-family home designs are available. (Both, author's collection.)

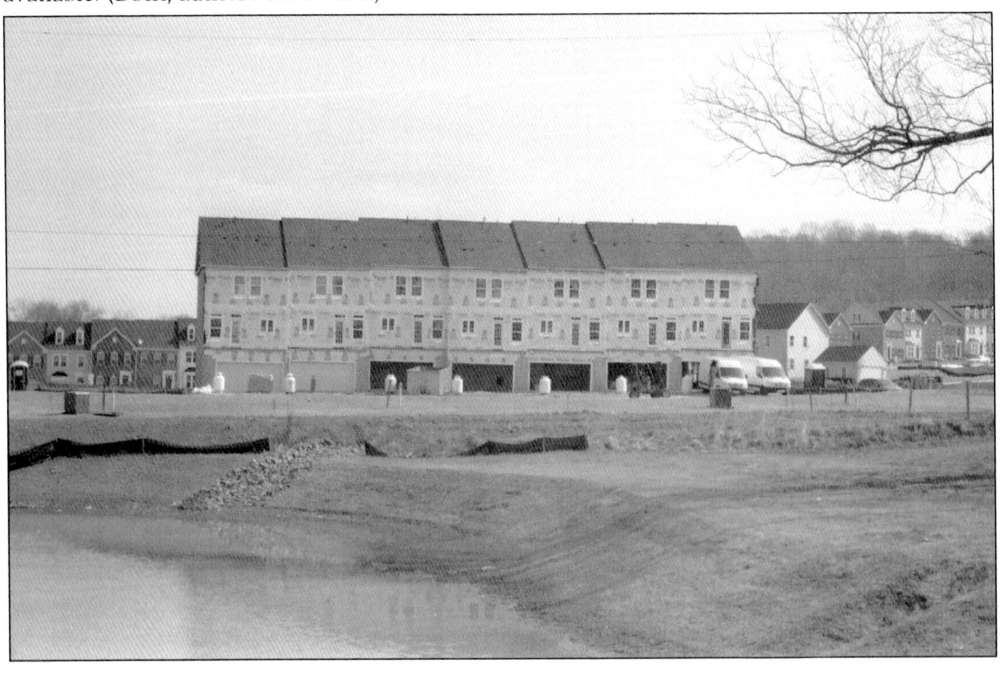

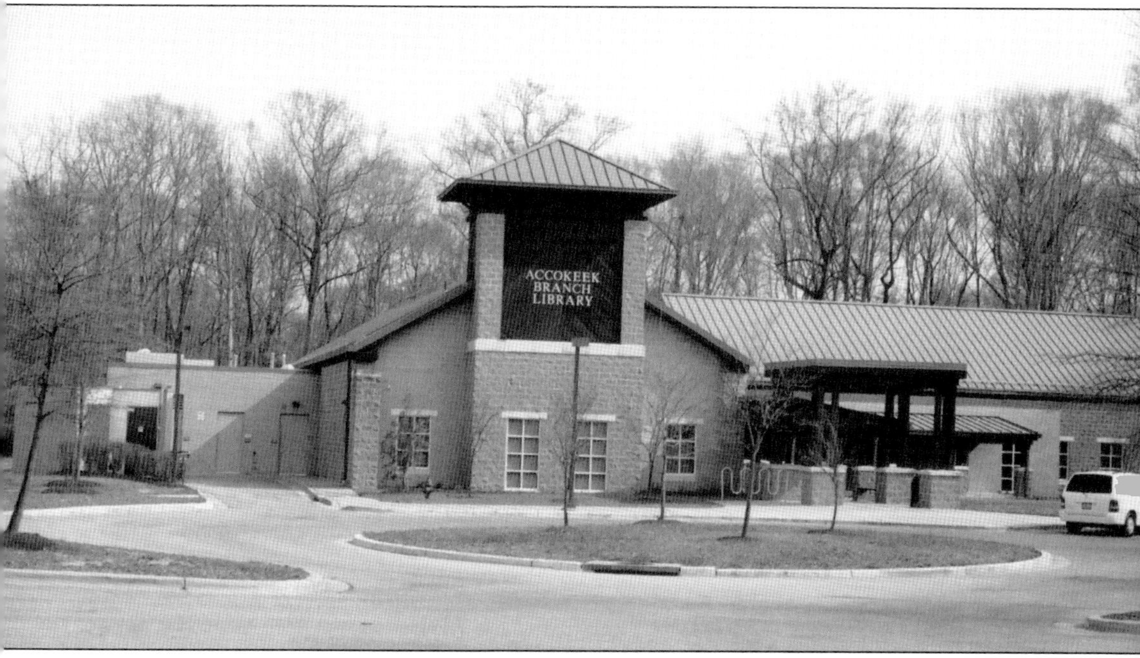

ACCOKEEK BRANCH LIBRARY. The Accokeek Branch of the Prince George's County Memorial Library system is a community gathering spot. It has wireless internet access, free computers for public use, adult, teen, and children's books, recorded books, music, magazines, and a friendly and helpful staff. While it is not a large library with a big collection, staff can help patrons reserve books that can be found in other public and academic libraries. The new library building seen here, east of Indian Head Highway, was built on land donated by Manning Clagett with the support of other members of the Accokeek community. Friends of the Accokeek Library is an organization with more than 100 members. Their efforts help to maintain the library's programs, which are important to more than 400 families who homeschool their children and to other working adults, senior citizens, and children and teens. The flourishing of the Accokeek Branch Library is due in large measure to the efforts of librarian Anne-Marie Ramsey, who retired in 2013. (Author's collection.)

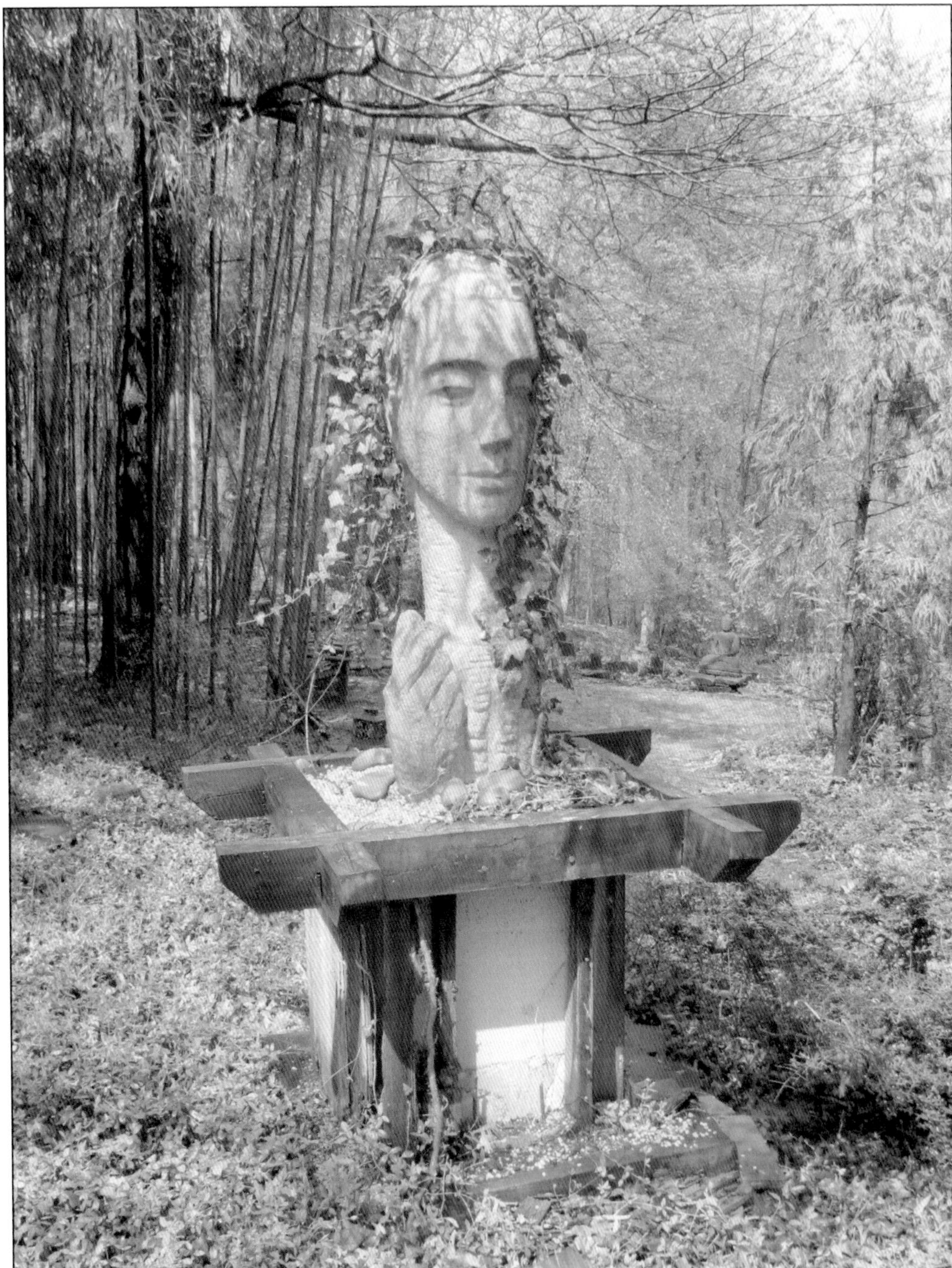

Preserving Accokeek Art. This sculpture by Lenore Thomas Straus is awaiting restoration after having been abandoned to the elements for years. Straus's son Eric is assisting these efforts. He would like the important sculpture to be displayed at the Accokeek Branch Library. (Courtesy of Eric Straus.)

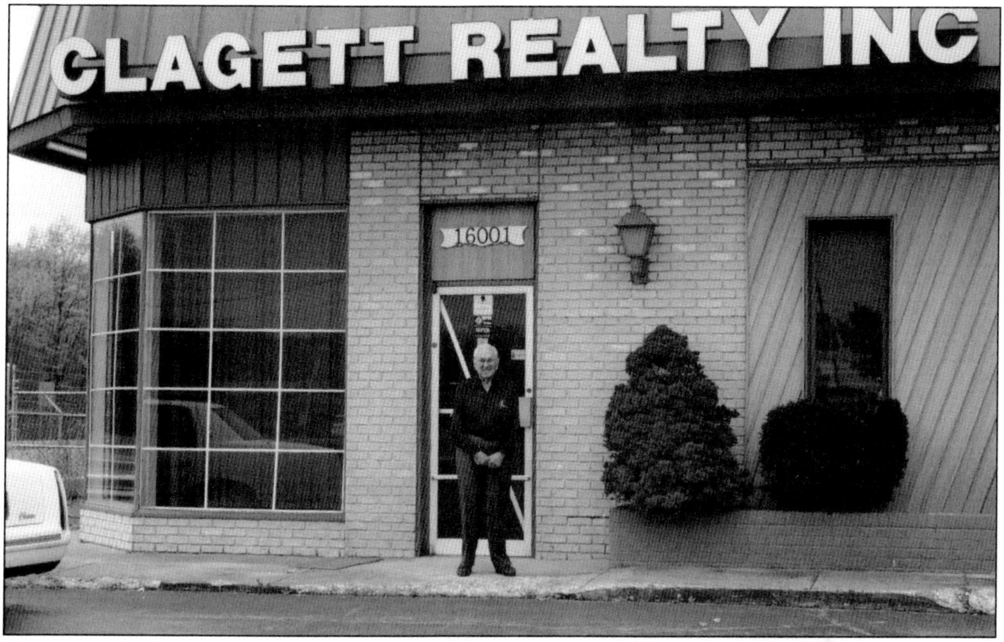

Manning Clagett. On April 24, 2013, the Greater Accokeek Citizens Association recognized Manning Clagett (above and right) as Accokeek Citizen of the Year. The certificate awarded to Clagett reads, in part, "A life-long prominent resident of Accokeek, Manning Clagett's roots in Accokeek extend back several generations. Among the highlights of his many accomplishments are his life-long membership and support of Christ Episcopal Church and his charter membership in the Accokeek Lions Club. His generous spirit and community commitment are illustrated by his selfless support of many local charities often through his business, Clagett Realty. This included donation of land for construction of the Accokeek Public Library." (Both, author's collection.)

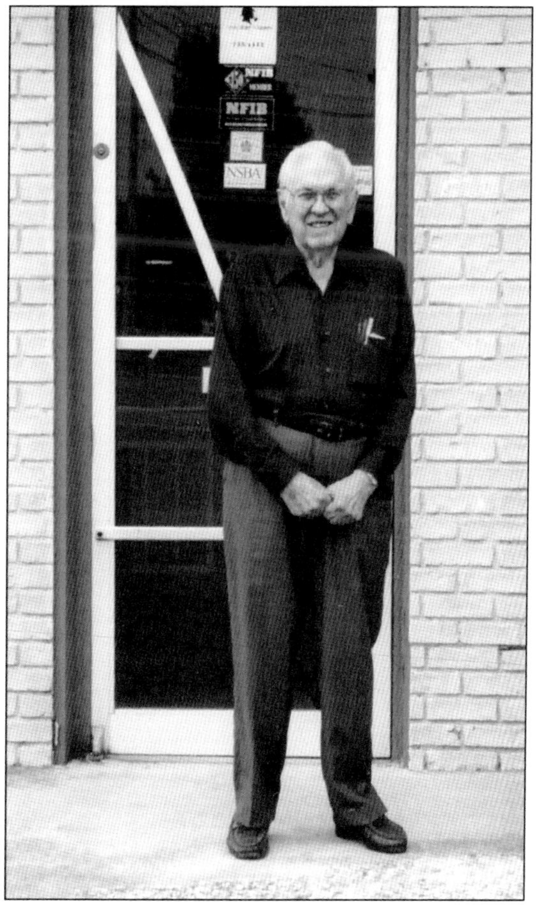

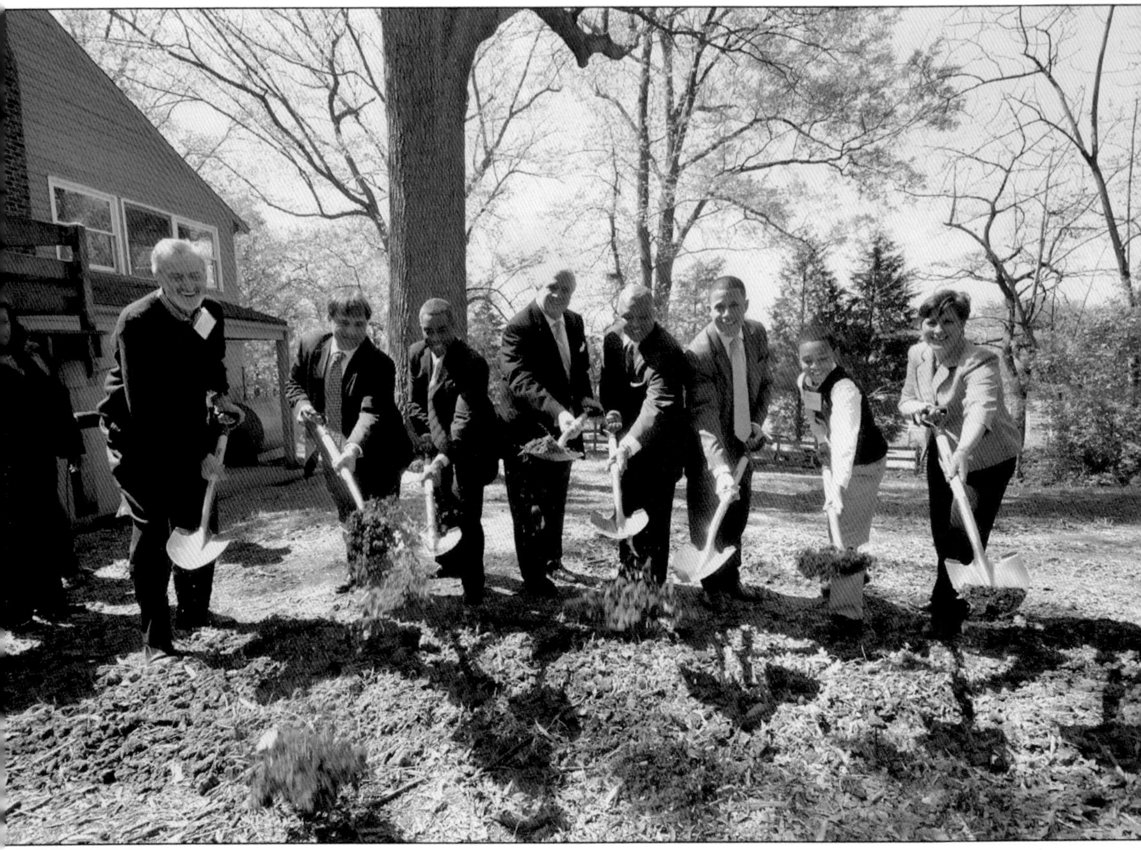

THE ALICE FERGUSON FOUNDATION'S "LIVING BUILDING." On April 25, 2013, Lt. Gov. Anthony Brown (third from right), Prince George's County Executive Rushern L. Baker III (fourth from right), and other dignitaries broke ground on one of the world's greenest, most energy efficient buildings—and the region's first "Living Building." The Alice Ferguson Foundation's Potomac Watershed Study Center will embrace the principles of the Living Building Challenge, making it among the most innovative and environmentally sustainable building projects in the world. Upon completion, the net-zero water, net-zero energy, and carbon neutral center will take green buildings to a new level. Currently there are only three certified Living Buildings in the world. The center will consist of a lodge providing overnight accommodations for students, a day-use education building, two sleeping cabins, and a wheelchair-accessible wetlands boardwalk. Energy for the facilities will be generated from photoelectric and solar thermal arrays and geothermal wells. Rainwater will be collected and purified for use throughout the center. Composting toilets, a zero-waste program, and a sustainable landscape will minimize outputs. (Courtesy of the Alice Ferguson Foundation.)

About the Alice Ferguson Foundation

The Alice Ferguson Foundation (AFF) was established in 1954 as a state-chartered nonprofit organization. The foundation's mission is to connect people to the natural world, sustainable agricultural practices, and the cultural heritage of their local watershed through education, stewardship, and advocacy.

The AFF promotes the education and preservation of the history, culture, and arts related to Alice and Henry Ferguson by interpreting the art, cultural artifacts, archival and other related objects, landscapes, and structures of Hard Bargain Farm for the benefit of children, adults, regional residents, and visitors.

The arts that Henry and Alice Ferguson so loved are continued today in the collections of paintings and sculptures by Alice and fellow artists at Hard Bargain Farm, as well as live plays and concerts at the outdoor amphitheater. Theater in the Woods productions by the Hard Bargain Players and performances by local musicians in the Concert in the Woods series carry on that Ferguson tradition.

AFF's Hard Bargain Farm Environmental Center's education program for elementary and middle school students is designed to promote understanding and stewardship of the natural resources in the Potomac River watershed and the legacy of farming in southern Maryland.

Bridging the Watershed is a middle school and high school outreach program, which, in partnership with the National Park Service and area schools, is designed to promote student academic achievement, personal connections with the natural world, lifelong civic engagement, and environmental stewardship through hands-on, curriculum-based outdoor studies in national parks and public lands.

The Trash Free Potomac Watershed Initiative seeks to address the trash problem with a comprehensive, watershed-wide approach that challenges regional leaders to work collaboratively, brings together key stakeholders to research and explore alternative, cost-effective solutions that have long-term impacts, and improves general education and awareness in order to shift individual behaviors.

Discover Thousands of Local History Books Featuring Millions of Vintage Images

Arcadia Publishing, the leading local history publisher in the United States, is committed to making history accessible and meaningful through publishing books that celebrate and preserve the heritage of America's people and places.

Find more books like this at
www.arcadiapublishing.com

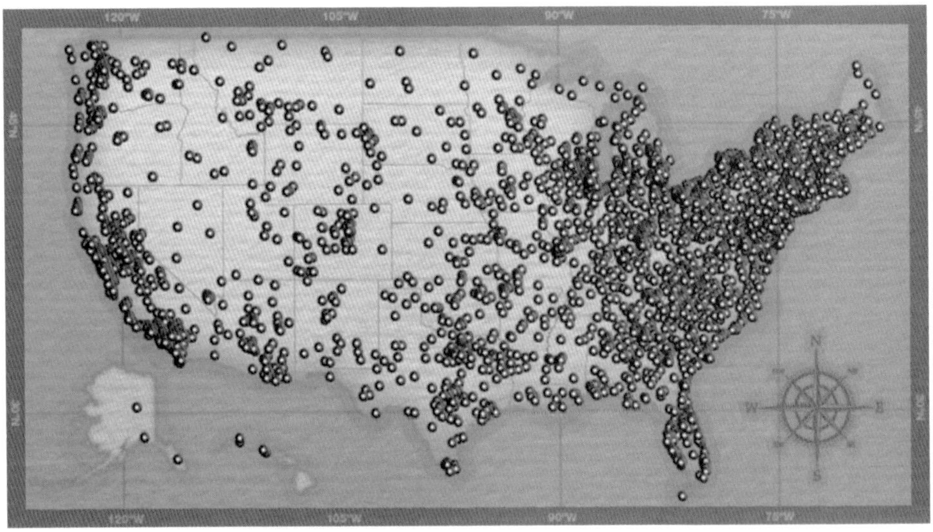

Search for your hometown history, your old stomping grounds, and even your favorite sports team.

Consistent with our mission to preserve history on a local level, this book was printed in South Carolina on American-made paper and manufactured entirely in the United States. Products carrying the accredited Forest Stewardship Council (FSC) label are printed on 100 percent FSC-certified paper.

MADE IN THE USA